THE BIG PICTURE

Reflections on our economic times

T T Ram Mohan

Viva Books Private Limited

New Delhi • Mumbai • Chennai • Kolkata • Hyderabad • Bangalore

First published 2004

VIVA BOOKS PRIVATE LIMITED

- 4262/3, Ansari Road, Daryaganj, New Delhi 110 002
  E-mail: viva@vivagroupindia.net
- 215-216 New Apollo Estate, 2nd Floor, Mogra Lane, Andheri (E), Mumbai 400 069
  E-mail: vivamumbai@vivagroupindia.net
- Jamals Fazal Chambers, 26 Greams Road, Chennai 600 006
  E-mail: vivachennai@vivagroupindia.net
- B-103, Jindal Towers, 21/1A/3 Darga Road, Kolkata 700 017
  E-mail: vivakolkata@vivagroupindia.net
- 7, GF, Sovereign Park Aptts., 56-58, K. R. Road, Basavanagudi, Bangalore 560 004
  E-mail: vivabangalore@vivagroupindia.net
- 101-102 First Floor, Mughal Marg Apartments, Narayanguda, Hyderabad 500 029
  E-mail: vivahyderabad@vivagroupindia.net

ISBN 81-7649-629-4

Published by Vinod Vasishtha for Viva Books Private Limited, 4262/3 Ansari Road, Daryaganj, New Delhi 110 002

Printed and bound in India by Sanat Printers, Kundli - 131 028.

To my parents

Foreword

I am happy to write the Foreword to this collection of articles by Professor TT Ram Mohan. These articles were published originally as a fortnightly column in a leading economic daily. Even as they were published, they were read with great interest by a wide cross section because of their quality and the unambiguous position taken by the author on various issues. Even though each article is short, given the constraint of space of a daily, taken together they constitute a veritable treasure-house of ideas and offer an informed commentary on the developments of the Indian economy.

Professor TT Ram Mohan supports liberalization. However, he differs from others of a similar conviction in terms of pace, sequencing and emphasis. This is what he calls in his Preface 'a contrarian position'. The financial sector is a major area of interest to the author and, therefore, gets his prime attention. He is happy about the progress made by the Public Sector Banks in the post-reform period. Banking sector reforms have led to improvement in viability without jeopardizing stability. It must be admitted that Professor TT Ram Mohan was more optimistic about the ability of the Public Sector Banks to transform themselves than many others. He was perceptive enough to recognize trends of improvement which were not obvious to others. Government ownership of banks is a double-edged sword. On the one hand it enabled some of the public sector banks that were making losses during the period of transition to prudential norms to enjoy credibility. On the other hand, the very public sector character also made induction of reforms more difficult because of the need for acceptance at various levels including political. Bringing about changes in the work culture needed patience. One has only to recall the difficulties faced in inducting computers into the system. Professor Ram Mohan has correctly identified three major sources of strength of Public Sector Banks—wide geographical reach, economies of scale and access to low cost deposits. Quite clearly, Public Sector Banks have shown striking improvement on several parameters.

However, customer service, particularly at the counter, is still a contentious issue. While prudential norms and greater accountability to a wider spectrum of shareholders have had a salutary effect, external interference beyond policy directions can be a throwback in time.

In the section on Indian economy, Professor Ram Mohan touches on many issues. While he recognizes the need to contain primary deficit, he takes a more benign view of fiscal deficit. The issue has never been whether or not there should be fiscal deficit. The question was about the level of fiscal deficit. The cause for concern arises only because the fiscal deficit at the centre and states taken together is closely approximating the household sector savings in financial assets. Presently, the nominal interest rate may not be under pressure. The ability of Government of India to borrow has been facilitated by the fact that corporate investment as a proportion of GDP has come down from 9.6% in 1995-96 to 5.9% in 2000-2001. Also, the ease with which the Central Government is able to raise funds from the market should not cloud the fact that several state governments are facing serious problems with respect to borrowing and repaying past loans.

The two other interesting sections in the book deal with privatization and international economy and they once again reveal the author's ability to think differently from others.

Professor Ram Mohan has given us a book that combines scholarship with readability. The style is lucid, the content rich and the arguments balanced. What more can a reader wish for!

July 27, 2004

DR C RANGARAJAN
Chairman, Twelfth Finance Commission

Preface

It can be a funny feeling in the stomach, a cold sweat or a vaguely felt irritability. Each fortnight as the deadline approaches—I have a self imposed deadline of Tuesday for my column which appears on Thursday—I go through hell. It's a struggle to find a topic. If a topic is at hand, saying something different is a challenge. What on earth can you say about the budget or about the credit policy if your turn falls a good 10 days after the saturation coverage of these events?

Often, I tell myself that this is my last piece and start thinking up a farewell to readers. Miraculously, at the last minute, a topic suggests itself. The trigger could be an item in the papers, a flash on the web or a chance remark at a meeting. Against all odds, the piece gets done. One lives to fight another day.

So it has been for over six years now. To be sure, it's not always a struggle. Sometimes, there is a piece waiting to be written and an event provides just the right provocation. The words come gushing out and the piece is done at one go.

Some of the pieces were written during stays in the United States but such is the power of the Internet that you can't tell—one's access to information about events is barely diminished by distance. I would venture to suggest that the pieces are at once a chronicle of key events in the period since 1997 and a summary of some of the central debates that have taken place.

Over the years, my column has ranged over five broad categories—the financial sector, the Indian economy, privatisation, corporate governance and the international economy. The pieces are thus arranged thematically rather than in the chronological order in which they appeared. I have corrected typos and minor errors in the originals but otherwise have retained the pieces as they appeared.

There is a brief introductory note to each of the five categories that sums up the main issues that were addressed and my principal ideas and concerns. There is also an interview in each category in which I have sought to ascertain the views of distinguished personalities concerned on the subjects that I have covered and their responses to some of my own views. I would hope that the introductory note, the interviews and my articles together would serve as a handy reference on some of the great debates of recent times.

The reader will notice that mine has been a contrarian position on many of the issues of the day—on privatisation, public sector banks and corporate governance mechanisms, for instance. This was by no means intentional. If anything, it stems from my rather unusual background. I was a consultant and banker before I turned to academics. Whilst I am appreciative of theoretical constructs, I would like to believe I have a keen sense of whether academically neat prescriptions would work on the ground or not. If I questioned some of the nostrums of the liberalisation brigade, it was out of a deep conviction that these would not work—or that better alternatives were available.

The debts I owe are many. I am deeply grateful to Dr C Rangarajan, for writing the foreword, amidst his many preoccupations. Dr Rangarajan preceded me at the Indian Institute of Management, Ahmedabad, by several decades and he remains a revered figure on the campus. We have another common association: Stern School of Business, New York University. I obtained my doctorate from Stern School and Dr Rangarajan taught there (again long before my time) before returning to India. He is fondly remembered by old-timers at Stern as well. To me, as to many others in academia, Dr Rangarajan has been an inspiring figure and his writings and speeches have been an important influence on our thinking.

The eminent personalities who have been interviewed for the five themes covered in this book—Bimal Jalan, N Vaghul, TN Srinivasan, GV Ramakrishna and Lawrence White—responded with alacrity and gave readily of their time. This compilation is greatly enriched by their insights. I am beholden to them.

I am grateful to the *Economic Times,* India's premier economic daily that is also something of a national institution by now, for its indulgence and for permission to compile my articles into a book. I have had a long association with the paper going back to my student days in New York when Manu Shroff, the then editor, offered me the position of stringer for the paper. This gave me the opportunity to cover major international events in

North America and to report on international economic affairs for an Indian audience. Mr Shroff's successors, TN Ninan and Swaminathan S Aiyar, leading columnists in their own right whose writings I have greatly admired, and Joideep Bose, too, have been kind to me.

I have also received much kindness from the two editorial page editors with whom I have had the privilege of being associated, TK Arun and Mythili Bhusnurmath. I make it a point to meet my deadline but am seldom satisfied when I reread a piece I have just despatched. I was in the habit of making niggling changes. Both Arun and Mythili bore these patiently. Until one day, Mythili pleaded with me not to insist on being a perfectionist as re-setting the column each time was creating problems at her end. I think I have not troubled her since.

In a way, my association with the *Economic Times* goes back even further. My father, TT Vijayaraghavan, was among the core group of journalists who helped found the paper and he was Senior Assistant Editor when he left the paper in 1981 after serving it for nearly two decades. I grew up with the smell of newspapers around me and pored over editorials and edit page articles fairly early on. So when people tell me that my articles have a certain journalistic fluency, that is entirely understandable.

My father would call me almost unfailingly the day my column appeared and give me his comments, which were by no means uncritical. One of the valuable suggestions he made was that in writing about international events, I should try wherever possible to bring in the Indian angle. My mother, Padmini Vijayaraghavan, a discerning reader of newspapers, also chipped in with useful comments.

My wife, Jayashree, was a big support. I would give her my piece to read and she would point out passages where the meaning was not clear or where the construction seemed clumsy. I dreaded the times when she would tell me, "Doesn't have the usual flow" or "Not your usual standard" but learnt to work on the piece after receiving her comment. I was very clear that if my articles didn't make sense to her, they would not make sense to the average ET reader. My wife and my son, Nandu, suffered stoically my spells of grumpiness as I wrestled with the rigours of column writing.

When I began to pen my column, I benefited from discussions with colleagues at IIM, Ahmedabad. I would particularly like to mention IR Varma, a man whose intellectual brilliance is matched by his generosity towards colleagues.

Finally, I must thank the readers of my column, those who wrote letters to the editors and also several others who wrote to me directly or called or gave me their feedback in person. Among the encomiums I value are the ones I received from RBI Governor, Dr YV Reddy. I seem to have appealed especially to the financial services fraternity. This does not surprise me greatly as I have tracked this sector closely both as a practitioner and as an academic.

Contents

Mergers and Universal Banking

Regulation

Investment Banking

INDIAN ECONOMY

Business Environment

CORPORATE GOVERNANCE

CEOs and Top Management

Policy Issues

Miscellany

PRIVATISATION

INTERNATIONAL ECONOMY

FINANCIAL SECTOR

Introductory Note

The financial sector accounts for the largest number of articles I wrote in my column. This reflects as much my interests as an academic as my background in both banking and investment banking. I have had an occasion to explore a variety of themes: ownership and performance in Indian banking, universal banking, regulation and investment banking.

Of all the positions that I have taken on policy issues, there is one for which I permit myself a little pat on the back. Quite early in the deregulation process, I was able to visualise the improvement in Public Sector Banks (PSBs). While many were sceptical of the ability of PSBs to turn around following the infusion of capital by government, I argued that the early trends showed that they were on the right track.

My assessment was based on a number of facts. PSBs had economies of scale, they had access to low cost deposits, there was no dearth of lending opportunities in an economy growing at 5-6 per cent (I flagged the potential for retail banking before it became all the rage), there was plenty of scope for cutting flab, and the systems at most banks were basically sound. Banks merely needed a clear profit orientation.

The international norms for bank capital and the government's inability to provide funding meant that politicians would necessarily have to allow the banks to pursue profit without too many distractions. The RBI's monitoring and supervision of banks would also not permit politicians to take too many liberties in the new, competitive environment. From being perceived as basket cases, PSBs have gone on to become darlings of the stock market.

I did not expect that banks would be able to improve their performance as dramatically as they have done and tap the equity market for funds so successfully. I had felt that banks would need a further modest infusion of capital from government before they could go the market. I had not bargained for the magic wrought by declining interest rates and the impact on treasury profits of banks.

I differed from the conventional wisdom on Indian banks in other ways as well. I was doubtful about the ability of many of the new private banks to succeed. I did not share the bleak view of the three weak banks propounded by the Verma committee. I pointed out that efficiency in the banking system as a whole was improving using conventional measures and that Indian banking had not witnessed the sort of collapse that has followed deregulation elsewhere. The presence of the public sector in the banking system, I argued, had conduced to the right trade off between efficiency and stability in Indian banking.

On universal banking, while I had no doubt that the divide between short-term and long-term funding must go, I was quick to point out that the advantages of the size and the benefits of mergers had proved delusional elsewhere. In any case, the scope for improvement in performance through organic growth was so great that it was not necessary for PSBs to contemplate mergers at the present stage.

I wrote about conflicts of interest in investment banking way back in 1997, long before the issue blew up in the faces of the world's leading investment banks in 2001. In my days in investment banking, I had had first-hand experience of such conflicts of interest and of management's willingness to ignore the interests of investors.

As for stock markets, I was unwilling to fall for the pretensions of fund managers, a vastly over-rated breed. Academic research has shown that most active funds, where managers pick and choose stocks, are outperformed by passive funds where managers merely mimic the market portfolio. It is not that fund managers have great insight into companies and are, therefore, able to produce superior returns.

On a slightly different note, I drew on an important research paper to make the point that, contrary to popular supposition, long-term returns to equities were rather modest. This, of course, meant that there was not much that fund management geniuses could do.

There is an all-too-common tendency to suppose that stock markets are a natural playground for rascals and shady characters, that manipulation and rigging are rampant in the Indian stock market. This tendency came to the fore following the high-tech collapse bubble of 2000 and the Joint Parliamentary

Committee probe that followed. The negative perception of the stock market ignores not only the strides made in regulation of the stock market in recent years but also changes in the micro-structure of the market, such as volumes traded in stocks, the multiplicity of players, etc. These render manipulation rather more difficult than in days past.

Politicians and media analysts need to curb the impulse to cry 'manipulation' each time there is a sharp dip in the market following the presentation of a budget or a change in government. Speculation is central to the stock market and viewing it with distaste is not helpful to the development of a vibrant stock market.

Interview: Bimal Jalan

Bimal Jalan, currently member of the Rajya Sabha, was educated at Calcutta, Cambridge and Oxford universities. He has been closely associated with the formulation of India's economic policies in a number of capacities: Chief Economic Advisor, Finance Secretary, and Member, Planning Commission. He has also been India's Executive Director at the World Bank and the IMF. Most recently, he was Governor, Reserve Bank of India, and has been widely credited with overseeing the turnaround in public sector banks and also the country's record accumulation of foreign exchange reserves.

1. *Financial sector reforms, most people would agree, are an astonishing success story. Looking back, does the success of financial sector reforms surprise you? Would you really have expected things to pan out so well?*

A. Yes, financial reforms have been reasonably successful. However, I would not go so far as to describe them as "astonishing success story". There is still a long way to go.

2. *There are many areas of success in the financial sector but the most important, perhaps, is the improvement in health and working of Public Sector Banks. The recapitalisation costs incurred so far on PSBs— around 2 per cent of GDP—must be the lowest anywhere in the world. As you have pointed out in one of your speeches, financial sector reforms have been a success because reforms were pre-emptive, not reactive. Would you agree that government ownership, to some extent, facilitated such pre-emptive action? How could government recapitalise banks that were privately owned?*

A. You are right that reforms were planned in advance. Our objective was to ensure that prudential, capitalisation, recognition, disclosure and auditing norms meet the best international standards over a period of time. This applies to both public sector and private sector banks. In the private sector, it is the responsibility of these banks and their shareholders to capitalise the banks, and not that of the government.

3. *The empirical evidence points to a high probability of a crisis within a decade of financial sector liberalisation. This has not happened in India. What factors do you believe have caused the Indian experience to be refreshingly different? Some would point to the absence of full capital account convertibility as a key factor. But I would like to pose a provocative question: to what extent has government ownership itself contributed to financial stability?*

A. Sovereign ownership, to some extent, does protect financial institutions or banks from becoming bankrupt or unable to meet their commitments to their depositors. Government can always rescue them or provide them with financing and that has happened in India with some sick banks. However, in a broader sense, financial stability must be reflected in the financial strength of banks and other institutions themselves to meet unforeseen contingencies or shocks rather than look to the government to rescue them from collapse.

4. *There is a sense that attempts at restructuring public sector units are a waste. Yet, restructuring has been an enormous success in banking and the government is richer as PSBs have become the darlings of the stock market. Are there any lessons to be drawn for the public sector as a whole from the successful restructuring of PSBs? For instance, does the interposition of an independent professional body such as the RBI between government and the public sector entity explain the success we have had with PSB restructuring?*

A. Yes, an arm's length relationship between Government, as the owner, and PSUs is certainly healthy so that unnecessary political interference is avoided. In that sense, it is true that RBI's regulatory and supervisory role over PSBs has helped. However, it is also important to ensure that there is a shared objective and harmonious relationship between Government and RBI.

5. *Did many people at RBI believe that the three weak banks could be turned around and that, too, with virtually no further financial support?*

A. It is not a question of belief or non-belief within RBI. Positive results were achieved because full support was provided to the management of these banks by the Government and RBI, and there was a very close supervision. Also, the right persons were appointed to head these banks.

6. *The more we come to think of it, the more it appears that getting the exchange rate has been, perhaps, the single biggest achievement of reforms as a whole. It has brought about the spectacular improvement in balance of payments, of course, but it has also contributed to a decline in interest rates with all the attendant benefits for the financial sector. Again, did many people at the RBI foresee the sort of interest rate declines that we have seen?*

A. Interest rate declines were supported by a low inflationary environment, and RBI's desire to provide maximum support to growth. This was a very deliberate policy and fortunately, it worked.

7. *Many people ascribe the turnaround in banks solely to the decline in interest rates and the windfall gains from investment in securities. They believe the interest-rate declines mask huge problems at PSBs. Yet, there is impressionistic evidence that operational efficiencies and service standards at PSBs have improved. What is your assessment?*

A. Operational efficiency and service standards have certainly improved. However, the transaction costs of PSBs are still high. Most PSBs have also created investment fluctuation reserves to provide for contingencies, such as, turnaround in interest rate. At present, there are no great worries on this account.

8. *Studies of trends in efficiency in the Indian banking system in the post-deregulation period reveal a mixed picture. Spreads have declined a little over the second half of the nineties relative to the first half but the real lending rate shows no consistent trend. Some would say that the decimation of the stock market has eased the pressure on the banking system to become more efficient and that the real test of banking system efficiency is yet to come. Any comments?*

A. The situation is more complicated than that. In any case, stock markets have been quite buoyant, recently. The real reasons why costs of banking have not come down more than they have is because of several constraints, e.g. too many non-remunerative branches, overstaffing, lack of adequate technology, infrastructure and managerial inefficiency in several banks. There is, of course, some progress; but the process of change in our country is generally slower than it should be.

9. *There is talk of lack of profit orientation in the public sector system. Yet, it is not realised that the Indian banking system is among the most profitable ones in the world, as statistics cited in the Report on Currency and Finance (2001-02) clearly show. Would you feel that there is also a tendency to magnify the issues of intermediation costs and NPA levels in Indian banking by comparing these with international levels? How does it matter that we compare unfavourably on these as long as the profitability is still high?*

A. Intermediation costs do matter particularly if profitability is also high. These make our interest rates higher than they could be, and thus affect the competitiveness of our products abroad.

10. *On the subject of NPA levels about which you have had a great deal to say yourself, do you have a sense that the concern with NPAs is translating itself into an aversion to lending and a preference for investment in government securities? More broadly, do you see trends in loan growth and especially growth in loans to small units, as an area of concern?*

A. The slow growth in credit, particularly to small and medium sectors, which do not have easy access to the corporate bond markets, is certainly a matter of concern. Banks must pay greater attention to the requirements of such borrowers, subject to normal banking parameters.

11. *The subject of governance at PSBs has rightly come to the fore. You have indicated that one of the problems is that the CEO cannot be removed by the board as he is appointed by the government. Suppose this was changed and the CEO became accountable to the board. Government would still have a say as government representatives would be on the board. Would you say that there should be no government representation on the board? Or that government should be represented by professionals and not by bureaucrats?*

A. Government as the owner should continue to have representation on the boards. That is not the problem. It is the question of accountability of CEO to the board as a whole, and not exclusively to government at the political level. Similarly, constitution of the board itself requires much more attention to professionalism than is the case now.

12. *You have observed that corporate governance is unsatisfactory at private banks as well. Some would say it is hard to tell where the problem is worse—at PSBs or private banks. Can we not effect significant improvements in governance at PSBs by ensuring that appointments to boards are drawn mainly from a pool approved by the RBI?*

A. I would also like RBI to stay at 'arm's length' from the process of board appointments. If the government so wishes, an independent committee of country's top serving or retired professionals from different fields (including central banking and judiciary) may be appointed to draw up a pool through a transparent process. Such a committee could be appointed, say, once in three years for a specified period and submit its recommendations to the Government.

13. *Part of the motivation for reducing government's stake in PSBs to 33 per cent was to free banks from some of the shackles that go with majority government ownership. If banks can turn around as effectively as they have done despite government ownership—and in the case of the three weak banks, perhaps because of the assurance provided by government ownership—does the case for dilution of government holding not become that much weaker today?*

A. No, not at all. The case of dilution is two-fold: (a) need for infusion of additional capital through the market in line with increase in assets rather than through higher fiscal deficit, and (b) greater public accountability for all banks, including good banks.

The case for dilution has very little to do with some banks being 'weak' in the public sector as some banks in the private sector are also weak.

14. *A constant refrain in any discussion of public sector units, including banks, is unattractive remuneration packages. This, it is said, would keep PSBs from attracting the right quality of top management talent. The Verma committee on weak banks wanted bankers from outside the PSB system to be brought in at market pay levels. In the case of UTI also it was said that without professional fund managers being inducted with an attractive compensation package, there was no hope. Yet, we have seen these institutions bounce back under leadership*

that was remunerated as per public sector norms. Is the issue of incentives, perhaps, overdone? Should we not be looking at incentives in broader, non-pecuniary terms as well?

A. The question of remuneration of PSB executives, including CEOs, being in line with modern-day requirements in a competitive environment is a real one. The minimum requirement is to delink the package from civil service pay scales—it does not make any sense any more. At the same time, going all the way to 'market' pay scales is also impractical because in PSBs there are vertical linkages among pay scales of different categories of staff, including clerical staff.

15. *The received wisdom at the commencement of reforms was that consolidation among PSBs was inevitable. Given that most banks are able to improve their performance as they are, would you see still see this as a pressing issue?*

A. It is not a pressing issue, but from a long-term point of view, the issue has to be addressed. There has to be rationalisation of the branch network and better focus on maximising the comparative advantage of different banks—large and small. Where there is unnecessary duplication of work or branches, without corresponding gain in terms of better customer service or credit delivery, consolidation is desirable.

16. *My last question to you—is there any aspect of financial sector reforms about which you are less than satisfied, where you feel that, perhaps, more could have been done in your tenure.*

A. By and large, I am satisfied. But whether, on balance, progress during my tenure was reasonable or not is for you, other experts and the public to judge.

Ownership and Performance

Tough call for Verma

Another committee, more recommendations? Talk about restructuring of public sector banks has been with us for so long that it's hard to stifle a yawn on news that the Reserve Bank of India has appointed a committee to consider the cases of weak banks in the system. Except that the job has been entrusted to a banker who commands great respect, MS Verma, former Chairman of SBI. It is a tough call for the Committee as it can't avoid ruffling feathers all round.

Narasimham-II had suggested that weak banks be recapitalized and then merged with strong banks. But after the experiences PNB and SBI have had with mergers foisted on them by RBI, the banking system has developed a proper horror of the prospect. It is not just a matter of differences in systems and processes; integrating the weak bank's personnel into the stronger bank has tended to sap the energies of top management. Narasimham-II had proposed a Restructuring Commission if mergers failed to make headway, and that's what the Verma Committee is.

The Tarapore Committee's proposal that weak banks be confined to narrow banking—that is, they invest incremental deposits in government securities and refrain from making further loans—has deservedly been given wide berth. Narrow banking would spell death by slow strangulation for the banks concerned, and, possibly, for some of their clients. Besides, there is no certainty that accumulated losses would be frozen at a given level; at best, losses would not rise as fast they would with continued lending. That doesn't solve the problem, it only postpones the day of reckoning.

What are the options open to the Verma committee ? One is to simply close down weak banks, with the government taking a huge hit. This option is not only unworkable, it is undesirable. Closures of big banks impose significant costs on the economy. When a bank is closed, the bigger firms, who are serviced by multiple banks, can get others to pick up the slack. But smaller firms suffer serious dislocation; besides, information embodied in financial assets is lost to the economy. It is not easy to accept the implied losses when you remember that bank capital is eight per cent of assets, and hence a mere 10 per cent drop in asset value can wipe out the bank.

So, the challenge in dealing with weak banks is to find ways in which good assets can be kept afloat. Recapitalization followed by a change in management is an obvious option. This may work for banks in which a few people at the top are the problem. But, in other cases, where the problem goes right down the ladder and encompasses collusive union leaders as well, more drastic surgery would be required. In such cases, is there any alternative to merger or outright closure ?

There is, if we stay focused on keeping good assets going. We need to consider sale of sound assets piecemeal to whoever is interested—public sector banks, private banks, foreign banks. If Bank of America can find buyers for its retail business in India, the idea of selling corporate loans should not appear far-fetched. Another possibility worth exploring is sale of select branches of weak banks to those interested in extending their retail reach at a price considerably lower than current costs.

Closure must happen only after the good parts of the bank have been sold. This will accomplish several things. *One*, it minimises externalities and preserves information built over decades. *Two*, it reduces the costs of closure to government, instead spreading these costs across all players in the system. *Three*, as some of the labour will be transferred along with assets sold, the numbers affected by closure will be lower, and also the cash garnered by asset sales could help sweeten severance packages. *Four*, it would be easier to interest other banks in pieces of a weak bank than to persuade them to swallow a whole bank.

Dealing with weak banks will not end the banking system's problems for all time. Addressing the factors that created the weakness is equally important. This means depoliticising appointments of bank Boards by creating an Appointments Board as recommended by Narasimham-II. Above all, as pointed out ad nauseum in recent years, it means overhauling a legal system in which recoveries are well nigh impossible. Hopefully, the Verma Committee will have something to say about these, too.

February 18, 1999

Public ownership the key

Three of India's public sector banks—Indian Bank, UCO Bank and United Bank of India—are bleeding badly despite capital infusions to the tune of Rs 6,740 crore since the onset of economic reforms in 1991-92. The knee-jerk response, in today's climate of liberalization, would be to prescribe one or other of the market solutions: closure, merger, privatisation.

It is to the credit of the MS Verma committee on weak public sector banks that it rejects these solutions in favour of comprehensive restructuring within the domain of public ownership. It does so on grounds that are economic rather than political. Closure would impose huge costs on the economy because of banks' well-known externalities. Merger would debilitate the stronger bank. Privatisation is infeasible because there would be no takers given the prohibitively high costs of restructuring.

The committee's proposal for restructuring weak banks at a cost of Rs 5,500 crore will draw howls of protest from those who believe it sidesteps the central problem of public ownership. It is well, therefore, to place the cost of shoring up Indian banks in perspective.

Adding the Rs 20,000 crore spent already on bank recapitalisation to the amount proposed by the committee, the total cost would amount to under 2.3 per cent of GDP in 1995, a rough middle point in the recapitalisation process. This cost compares very favourably indeed with the costs of recapitalising banks in East Asia following the 1997 crisis, estimated to be in the range of 18-34 per cent of GDP, and with the average cost of 10 per cent of GDP in the period 1981-94 in 14 countries where banks were predominantly under private ownership.

At the very least, these comparisons indicate that private ownership is no insurance against banking crises. Banks are inherently crisis-prone and few countries have been free from problems in the banking sector over a longish period. The test for these very fragile institutions is whether they have contributed to the overall economic performance without inflicting disproportionate costs of reconstruction. India's public sector banks would not fail this test.

It is not just that public sector banks shoulder enormous social obligations. The more remarkable thing about their performance is that the Indian banking system has defied the correlation seen elsewhere between financial liberalisation and banking fragility. The evidence is that bank deregulation, by lowering franchise values and inducing banks to take greater risks, makes a banking crisis highly probable.

If this has not happened in India, is because public ownership, far from being the bane of the banking system, has helped contain systemic risk following deregulation. Government ownership of banks made possible their swift recapitalization even as deregulation was set in motion and this ensured that growth in assets was not hobbled by requirements of capital adequacy. It enabled banks to retain depositor confidence in the wake of poor financial results in the initial years of reform. Above all, the cautious attitude towards risk-taking that goes with government ownership has helped stave off the excesses that have proved the undoing of banking systems elsewhere.

While making for stability in the banking system, government ownership has not come in the way of improved financial performance either. Profitability at 27 public sector banks, measured by the ratio of net profit to total assets, went up from -1 per cent in 1992-93 to 0.77 per cent in 1997-98 despite losses incurred by the weak banks. This again is in stark contrast to the experience in other countries where franchise values have tended to decline following deregulation.

It is necessary to view the weak banks' problems in this broader perspective in fielding breezy generalisations about public sector banks and demands for whole-hogging privatisation. Some banks may have to tap the markets down the road in order to augment capital and this may mean letting government ownership fall below 51 per cent. In general, however, it is not obvious that reducing the government's stake below 51 per cent should be a priority in a context in which performance is showing an upswing.

Banking sector reform must be informed by the heightened recognition today of the trade-off between stability and efficiency in banking. It must also be informed by the realisation that the present market structure—of dominant public sector banks, private sector banks and foreign banks—conduces to a desirable trade-off. The pursuit of privatisation in disregard of the overriding requirement of financial stability is the last tning we need at the moment.

October 14, 2003

Make it bank-specific

Given the position of the fisc, the newly elected government could have done without the bill for Rs 5,500 crore presented by the MS Verma committee for resuscitating the three weak public sector banks—Indian Bank, UBI and UCO Bank. Unless the government wishes to pursue other options, the best it can now hope for is that the restructuring exercise resolves the problems at the weak banks once and for all.

That said, there is no reason for the government to stick to the specifics in the report. While the basic framework is unexceptionable, the package for each bank must be designed so as to achieve a turnaround in a reasonable timeframe, say, five years. This may require making departures from the committee's broad recommendations in each case.

In addressing the question of future viability, it is necessary to identify the central factor that has led up to the present weakness in each instance: is it mismanagement or weak business fundamentals? The Verma committee report is not terribly helpful in this respect.

Much of its litany of the causes of weakness—lack of succession planning, short tenures for management, poor risk management, etc.—would apply to most public sector banks. The Verma report does not tell us why these created serious problems only at the three banks in question. If only the committee had framed the problem in these terms, it would have understood that at all the three banks NPAs got out of hand at some point for reasons *other than the ones it has listed.*

So what caused NPAs to get out of hand? At least Indian Bank is paying for the sins of one top management dispensation. The bank went on a lending boom in the period 1988-92; the related NPAs started showing up in the mid-nineties. The fundamentals of Indian Bank, which has a strong franchise in the attractive southern market, are sound. The strategy for the bank must be to rebuild its book with quality assets. The bank needs to cut its workforce to gain breathing space although such a reduction must factor in the required growth in assets in the future.

As for UBI and UCO Bank, neither has suffered a particularly bad episode of mismanagement. Locational disadvantages are undoubtedly a big factor in their NPA problem (UBI has 87 per cent of its branches in the eastern region and UCO Bank 43 per cent). So the plight of these two banks raises a fundamental issue: is it possible for banks whose exposure is predominantly in the eastern region to be viable at all?

The east provides deposits in abundance but not quality borrowers. Geographical expansion is an obvious option but both the banks have failed at this. Their best bet now is to become regional specialists. In this role, they will have to focus on the lower and middle segments as the committee suggests.

For one thing, they cannot hope to compete with the bigger banks for the larger borrowers. Secondly, if they are to build a diversified portfolio within the east itself, they cannot afford a concentration of large accounts. From the standpoint of managing banking risk in a low-growth area, it makes more sense to have large accounts in the east as part of diversified portfolios at banks that can compete nationally. This means the two banks may have to shed many of their larger accounts in favour of the bigger banks.

If this principle is accepted, the government may need to go beyond the recommendations of the Verma committee where these two banks are concerned. Not just the workforce and the branch network but also the loan book will have to be downsized with UBI requiring more downsizing than UCO Bank which has a sizeable presence outside the east.

If this is not to translate into a bigger hit for the government than estimated by the Verma committee, pieces of the banks' assets will have to be sold with some of the staff being transferred with the assets. These assets could be big loans as well as branches that mainly garner deposits. The proceeds could be used to gradually increase exposure in the lower and middle segments and to fund VRS schemes along more generous lines than proposed by the committee.

The focus must be on finding lasting solutions while minimizing the pain to the workforce. Success in meeting these twin objectives may well hinge on refining the Verma committee's generic prescriptions into bank-specific strategies.

October 21, 1999

Questionable ranking

Bankers are not amused. The Verma committee's ranking of public sector banks on weakness is distinctly unflattering to many. There is consternation over the low rank accorded to SBI. Some banks that are due to tap the capital markets shortly are miffed at the suggestion that they are close to distress. The Verma committee's approach to ranking banks, therefore, merits scrutiny.

A bank is weak in the sense of being close to failure if it does not have capital in excess of the likely drop in the value of its assets, the drop being measured by accumulated losses and net NPAs. It runs the risk of reaching this state if it has made operating losses for, say, three years consecutively. Hence the suggestion made by the Narasimham Committee-II that banks be characterised as weak if they satisfied either of these two criteria.

The Verma committee recommends that a broader assessment of weakness be used in conjunction with these two criteria. The committee evaluates the 27 public sector banks in respect of seven parameters for 1997-98 and 1998-99 based on whether they satisfy the following: capital adequacy ratio of 8 per cent for both the years; coverage ratio of 0.50 per cent; and the median level of five efficiency parameters. Banks are then classified into five categories. At the extremes are those that satisfy all parameters and those that satisfy none. In between come three categories based on how many of the six parameters a bank fails to satisfy after complying with capital adequacy: one or two; three or four; and five or six.

Consider some results. SBI falls in the second category from the top in 1997-98 (and in the third in 1998-99). For 1997-98, it satisfies all parameters except one, net interest margin, while Dena Bank meets all seven parameters and is placed in the highest category. Yet SBI's return on assets (ROA) in that year, 1.04, is way above Dena Bank's 0.86. Was SBI weaker than Dena Bank in 1997-98 ?

Or take the public sector's outstanding performer, Corporation Bank. It had the highest ROA (1.43) in 1998-99. Yet, it is ranked one category below Oriental Bank of Commerce (ROA: 1.20) and State Bank of Patiala (ROA: 0.99) just because its value on one parameter, net interest margin, is below the median value. For 1998-99, State Bank of Bikaner and Jaipur is placed below PNB athough the former is superior on three critical parameters: capital adequacy ratio, coverage ratio and ROA.

The substantive issue here is this: are all parameters relevant (or equally relevant) to ranking a bank? SBI might opt to have a lower net interest margin as it has the advantage of higher volumes. If it ends up with a higher ROA than competitors such as Dena Bank, that means it has a winning strategy. Similarly, for a bank that is strong on fee-based services, a relatively lower net interest margin arising from lower loan rates could be a source of competitive advantage; it would signify strength, not weakness.

Parameters such as ROA are resultants that come out of managing a number of discretionary parameters such as net interest margin, cost ratios etc. Evaluating a bank on the basis of the number of discretionary parameters it satisfies can be misleading. What matters, ultimately, is that a bank has adequate capital and ends up with a desired ROA consistent with an acceptable risk profile. Most other parameters are to be managed in ways consistent with a bank's strengths and its strategy; their values need not be superior to median values.

The examples cited earlier indicate that the Verma committee's ranking of banks is questionable. But the bigger concern must be that, by adopting a methodology that suggests that as many as 15 banks are in distress or a notch away from it, the Verma report might create a gratuitous impression of pervasive weakness among public sector banks. Union Bank of India has a capital adequacy ratio of 10; its post-tax ROA of 0.51 is comparable to the average pre-tax ROA of 0.63 for 44 banks in the Euro area in 1998. To call it an underperformer is a fair characterisation. But "showing strong signs of distress"?

There *is* an issue of underperformance and it needs to be addressed. Nothing is to be gained, however, by undermining confidence in a sector in which confidence is everything. The RBI needs to review the Verma committee's methodology.

October 28, 1999

More than a banking problem

The RBI is keen to shore up banks' profits—or at least prevent an erosion of these. That is the unstated motivation behind the reduction in the Cash Reserve Ratio (CRR) in the latest credit policy. The Rs 7,000 crore released by the CRR cut will boost banks' bottomlines by fetching them about Rs 250-350 crore on short-term instruments.

More importantly, the CRR cut will keep rates from hardening as the government concludes its borrowing programme for the year. At least the RBI must hope it does. Any rise in interest rates would dent banks' profits because of the depreciation to be provided on securities marked to market. The impact would be particularly severe on the three weak banks whose holdings of government securities are a way above the statutory requirement of 25 per cent of liabilities.

The RBI is right to be concerned about banks' bottomlines. Figures provided by the Verma committee reveal that profits at the 27 public sector banks (PSBs) declined by 35 per cent in 1998-99 relative to the previous year. But the RBI's pre-emptive strike against a rise in interest rates can at best stem the decline in banks' profits. This is not enough. The decline needs to be reversed. For this to happen, the factors depressing profits at PSBs in the wake of deregulation need to be understood.

The fall in spreads—from 3.22 per cent of total assets in 1991-92 to 2.91 per cent in 1997-98—is one factor. Loss of market share is another: PSBs' share of total credit dropped from 56 per cent in 1991-92 to 50 per cent in 1997-98. Both of these are wholly expected consequences of—and indeed part of the rationale for—bank deregulation. The trouble is that the third factor has failed to materialize. The overall loan cake has not grown fast enough to compensate for either declining spreads or diminished market share.

In its annual report for 1998-99, the RBI draws attention to signs of a deceleration in non-food credit that mirrors the pronounced slowdown in industrial growth over the past three years. Between 1995-96 and 1998-99, non-food credit grew at a compound annual growth rate of 13 per cent compared to

17 per cent in the period 1991-92 to 1995-96. Taking the nineties as a whole, the surge in credit on which deregulation is predicated has not happened. On the contrary, growth in non-food credit has slowed to 15.4 per cent compared to growth of 16.8 per cent in the period 1981-91. The experience elsewhere has been that credit expanded sharply once financial liberalization was set in motion and indeed the problem in many countries was a runaway boom in lending.

Whether the decline in loan growth is the cause or the effect of the slowdown in industry has been debated. The RBI annual report does mention supply-side factors such as stiffer prudential standards for lending as part of the explanation for tardy loan growth. But it is quite emphatic that it is demand-side factors that are mainly responsible. It finds strong evidence in the period April 1995 to March 1999 of industrial growth (with one quarter lag) leading the expansion in non-food credit growth rather than otherwise.

The RBI annual report notes that another factor holding down loan growth is the depressed state of the capital market. With corporates unable to raise resources from the capital market, the debt-equity ratio of 807 large public limited companies increased from 56 per cent in 1995-96 to 60 per cent in 1997-98. A rising debt-equity ratio leads to slower loan growth in two ways: it makes corporates wary of taking on more loans and it discourages banks from increasing loan exposures to corporates.

So, if the financial health of public sector banks today is unsatisfactory, an important causatory factor is sluggishness in the economy at large which translates into slower growth in loans. It follows that weaknesses in banking cannot be tackled without addressing the very real problem of disappointing industrial growth.

The focus today is on improving operational efficiencies through reforms such as lowering the government's ownership to below 50 per cent and reduction in manpower. But how much can be achieved and how quickly is open to question. Reformist ardour—and certainly any impulse towards bashing public sector banks—must be tempered by the realization that the fundamental solutions to banks' problems lie beyond the purview of bank management.

November 11, 1999

Now, for some bouquets

The Finance Minister has been receiving more than his fair share of brickbats for his latest budget. He deserves bouquets for at least one item: clarity on bank privatisation.

The budget is unambiguous about what the present government intends this to mean. The government will bring its shareholding in nationalised banks down to 33 per cent in line with the recommendations of Narasimham Committee (II) but this will be done without "changing the public sector character of banks and while ensuring that fresh issue of shares is widely held by the public".

In subsequent utterances, Yashwant Sinha has elaborated on this pronouncement. The government's stake will be lowered through fresh issue of stock and not by divestment of the government's shareholding. There will be no transfer of controlling interest to any private entity. Not least, the government will retain the right to appoint bank Chairmen and may even reserve veto powers for itself through the mechanism of a 'golden share'.

Now that the government has revealed its mind on bank privatisation, two things need to happen. *One*, the government must come up with a similar statement of intent on financial institutions (FIs). *Two*, the government and the RBI must put in place structures that make for improved governance in public sector financial intermediaries. As banks and FIs hold the key to governance in the non-financial sector, these are matters whose importance goes well beyond the financial sector.

RBI Deputy Governor, Y Venugopal Reddy, has dissected the subject with characteristic thoroughness in one of his speeches (Corporate Governance in Financial Sector, June 14, 1999). Dr Reddy points to a number of areas where changes could make for qualitative improvement.

The corporatisation of banks and FIs must rank high on the agenda. This means, for instance, that SBI and IDBI would be governed by the Companies Act instead of by separate statutes, as is the case today. Conflicts between the RBI's ownership and regulatory roles must be resolved, implying such things as removal of RBI nominees from bank boards. Bank boards need to be strengthened. Regulation must be adapted to the requirements of globalisation and universal banking.

The broader point of Dr. Reddy's exposition, of course, is that the issue of governance at public sector banks and FIs need not be viewed in either/or terms: complete removal of government control or nothing. Enormous scope for improvement in governance exists with the government's retaining a 33 per cent stake, without the downside risks that go with taking away the public sector character of the institutions.

The point seems to be lost on those clamouring for a wholesale withdrawal of government control in the financial sector. The issue the government's critics need to address is whether we can afford a monitoring vacuum in the transition to autonomous professional management. A transfer of control to a dominant private sector owner is not on, given the RBI's reluctance to allow industrial houses into banking. To expect government to transfer control to foreign banks in as strategic a sector as banking is unrealistic. The only alternative to having a modicum of government control is leaving things entirely in the hands of professionals, a course that is fraught with risk.

Some of the risks are exemplified by the problems uncovered by the RBI inspection report on the high-flying ICICI, whose management is today neither accountable to government nor faced with demanding institutional shareholders. The RBI has reportedly drawn attention to inflation of profits through understatement of NPAs, questionable risk management practices, concentration of sanctioning authority in a few hands, etc. One shudders to think of what the outcome might be if these practices were to become the norm at nationalised banks once they lost their public sector character.

Another serious risk is the possible impact on banks' bottom lines of ICICI-style compensation packages. A moral hazard that goes with conferring greater autonomy on management in the public sector is that those at the top and planning their retirement are liable to raise compensation steeply in the name of 'retaining talent' and with scant regard for long-term viability—the 'after me, the deluge' syndrome.

As management everywhere regards itself as extremely talented, the most outrageous increases are apt to occur at the top—as happened in British privatisation. If, by retaining the public sector character of banks, compensation can be kept within reasonable bounds, that is no small blessing.

March 16, 2000

Bolster banks' capital

Commercial bank lending to business has slowed down in the nineties. Non-food credit has grown at 15 per cent compared to 18 per cent in the eighties. The deceleration, as the RBI's *Annual Report* for 1998-99 points out, owes to both demand-side and supply-side factors, with the former dominating. With signs of an industrial recovery in recent months, it is important now to focus on the supply side—and to act boldly to remove constraints on credit expansion.

A key constraint is banks' marked preference for investment in government securities. Such investment is nearly Rs 60,000 crore in excess of the SLR requirement. The *Report on Currency and Finance* (1998-99) cites two possible reasons for this preference. *One,* banks' aversion to risk at a time when reducing NPAs is a priority. *Two,* the narrowing differential between the PLR and the weighted-average interest rate on government securities, which diminishes banks' appetite for loans. The differential fell to 0.14 percentage points in 1998-99 from 2.75 percentage points in 1995-96.

How valid are these propositions? Going by PLR reductions can be deceptive. Banks may announce headline—grabbing reductions in PLRs in order to humour the RBI (which, in turn, would like to humour the Finance Minister) while simultaneously pruning the list of prime borrowers. They may leave rates untouched for borrowers below prime grade (effectively increasing the spread over PLR for them) or they may lower the grades of some borrowers at the time of renewal. Any of these moves would be reflected in a relative increase in exposures to borrowers in lower grades.

There is reason to believe that this is indeed happening. *The Report on Currency and Finance* mentions that as high as 28.5 per cent of bank advances fell in the interest range of 18 per cent or more in March 1998—or a spread of at least four per cent over the five major banks' PLR of 14 per cent at the time. Prior to 1993, the report notes, the corresponding proportion was a mere 2 per cent!

This does call into question the first proposition, about banks' increased aversion to risk. It also suggests that the weighted-average interest rate across different classes of borrowers may not have declined as much as the PLR. So, the proposition that loans have become unattractive relative to government securities is not convincing either.

It is more plausible that excess investment in securities today has to do with capital adequacy requirements. One-third of the 27 public sector banks had capital adequacy ratios of 10 or less and two-thirds 11 or less in 1998-99. My discussions with bankers suggest that most of the latter may fail to meet the minimum capital adequacy ratio of 9 if their investment in government securities declined to the mandatory level of 25 per cent.

In such a situation, banks are bound to have excess investment in government securities. Banks everywhere would like a minimal cushion in respect of capital adequacy. Here they have little choice as they are in no position to source capital from the market at a pinch.

It follows that if supply-side constraints are not to inhibit the ongoing recovery, bolstering banks' capital is of vital importance. Three steps are required—*First,* the government must swiftly recapitalise the three weak banks. *Secondly,* now that the government is committed to reducing its equity in banks to 33 per cent, banks must be enabled to tap the market at the earliest.

It is unrealistic, however, to expect a whole lot of banks to do so quickly enough. The government must, therefore, seriously consider a *third* step, namely, augmenting capital at banks with capital adequacy ratios of 10 or less. This undoubtedly goes against the government's grain but there is a strong case in favour of it.

Recapitalisation does not entail any immediate cash outflow for the government as the proceeds are invested in government bonds. On a modest infusion of Rs 3,000 crore, the annual interest outflow would be, say, Rs 300 crore. This is a negligible cost compared to the impact on industrial activity of Rs 35,000 crore of additional loans (and would easily be recouped through higher tax collections). Moreover, banks so recapitalised would have stronger balance sheets when they approach the market and this would get reflected in higher values for the government's shareholdings.

The industrial recovery must be sustained but, also, it provides an opportunity to strengthen public sector banks. The government must grab it with both hands.

May 11, 2000

No dithering, please

Once the ritualistic hoopla over the latest credit policy statement dies down, the RBI will need to confront a fundamental issue: how to bolster capital at Public Sector Banks (PSBs).

In the last budget, the government had committed itself to retaining the public sector character of banks even while reducing its stakes to 33 per cent. The reduction, it said, would take place through fresh public issues rather than through sale of government stakes to private parties.

However, only one PSB has since tapped the market. If PSBs cannot mobilise capital from what appears to be a doomed primary market and they will not get additional capital from the government either, strategic sales—most likely, to foreign banks—will become inevitable.

If foreign players were eventually to enter the banking sector through the privatisation route, that would be no surprise. Indeed, the surprise about the Indian banking system is that, seven years into financial sector liberalisation, this has not already happened.

The IMF's *International Capital Markets* (September 2000) has a chapter, "The role of foreign banks in emerging markets", that shows how unique the Indian experience is. In the 1990s, foreign bank ownership increased dramatically in Central Europe and Latin America and significantly in Asia.

In 1999, foreign control (defined as foreign ownership of more than 50 per cent of equity) averaged 52 per cent of bank assets in three countries in Central Europe, up from 8 per cent in 1994. Foreign control rose from 8 per cent to 25 per cent in seven countries in Latin America and from 1.6 per cent to 6 per cent in three East Asian countries.

As important are the reasons why this happened. The report notes that in several countries restrictions on foreign bank entry were eased in order to improve efficiency in the banking system. However, such easing was "often triggered by the need to help reduce the costs of restructuring and recapitalizing banks following a major crisis".

The Indian experience with financial sector liberalisation has been refreshingly different. Although studies point to a high probability of a full-blown crisis within five to seven years of financial sector liberalisation, the Indian banking system has not run into one.

One reason is that, unlike in many other countries, financial sector liberalisation was not accompanied by capital account convertibility. Another is that government ownership facilitated the swift recapitalisation of PSBs ahead of liberalisation and this, along with prudential safeguards, helped pre-empt excessive risk-taking in the banking sector.

Then, several factors ensured that declines in margins were not unduly steep in the aftermath of liberalisation: the prior existence of private (including foreign bank) competition, the relatively low level of disintermediation and PSBs' access to large volumes of low-cost deposits.

At the same time, the banking sector has seen an improvement in efficiency: one measure, the ratio of net interest income to assets, declined from 3.22 per cent in 1991-92 to 2.81 per cent in 1998-99 at PSBs. The ratio declined at private and foreign banks as well. In other words, an improvement in efficiency has gone hand in hand with stability in banking. The compulsions for privatisation—and especially for a bigger role for foreign banks—are thus hardly as strong as they were elsewhere.

However, PSBs will need capital going forward. Of the 22 out of 27 PSBs with capital adequacy of over 10 on March 2000, quite a few must have slipped below by now. The government must decide whether, in meeting their requirements, it intends to build on the demonstrated strengths of PSBs. Or, whether it wants to go down the privatisation route.

If the former, it will need to recapitalise some of the PSBs. The costs incurred thus far on bank recapitalisation (under 3 per cent of GDP), it is worth emphasizing, are extremely low by international standards. Alternatively, if the government is not sanguine about PSBs' prospects, it must prepare them for privatisation.

The worst outcome would be to dither and create conditions for distress sale of banks. The current policy owes to the RBI's low-key articulation of the case for retaining the public sector character of banks. It is up to the RBI now to spell out how this policy can be made compatible with the need to augment capital.

October 12, 2000

Recapitalisation blues

The government is reportedly set to amend the statute in order to lower its stakes in Public Sector Banks (PSBs) to 33 per cent, thereby enabling banks to raise additional capital. Any jubilation on this count would be misplaced. It is virtually impossible for banks to source their requirements entirely from the market. This begs the question whether the issue of bank recapitalisation has been thought through carefully enough.

According to a recent news report (*Times of India*, October 22), the RBI estimates the current risk-weighted assets of PSBs at around Rs 3,35,000 crore and expects this to double over the next five years.

The general reckoning is that today the majority of PSBs must be close to capital adequacy of 9. Even this level is attained only because banks hold excess SLR securities that require considerably lower capital than loans.

If banks are to shed excess SLR securities and operate comfortably at the future capital adequacy norm of 10, they would need additional capital of at least two per cent of risk weighted assets—or Rs 6,700 crore today and another Rs 6,700 crore over the next five years. Add the Rs 5,500 crore budgeted for the weak banks and the estimate of Rs 20,000 crore mentioned in the TOI report seems credible.

Excluding the weak banks' requirements (which the government is committed to meeting), we are talking of an immediate capital infusion of Rs 6,700 crore. It requires extraordinary naïvete to suppose that PSBs can raise capital of this order under the present market conditions, leave alone raise it at prices that bank management finds reasonable. (The chairman of SBI balks at raising capital at SBI's current multiple of under five).

It follows that if the government wishes to retain the public sector character of PSBs, it must seriously consider another bout of recapitalisation. The suggestion will cause many to recoil in horror but that is because misconceptions on the subject abound. It may be useful to address some of these.

Recapitalisation of insolvent banks does not constitute deadweight or economic loss. It is only a transfer within the economy. The 'cost' of recapitalisation here is meaningful only as a measure of the severity of problems in the banking sector. The economic cost is, in fact, the output lost because loans are not available or are not properly allocated.

Nevertheless, recapitalisation of insolvent banks and also in general by government is opposed on grounds of fiscal stringency. The argument is rather weak. Because the proceeds of recapitalisation are invested in government securities, there is no immediate cash outflow. There will be an impact down the road on account of interest costs on recapitalisation bonds (say, 10 per cent of the capital infusion). On Rs 6700 crore of recapitalisation, this would amount to Rs 670 crore annually-hardly fisc-shattering.

The fiscal impact becomes significant when recapitalisation costs as a proportion of GDP are high. The costs of recapitalisation incurred thus far in India (2 per cent of 1996 GDP) are way below than the average cost of 6 per cent of GDP for the industrial countries and the cost of over 10 per cent of GDP in a range of emerging markets. Another Rs 6,700 crore (or Rs 12,200 crore, the weak banks included) would not disgrace the Indian record—or unduly strain the fisc.

A weightier objection to recapitalisation by government is that it accentuates moral hazard in banking. But this argument holds mainly in contexts in which banking systems have been devastated and the real economy, in turn, has suffered a major shock in consequence.

Such is not the case here. If we leave aside the three weak banks, recapitalisation is needed today not because banks have collapsed taking the economy down with them. It is needed in order to comply with increasingly onerous international capital norms. It is the future loss of output arising from the failure to recapitalise that we need to fear more than any moral hazard caused by recapitalisation.

The situation thus cries out for a further bout of recapitalisation. To oppose this, you need to contend that the end result will be a weaker, not stronger, banking system. This contention can be sustained not by the post-reform record of PSBs but by hostility towards the public sector per se. It would be folly to allow such ideological bias to prevail over economic sense.

October 26, 2000

Pessimism not warranted

Living as do in the globalised village, with its instant transmission of information, it is easy to make the mistake of supposing that trends in evidence elsewhere must have major implications for us, too. This often results in flawed perceptions of the realities here and in inappropriate prescriptions.

The tendency is discernible in discussions on Indian banking. In the industrial world, increased competition for household savings and disintermediation have compelled banks to remake themselves. From this, it is but a short step to suggesting that Indian banks are likewise under siege and must adapt or perish. Yet the threat from these forces in the immediate future can be exaggerated in our context.

The core banking functions, taking deposits and making loans, have been severely undermined in the industrial world. Non-bank financial institutions have lured savings away from depositors. In the US, where this trend has gone farthest, banks' share of household financial assets declined by 50 per cent to 18 per cent between 1980 and 1995. (*International Capital Markets, September 1998, IMF*). This has translated into a steep decline in bank deposits as a share of liabilities in the industrial countries (except Japan and the UK). In the US, the ratio declined from 76 per cent to 59 per cent.

On the asset side, disintermediation, that is, firms accessing the capital market for funds, has caused loans as a proportion of assets to decline. The ratio fell from 63 to 59 per cent in the US between 1980 and 1995, with interest income to total income declining even more steeply.

How serious is the threat to the core banking functions in India? To take deposits first. True, the ratio of bank deposits to household financial assets has been declining but at 37 per cent in 1998-99 it is still twice the ratio in the US. True also that another measure of banks' dominance, share of deposits in resources mobilised, shows a decline—from 77 per cent in 1991-92 to 59 per cent in 1996-97.

But the key issue, from the standpoint of banks' profitability, is how these declines in market shares are reflected in the share of deposits relative to costlier funds. The RBI's *Report on Trend and Progress in Banking* has only recently started providing data on consolidated balance sheets of banks, so it is not possible to compare over time. What can be stated confidently is that the ratio of deposits to total liabilities of 83 per cent for public sector banks (PSBs) in 1998-99 is much higher than in the industrial world. With the ratio at this level, it is hard to argue that there is a serious competitive threat to banks arising from loss of deposits.

It is on the asset side that Indian banks compare unfavourably with their counterparts in the industrial world. Loans constituted 39 per cent of assets at PSBs, which is much lower than in the industrial world. Indian banks' holdings of securities are higher (36 per cent at PSBs compared to 20 per cent in the US).

But this is not on account of disintermediation. It is mainly on account of reserve requirements, but also, as this column has argued earlier, because banks lack capital to back loan expansion. The positive side to this must not be overlooked: unlike in the industrial world, the potential is for the loan-to-assets ratio to rise once the fetters on credit expansion are eased.

Not only are the core banking functions under no serious threat but also spreads have held up remarkably well in the face of deregulation. Net interest income as a percentage of total assets at PSBs fell sharply from 3.22 in 1991-92 to 2.39 in 1992-93, but has risen since to 2.81 in 1998-99, despite the dip at SBI on account of one-off factors. This spread, it must be emphasised, is well above that in 15 out of 17 advanced economies for which the BIS provides data.

The preceding analysis points to two conclusions. *One,* pessimism about the outlook for Indian banks, especially PSBs, is not warranted. The potential combination of rapid loan growth and relatively high spreads provides an altogether more benign environment for banking than is available elsewhere today. *Two,* the prescriptions touted for PSBs-consolidation, diversification-can at best provide thin icing on the cake. At worst, these can be debilitating distractions. Indian banks' best bet is to focus in better ways on the core banking functions.

June 8, 2000

Sitting pretty for now

When the capital markets weep, banks laugh their way to, well, the bank. Much has been made of the challenge posed to banks in India by the rise of the capital market—or what is characterized as disintermediation. In reality, the disappointments occasioned by the capital market have meant that this challenge has remained muted so far. This does put Indian banks on a stronger wicket relative to what banks elsewhere had to cope with at the advent of financial liberalisation.

Banks face the threat of disintermediation on both the liability and asset sides. They may lose depositors to capital market-related savings instruments and they may lose borrowers as well to the capital market. The RBI *Annual Report* (1999-2000) devotes a box to the phenomenon. Its judgement: "the overall scenario does not still favour the view of financial disintermediation in motion".

The RBI report observes that, on the liability side, disintermediation has actually declined: a key measure, the ratio of aggregate bank deposits to GDP, increased from 40.3 per cent in 1990-91 to 41.7 per cent in 1999-2000. What is, perhaps, more material to banks is that deposits grew at a healthy 17.4 per cent per annum in 1991-2000, only slightly below the 18.1 per cent growth rate recorded on the lower base in the period 1981-90.

How does this square with the perception that banks have their work cut out for them in holding on to deposits? The RBI report notes that in the immediate post-reform years (1992-93 to 1996-97), banks did lose out to NBFCs, new public issues and mutual funds. Subsequently, however, "the disintermediation process dampened". (NBFCs are also intermediaries but here the focus is on bank-based intermediation versus the rest).

The *Report on Currency and Finance* (1998-99) provides detailed data on this up to 1996-97. Between 1990-91 and 1992-93, banks' share of resources mobilised dropped sharply from 78 per cent to 60 per cent. From 1992-93 to 1996-97, however, the decline was much smaller—1.6 percentage points. The annual report's observations suggest that in the three years since banks have regained some of the share lost earlier. But, taking the nineties as a whole, banks undoubtedly lost share.

However, the savings cake itself grew over the same period: the gross savings rate in the nineties averaged 23.9 per cent compared to the average of 20 per cent in the eighties. The combined effect of the two factors—banks' share of resources mobilised and the overall savings rate—has been that deposit growth has been running at close to the eighties' level. On the liability side, banks are sitting pretty for now.

Turn to the asset side. The RBI annual report notes that bank credit as a proportion of GDP declined from 24.3 per cent in 1990-91 to 22.4 per cent in 1999-2000. But this is because banks' investment in government securities (34.5 per cent) is in excess of SLR requirements (25 per cent).

While the RBI had in the past ascribed this excess to 'risk-aversion', it now concedes that higher capital adequacy norms are largely responsible—a point this column has long been hammering away at. In other words, the ratio of bank credit to GDP could be higher if banks were not constrained by lack of capital. Disintermediation is thus not a threat to the asset side of the balance sheet either.

That said, the structural shifts taking place in the economy do imply that banks could lose out on asset quality unless they are sufficiently agile. The large, old economy companies to which banks are exposed have declined in quality. At the same time, banks lack exposure to high quality, new economy companies.

Going by the *Annual Report*, the software and telecom sectors account for a mere Rs 3,000 crore out of total loans outstanding of Rs 200,000 crore for 50 selected scheduled commercial banks. Banks will need to step up exposure to the new economy while also becoming more adept at locating opportunities in the small and medium categories in the old economy.

Overall, the deposits are there and so are the lending opportunities. Elsewhere, rising disintermediation called forth dramatic responses to financial liberalisation—merger, diversification into investment banking, asset management etc. Banks here do not need as yet to mimic their counterparts elsewhere. They simply need to get better at the old, boring business of taking deposits and making loans.

November 9, 2000

Privatisation by stealth?

Following last week's bank strike, the government must hope that the clarifications it has provided on the proposed amendments to the Banking Companies Act will allay unions' fears about privatisation and fend off further disruption.

The government has emphasised that with its minimum stake pegged at 33 per cent and with no investor allowed to hold more than one per cent voting rights in a Public Sector Bank (PSB), it will retain control.

What will not be missed, however, is that the government is putting in place provisions that will facilitate a transfer of control at a future date and a change from the public sector character of banks. One provision will allow it to transfer its equity holding (not permitted under the present statute). Another will allow it to convert banks into companies under the Companies Act. So converted, banks in which the government's holding is less than 51 per cent will lose their public sector character (which does not happen under the Banking Companies Act).

The government says the planned dilution in its stakes is driven entirely by the need to augment capital at PSBs. It does not have the money to fund banks, so banks must raise capital on their own. The issue is whether the government's stance is at all based on a rigorous evaluation of the relative costs of the two alternatives.

To make such an evaluation possible, the government must first present a detailed estimate of banks' requirements over the next five years. Rough estimates point to a requirement of external capital for the nationalised banks (other than for the weak banks) of Rs 13,000 crore. The immediate requirement would be, say, Rs 3,000-4,000 crore.

Nobody can pretend this is a staggering sum in relation to the vital task of shoring up regulatory capital in the banking system. Besides, it makes little sense to judge the impact of such a provision by looking at the immediate change in the numerator in the fiscal deficit to GDP ratio. An infusion of Rs 3,000 crore of capital translates into incremental loans of Rs 33,000 crore. These, in turn, would generate commensurate output over a time horizon extending beyond a given fiscal year. It is hard to see how the fiscal deficit to GDP ratio can worsen over the entire time horizon.

More importantly, it is not as if the alternative, banks going to the market, is without cost under the present market conditions. This year, only Indian Overseas Bank has made bold to approach the market, raising Rs 110 crore with a par issue. Others such as Canara Bank and Allahabad Bank chose to defer their issues. This is because bank management reckons that issues will be heavily under-priced.

Under-pricing of stock transfers wealth from existing shareholders to new ones—in the case of PSBs, from tax payers (and existing shareholders, if any) to new shareholders. The consequent loss to tax payers ought to worry the government as much the future impact on tax payers of a rise in the fiscal deficit. Does the government really want Bank of India and Bank of Baroda to go to the market at their current price-earnings multiples of around 3? Which private firm would entertain the idea?

Excessive under-pricing is an invitation to individuals and groups to corner a big chunk of issues in anticipation of privatisation. They can then bid for more when the government decides to transfer its shares and acquire control. If the government does want to privatize any of the PSBs, this would be a poor way of going about it because private parties would end up gaining control at ridiculously low prices.

The preferred route to privatisation in general must be a move first towards a genuine board-driven culture accompanied by financial restructuring and a modest infusion of capital where required. Having provided adequate scope for improving performance, the government can judge which banks need to be privatised and try to obtain the best price. Alternatively, if the government cannot shed its fiscal blinkers, it should declare its intentions for the concerned banks right away and see how it can get the best price instead of allowing private parties to get in at absurd valuations.

The government may not want to talk privatisation now because it wants to buy time with unions and political parties but its tactics could cost the nation dearly. Privatisation by stealth may be astute politics but it is poor economics.

November 23, 2000

Convenient myths about Public Sector Banks

When the government announced that it would lower its equity stake in Public Sector Banks (PSBs) to 33 per cent, shares of some of the listed PSBs rose smartly. Many were quick to interpret this to mean that perceptions about PSBs are negative and that the market viewed privatisation as having the potential to improve performance.

Herein lies a conundrum: while performance at PSBs has improved, myths about the banks persist, mostly rooted in an era in which banks lacked clear commercial goals. It is worth examining some of these myths.

Myth 1: Profitability at PSBs has taken a beating following deregulation and PSBs cannot hope to compete with the private sector.

Reality: Profitability at PSBs, defined as the ratio of net profit to total assets, has improved from minus one per cent of assets in 1992-93 to 0.6 per cent in 1999-2000. This is for 27 PSBs including the three weak banks that await restructuring. If we exclude the three weak banks, the ratio rises to 0.7. This compares with profitability at 34 private sector banks (old and new) of 0.9.

The figure for private sector banks does seem to be inflated because it includes two high values, 1.44 for Global Trust Bank and 1.35 for IDBI Bank, that fly in the face of current perceptions of these banks. If we also factor in the fact that the nine private sector banks (it is a mystery why IDBI Bank and UTI Bank are so categorized) have been around only for six years and hence the NPAs are yet to show up fully, the gap between the PSBs (minus the three weak banks) and the private sector banks would probably vanish.

Note also that aggregate comparisons can be misleading. Profitability at the top 10 PSBs (including SBI and three of its associates) is 0.96, equal to that for the nine new private sector banks.

Myth 2: PSBs could survive in the regulated era because of cosy spreads on loans. Deregulation and narrowing spreads spell doom for PSBs.

Reality: The spread of 2.7 per cent of assets in 1999-2000 at PSBs was higher than the spread of 2.4 in 1992-93, although it is lower than the peak of 3.2 attained in 1996-97. It is interest spread at private banks that has declined sharply—from 2.9 per cent of assets in 1992-93 to 2.1 per cent in 1999-2000.

For banks to hold on to spreads in the wake of deregulation is rare; indeed, it is the pressure on spreads, consequent to deregulation, that pushed banks elsewhere to take on big risks and brought whole banking systems crashing down. The ability of PSBs to maintain spreads does diminish the risks to stability in banking, which is as important an objective for policy-makers as improved efficiency.

Myth 3: High intermediation costs (wages and salaries and high establishment costs) undermine profitability at PSBs.

Reality: At 2.5 per cent of assets, intermediation costs at PSBs are higher than those at private sector banks (1.85 per cent) but they are way below that for foreign banks (3.85 per cent). American banks are the most profitable in the world today and they have the highest intermediation costs thanks to high technology spend.

It is possible, therefore, for high intermediation costs to go hand with hand with high profitability. It all depends on whether the costs are consistent with revenue opportunities. It could be plausibly argued that many PSBs will need all their manpower if they are to aggressively pursue revenue opportunities. It is not the size of the workforce so much as lack of flexibility in deployment that has been a problem.

Myth 4: PSBs cannot control NPAs, given interference from outside.

Reality: Net NPAs at PSBs have declined from 3.7 per cent in 1996-97 to 3 per cent in 1999-2000. The present figure does not compare unfavourably with NPAs at private sector banks, which was 2.3 per cent in 1999-2000 (again understated on account of the presence of new private banks).

In short, profitability at PSBs has been rising, spreads are still healthy, NPAs are declining and rising efficiency has not been achieved at the expense of stability. So how come the myths endure? One reason surely is that management at PSBs have not articulated facts about PSB performance or their intrinsic strengths. They have not cultivated the fine art of managing investor relationships and market perceptions. Another, of course, is that the myths prove convenient to those intent on pursuing an ideological agenda.

December 7, 2000

Lack of perspective in debate on the financial sector

The recent debate on the problems in the financial sector has been characterised by a lamentable lack of perspective. By highlighting particular investment decisions that seem unwise with the benefit of hindsight, both the government and the opposition have lent weight to the perception that there has been gross mismanagement at UTI.

The finance minister, who defended himself ably during the debate in Parliament, could have contributed to a fairer assessment by staying focused on his other main theme, namely, that the seeds of today's problems were sown when UTI decided to weight the US-64 portfolio heavily in favour of equities in the early nineties. Two factors ensured that UTI, having increased its equity portfolio, could not exit. *One*, the absence of a long enough bull phase in the market. *Two*, the sheer size of UTI's holding.

UTI's predicament was similar to that faced by the infamous hedge fund, Long Term Capital Management: it is well nigh impossible for a large player to exit a market. Remember. LTCM, even though a private fund, was bailed out by a rescue operation orchestrated by the Fed in order to avert a global meltdown.

Surely, the decision to tilt towards equities in the US-64 scheme points to mis-management? After the event, this seems self-evident. It could be plausibly argued, however, that had UTI not maintained its returns at a level above that offered by a pure debt fund, it would have come under redemption pressure and forced into large sell-offs. It would have then been blamed for snuffing out a bull rally in the early years of reforms. Besides, in the heady, initial years of reforms, who could have supposed that stock market returns would disappoint over a whole decade?

The transition from administered returns to a net asset value regime would have thus proved a headache at almost any time over the past decade. It would have conceivably required a bailout at almost any point, albeit of varying magnitude, given that the performance of the stock market belied expectations.

Nor is the need for bailouts, in the aftermath of deregulation, in itself proof of mis-management. At the aggregate level, the test is whether bailouts can be kept within reasonable bounds. Bailouts are an almost inevitable sequel to deregulation of the financial sector, although these are most common in banking. Studies show that financial systems have a high probability of lurching into crisis within seven years of the advent of deregulation and end up requiring bailouts in the range of 5 to 40 per cent of GDP.

This happens typically because, with returns being squeezed by deregulation, financial institutions take on higher levels of risk in order to meet return expectations. UTI, too, went down this route but it can at least plead in extenuation that any other course might have equally exposed the system to risk.

In the banking sector, government ownership facilitated recapitalisation at the very onset of reforms and arguably pre-empted costlier bailouts down the road. (The finance minister is right to make a distinction between recapitalisation and a bailout; the latter entails recapitalisation of an institution that has become insolvent.) The total recapitalisation costs to date, including those involved in UTI and IFCI, would not exceed four per cent of GDP, which is way below that experienced by any emerging market. The allegations of mis-management in the financial sector must be viewed in this broader context.

It is a different matter that the government today finds it difficult to bear the minimal costs of recapitalising the financial sector. When financial sector reforms were set in motion alongside macroeconomic and structural reforms, the presumption was that macroeconomic imbalances would be brought under control over a reasonable time frame and industrial growth would accelerate. The financial sector could then be restructured through a combination of further recapitalisation by government and consolidation among domestic banks. But with the fisc spinning out of control and banks weighed down by sluggishness in industry, the financial sector has been left in the lurch.

It is precisely such a perspective that is missing today in the hysterical denunciation of the nation's financial institutions. Any dip in returns to the investor, every bad investment or loan decision seems to trigger a lynch mob mentality in which people are ready to believe the worst about our institutions. As the obligatory cry of 'scam' goes up, the government responds with raids, arrests and other intimidatory actions, the only effect of which can be to discourage risk-taking at a time when this is a requirement for survival in the financial sector. These are events that cannot but fill those interested in the orderly development of India's financial system with grim foreboding.

August 16, 2001

Why it is a good idea to leave UTI alone

Contrary to the impression created by some press reports, the YH Malegam committee on the 'corporate repositioning' of UTI has not recommended the privatisation of UTI. It has merely presented as an 'option for consideration' the induction of a strategic partner in the new structure it envisages for UTI.

The report says guardedly, "It is for consideration whether UTI should be wholly-owned and managed by the government . . .". One would have thought this was precisely for the consideration of the committee. But the five signatories to the report have fought shy of making an unambiguous recommendation.

Much of the report revolves around the central recommendation about moving UTI towards the structure that is the regulatory norm for mutual funds, namely, a Sponsor, a Trustee Company and an Asset Management Company.

The committee wants 40 per cent of the equity in the Sponsoring Company to be held by the Sponsoring Institutions (that is, institutions such as IDBI and SBI that hold the initial capital) and the remaining 60 per cent by the government or a strategic partner. The Sponsoring Company, in turn, would have a 40 per cent stake in the AMC, the balance being held by the public. The total capital infusion from the strategic partner (or government) would amount to Rs 570 crore.

A truly meaningful case against continued government control must rest on proven under-performance. It is surprising that the committee did not think it necessary to compare returns on UTI's schemes with those of other players. If UTI has not done badly, ownership is not the pressing issue and UTI should simply focus on getting its structure right and on streamlining internal processes.

But that is not how the committee views matters. The argument against government control, the report suggests, is the implied responsibility on the government for periodic bailouts. Yet it must understood that such a responsibility has existed only in the case of US-64, which accounts for 23 per cent of domestic funds managed by UTI. Investors have experienced losses in other UTI schemes but have not clamoured for bailouts. This is true also of mutual funds promoted by government-owned banks.

US-64 is a special case where certain return expectations had become deeply ingrained in the public mind. But even with US-64, there is little reason to suppose that an expectation of a bailout would continue even after a switch to an NAV regime.

Still, suppose we go along with the argument for government withdrawal on grounds of "de-risking the government from the operations of UTI", to quote the inelegant phraseology of the committee. The alternative, inducting a strategic partner, bristles with problems.

With an investment of just Rs 570 crore ($ 116 million), a private investor would gain control over domestic funds worth Rs 56,000 crore ($12 billion) and 41 million investor accounts. The investor will also end up with significant equity holdings and a presence on the board in a wide swathe of Indian companies. This must seem unconscionable to many.

There are practical difficulties as well. Who is to be the strategic partner? It cannot be an Indian industrial house—that would be too controversial. It cannot be government-owned financial institutions—that defeats the basic purpose. It cannot be HDFC or ICICI—both are relative newcomers to the mutual fund industry and may also lack the requisite capital.

Foreign mutual funds would have capital and expertise but handing over UTI to them for a pittance will be fiercely opposed; besides, it may not be fair to domestic players. That leaves us with multilateral institutions such as IFC and ADB. One report has indicated that this is being viewed as the most feasible option, but this begs the question whether such a player brings anything to the table apart from capital.

If the government, nevertheless, chooses to privatise UTI, there is no call to retain UTI in its present monolithic form. Far better to house UTI's schemes under, say, three AMCs and to look for a strategic partner for one of them. Let a start be made with a strategic partner for an AMC assigned to manage the troubled US-64. This will enable us to judge the value added by a strategic partner and also the public's willingness to subscribe to a stock issue from UTI. The government could provide capital for the other schemes and move UTI quickly towards the new structure.

The worst prospect is that the government dithers on the ownership issue, a possibility that is unfortunately enhanced by the Malegam committee's own tentativeness on the subject. The last thing we need now is to a spell of protracted uncertainty at the nation's biggest mutual fund on top of a comatose stock market.

November 8, 2001

Before recapitalising banks, thrash out the issues

India's Public Sector Banks (PSBs) need to be recapitalised. On whether this can be accomplished quickly—and how it is accomplished—hinges the health of Indian banking and of the economy at large. Several other issues in banking- privatisation, improved governance, higher credit disbursal- flow directly from this issue.

In its latest *Report on Trend and Progress in Banking,* the RBI has finally put a number on the recapitalisation needs of PSBs (other than the weak banks)—Rs 10,000 crore over a five year period. But its treatment of the subject fails to do justice to its importance.

The estimate itself requires clarification. If it includes the requirements of the SBI group, then it is not such a staggering figure because the SBI group is quite capable of meeting its requirements. Secondly, it is unclear whether the estimate pertains only to external funds or includes a component that can be met by retained earnings. Thirdly, the aggregate figure may intimidate needlessly. For some PSBs, the immediate recapitalisation requirement may be low enough to be met without fuss whether by the government or through a public issue. The RBI would do well, therefore, to provide a bank-wise projection.

More critical than any estimate, however, is how the Central Bank views the results of recapitalisation to date. The report observes, " The experience of bank recapitalisation in several parts of the world has demonstrated that the exercise of recapitalisation does not necessarily prevent banks from getting into trouble again". True. But what has been the experience in the Indian context? That is the key question for us.

It is fair to suggest that the Indian experience has been refreshingly different from that elsewhere. *First,* the big chunk of recapitalisation costs was incurred not in response to failures in the wake of deregulation. It was incurred in the first three years of the transition to deregulation when a whole new set of prudential and accounting norms was put in place, which blew a huge hole in banks' balance sheets. *Secondly*, as the report notes, the recapitalisation costs incurred to date by the government have been just around two per cent of GDP over a seven-year period, which must be among the lowest in the world.

Thirdly, consequent to recapitalisation, the profitability of PSBs has improved from minus one per cent in 1992-93 to 0.57 per cent in 1999-2000, except for a setback in 1995-96. In the aggregate, therefore, it is hard to sustain the proposition that PSBs have been "getting into trouble again" following recapitalisation.

The RBI, whose stewardship of the banking system in the deregulated era has been astute, need not be shy of affirming this. It could better make the point by using a little finesse in its analysis of bank performance. In the first place, the RBI must separate out the three weak banks in compiling aggregate ratios for PSBs.

Secondly, it must highlight one-off factors impacting on profitability of PSBs. The report shows a decline in profitability for PSBs in 2000-01 over the previous year, mainly on account of an increase in operating expenses as a proportion of total assets. This latter increase, which bucks the declining trend in the ratio over the previous five years, seems to be the effect of VRS charges incurred by several banks.

If we adjust for this, the profitability of PSBs in 2000-01 is seen to have improved over 1999-2000. More compelling, the adjusted ratio of net profit to total assets for PSBs (including weak banks) of 0.61 turns out to be quite close to the figure of 0.71 for private sector banks (including new banks). PSBs have thus improved their performance not just in absolute terms but in relative terms as well.

"Recapitalisation of weak banks using public money is also a costly and unsustainable option", the RBI report says, given the strains on the exchequer. But recapitalisation of reasonably strong banks where the capital market is moribund? This is the issue the RBI and the government need to face squarely.

It must be a brave soul who can suppose that the capital market can support Rs 2,000 crore in bank issues each year even if banks are willing to under-price themselves. The more cautious reckoning must be that a combination of recapitalisation by government and recourse to the market will be required, the former preceding the latter. In the alternative, the government will have to allow acquisition of PSBs by foreigners.

The subject calls for the widest debate. It would be best if the RBI came out with a Discussion Paper with detailed estimates set in the broader context of the impact of past recapitalisation on PSBs' performance.

November 22, 2001

Privatising banks but for the wrong reasons

So the sleek, seductive, jungle cat is set to leap out of the government's bag. Slowly but inexorably, the ground is being prepared for a bigger foreign presence in India's financial sector.

The indications have been everywhere in recent days. Speculation about Bank Belgium's interest in increasing its stake in Vysya Bank was followed by reports about the government mulling over an increase in the 20 per cent limit on foreign direct investment in banking. IFCI is said to be scouting for a strategic partner—there is virtually no chance of this being a domestic party.

A less obvious but surer indication of the shape of things to come is the reported decision to ask Public Sector Banks (PSBs) to go in for yet another round of VRS aimed at reducing the workforce by as much as 50 per cent (ET, February 9). This will follow the VRS offered last year and that resulted in the workforce being pruned by 1.2 lakh.

Those sections of the middle-class that have held on to their jobs thus far will, no doubt, cheer the planned bout of downsizing as yet another sign that 'second generation reforms' are on track. But there will be few takers in the banking industry today for the notion that such downsizing is required in order to make PSBs more competitive- and indeed some banks are said to have already expressed their reservations over the proposed move.

PSBs' profitability is lower than that of foreign banks (although not very much lower than that of domestic Private Sector Banks). The difference is widely ascribed to 'overmanning' at PSBs. This is a specious argument to make for two reasons. In the first place, given their vastly differing sizes and scope of operations, a comparison of the two categories is utterly inappropriate. But even if we were to go along with the comparison, it is not the cost side that is making the difference.

True, PSBs have a higher wage bill. But the ratio of operating expenses (which includes all expenses, including wages) to assets at PSBs in 2000 (2.53 per cent) is way below that of foreign banks

(3.22 per cent). Foreign banks end up having higher profitability because they have a higher spread and a lower proportion of non-performing assets. These latter, in turn, arise from focusing on treasury operations and on a small slice of the loan market.

PSBs can improve their profitability in two ways. They can increase their revenues while taking their present cost base as a given—most PSBs would regard this as perfectly feasible. Or they can cut back radically on their operations, which means closing branches wholesale, not just trimming the workforce, and using technology to scale up volumes in their more profitable branches.

PSBs are in no position to move towards the second model on their own. They cannot expend resources on another major bout of VRS without undermining their immediate growth prospects, nor can they fund the requisite infusion of technology.

So, any move towards a radical VRS of the sort contemplated cannot be about shoring up PSBs' competitiveness. It can only be about readying them for privatisation. Having tasted success with big public sector companies recently, the government seems to be preparing for an assault on the public sector's last bastion, the banking industry. Halving the workforce will help weaken bank unions that are opposed to privatisation. It will meet the requirements of foreign suitors who are uncomfortable with a large labour force. It will drive down valuations of PSBs and make acquisitions of these easier.

It must be asked: to what purpose? PSBs' performance has shown an improving trend in recent years. It is legitimate to seek further improvement but to focus on profitability alone in banking is to be myopic. RBI Deputy Governor YV Reddy posed the issue in stark terms in Kolkata recently: if 20 per cent of the branches of PSBs produced 80 per of their profits, did that mean that 80 per cent of the branches deserved to be closed?

Foreign ownership may push up PSBs' profitability through a massive retrenchment of banking operations but it will lead to vital sectors and regions being starved of credit. Those who are dismissive of such concerns must heed the point Joseph Stiglitz made in this paper recently: the reluctance of foreign banks to lend to small and medium enterprises in Argentina was an important factor underlying the collapse of that economy.

Merely improving profitability in banking is a mug's game. The challenge is to produce a banking system that is profitable, that is stable and that meshes the requirement of profitability with larger socio-economic requirements. It is a challenge that we dodge at great peril to the economy.

February 14, 2002

NPA levels must be managed, not necessarily lowered

Is the current preoccupation with reducing NPAs at Public Sector Banks (PSBs) becoming too much of a good thing? It is important to ask because there is no let-up in banks' aversion to lending and their preference for government securities. Left unchecked, this could not only undermine banks' long-term viability but also end up limiting growth in the economy.

PSBs have made much headway in reducing NPA levels since 1996-97. NPAs, whether measured in gross terms or net terms, have declined as a proportion of assets as well as of advances. The ratio of net NPAs to total assets for PSBs of 2.72 per cent in 2000-01 does not compare unfavourably with the private sector's 2.26 per cent although it is much higher than foreign banks' figure of 0.79 per cent.

One reason for the decline in NPAs relative to total assets is the change in composition of assets in favour of investment in government and other approved securities in recent years. This is reflected in the ratio of investments to credit. The ratio has risen for all banks from 59 per cent in 1996-97 to 72 per cent in 2000-01. With loans going down as a proportion of total assets, one must expect the NPA to total asset ratio to decline.

But the more important reason for the decline in NPA levels is banks' unwillingness or inability to assume higher exposures to small and medium enterprises. It is not possible to track exposure to this category as a whole because the RBI clubs medium enterprises with large ones in its data on the sectoral deployment of bank credit. But an indication is available from data on banks' exposure to small enterprises. This, according to the RBI Annual Report (2000-01), was 14 per cent of non-food gross bank credit in 2000, compared to the sector's share in industrial output of 40 per cent. This does suggest that banks are under-exposed to a dynamic segment of the Indian economy.

An economy that is growing at 5.5–6 per cent cannot be bereft of lending opportunities. Yet banks have responded to the pressure to reduce NPAs by simply forgoing such opportunities and parking their funds instead in risk-free securities. While this approach has paid off in a context of falling interest rates, it exposes banks to serious risk in the event of interest rates rising in the future. Moreover, such an approach cannot fully tap the growth potential in the economy because it cuts off firms' access to bank credit.

Part of the problem is that banks' NPA levels are all the time being compared to those obtaining elsewhere. Banks dare not contemplate a rise in NPA levels. To do so in today's charged climate is to invite cries of 'scam'. What is overlooked is that in a high-growth, high-return context, a higher level of NPAs is perfectly consistent with profitability.

Provisioning against NPAs is but one item in the computation of profit, the other key items being spread, operating expenses and other income. Indian banks need to take a view on what is an acceptable level of NPAs by factoring in all the relevant variables—and this level could well be higher in relation to international standards.

One reason banks can afford to lend to riskier businesses is that they have woken up to the potential of retail lending. A big chunk (39 per cent) of outstanding retail loans is housing loans and advances against fixed deposits, both of which have low levels of risk. This changing mix of business and retail lending will contribute towards keeping NPA levels within acceptable bounds.

But for banks to get into riskier lending, they will need an adequate cushion of capital. The capital adequacy ratio today is nine, and is expected to rise to 10 in the near future. Banks will need a cushion of at least two percentage points above the minimal capital requirement in order to operate comfortably. So we are talking about a capital adequacy ratio of around 12.

Today, out of 27 PSBs, ten have a capital adequacy ratio of over 12. Thus, 17 PSBs are undercapitalised in relation to risky lending. Banks will need more capital than the Rs 100 billion projected by the RBI over the next five years, which is presumably based on a capital adequacy ratio of 9 or 10. They will also need to upgrade their appraisal skills and their techniques of loan pricing.

Indian banks have had their share of luck in recent years. The fall in interest rates has meant easy pickings through investment in government securities. The collapse of confidence in the stock market has meant a steady flow of deposits even at lower rates. But they cannot expect to ride their luck forever. There is no escape from riskier lending, backed by capital. And this would mean higher, not lower, levels of NPAs.

March 28, 2002

Myth of 'weak' banks

Confounding sceptics and believers alike, the three 'weak' banks –Indian Bank, United Bank of India and UCO Bank—have stormed back into the black in less than three years after they were so categorised by the MS Verma Working Group. (At the time of the Verma report, UBI had shown the barest net profit.) In consequence, a much propagated myth about Public Sector Banks (PSBs), namely, that many are incurable basket cases may be about to get debunked.

The Verma committee, which came out with its recommendations in October 1999, was scathing in its assessment of the three banks and pessimistic about their prospects. The committee's litany of weaknesses at the three banks was most damning. Decision-making processes were slow. There was no cost control. Information systems were poor. The banks suffered from excess manning, low skill levels and poor motivation. Top management was unstable.

This column was almost alone in pointing out that it was incorrect to suppose that in the nationalised bank fraternity, there was a set of weaknesses peculiar to the three banks. While SBI and its affiliates had always been a class apart, the culture and systems in the 19 nationalised banks were broadly similar. The quality of people could not be very different either considering that they were drawn from the same talent pool. The three banks' problems were thus the product, not of inherent managerial deficiencies, but of adverse circumstances over which the banks had no control.

Indian Bank had suffered under one top management dispensation, and both the political leadership and the RBI were responsible for not addressing this problem much earlier. As for UCO Bank and UBI, their high NPA levels, the fundamental problem at both banks, were the result of their operations being concentrated in the east and the north-east.

The Verma report had compared the NPA levels of UCO Bank and UBI with those of other Public Sector Banks (PSBs). The writer had occasion to ask Mr Verma whether the committee had compared the two banks's NPA levels with those of the PSBs in the Eastern Region alone. Mr Verma replied that the committee had done so and, in this comparison, the two banks were not seen at a disadvantage. That was precisely the point.

The turnaround at the three banks has vindicated this column's assessment and proved the Verma committee wrong. Indian Bank has reported a net profit of Rs 33 crore in 2001-02, its first in six years, while UCO Bank and UBI have reported net profit of Rs 165 crore and Rs 129 crore respectively. The Verma committee had contended that, even with fairly drastic restructuring, Indian Bank and UBI were unlikely to show net profit by 2004, while UCO Bank would not be able to reach a 'reasonable level' of net profit before 2003.

Cynics will ascribe the turnaround at the weak banks entirely to windfall trading gains at a time of falling interest rates. This is not true. To be sure, with the profit orientation that has come into the public sector, the three banks, like other PSBs, have woken up to opportunities in securities trading, for long the principal source of profit for foreign banks. But it as not as if the banks have been engaged in narrow banking over the past three years.

While deposits at Indian Bank have increased by Rs 70 billion between 1998-99 and 2001-02, there has been an increase in credit of Rs 33 crore; for UCO Bank, the figures for increase in deposits and credit are Rs 90 billion and Rs 72 billion respectively; and for UBI, Rs 50 billion and Rs 37 billion respectively (estimates for UBI and UCO Bank are based on newspaper reports).

So where did the Verma committee go wrong? First, the committee was sceptical about the ability of these banks to grow their credit business in a competitive environment. What it overlooked was the enormous potential in retail credit, especially housing loans, which had been ignored by PSBs.

Secondly, it seems to have under-estimated the ability of the banks to cut costs, chiefly labour costs. Faced with the dire prospect of closure, the banks have been able to push through greater reductions in costs than had seemed possible. Thirdly, the banks seem to have done better than expected in respect of NPA recoveries.

What is most striking is that the banks have successfully restructured themselves without any recapitalisation support from the government, without any managerial talent having to be imported from outside the public sector and without any great incentives for performance. In the process, the notion that some of the PSBs are beyond salvation has taken a hard knock, while the notion that consolidation among PSBs is inevitable may need to be revisited.

June 20, 2002

Hiving off UTI-II may be ill-judged

In the barrage of comment about UTI's woes, several points have been made. The promises made to investors in US-64 in December 2001 and reiterated recently were motivated overwhelmingly by the government's desire to woo the middle class. The package announced constitutes a moral hazard. In order to avoid similar bailouts in future, it is necessary to hive UTI-II off to private management. Every one of these propositions is incorrect.

To take the offer made in December 2001 first. The decision to assure investors the face value of Rs 10 is seen as motivated by the desire to keep the middle classes happy. But was any other course feasible?

Had the government announced a shift to NAV–based prices without its assurances, there would almost certainly have been a stampede towards the exit. A downward spiral of lower market prices–lower NAV–lower market prices would have resulted. The collapse in equity prices would have been the lesser of the government's worries. There would have been a firesale in fixed income securities as well, which would have caused interest rates to rise.

The government would conceivably have lost through higher interest rates on its borrowings far more that it could have saved by refusing a rescue package. (In theory, the RBI could intervene massively in the securities market, but that would mean its straying far from its mandate, quite apart from the impact on money supply.) In other words, the rescue of US-64 investors was dictated by considerations of systemic risk and the costs thereof. It was the fact of US-64's bigness (as in the case of LTCM), and not just concern for middle-class investors, that necessitated government intervention.

Does the package constitute moral hazard, meaning schemes promoted by government–owned funds can merrily lose value in the knowledge that investors would be rescued? Most certainly not. Both at UTI and at other government–owned mutual funds, there are several schemes in which NAVs have fallen far below face values without this generating a clamour for bailouts. US-64 was unique among equity schemes in that a perception, however misplaced, was created of assured returns. No such perception obtains in the cases of other schemes offered by government–run institutions including UTI.

This brings us to the third point, the hiving off of UTI-II to professional' management. If the implication is that those managing the schemes that will fall under UTI-II have been unprofessional, nothing could be more absurd. According to UTI Chairman, M Damodaran, nearly half the 20 open-ended equity schemes that will belong to UTI-II belong to the top quartile in terms of performance and seven in the second quartile. It would be the ultimate irony if, in the name of bringing in 'professionals', UTI-II ended up in the hands of a private sector mutual fund whose performance has been inferior to that of UTI-II.

The decision to privatise UTI-II- it's best to call a spade a bloody shovel—is in keeping with an approach that has seen the disinvestment programme grind to a standstill: sell off the better performers, let government tend the discards. Unlike in the case of the better–performing PSUs, the privatisation of UTI-II will not even fetch big revenues. On a valuation of 2-4 per cent of assets under management, UTI-II will fetch around Rs 400-700 crores, plus something for real estate—a sum that contributes little to the rescue package for UTI.

The international agencies have long harped on the fact that the presence of UTI was inhibiting the growth of private mutual funds. It is hard to resist the conclusion that the unavoidable rescue of US-64 investors has provided a pretext for pushing through a pre-determined agenda for privatisation of the nation's biggest mutual fund.

There is a plausible rationale to privatising UTI in its entirety along with the rescue package for US-64 and the assured return schemes. But no, it is only the better-performing part that is to be sold. Going by the rising sentiment against strategic sale of well–run enterprises across the political spectrum, we should not be surprised if the government's proposal fails to win approval in parliament.

If that happens, all that will have been achieved by the move to split UTI into two parts is to erode confidence in UTI-II as well. The public cannot be faulted for drawing the conclusion that UTI-II was sought to be taken out of UTI's fold because it could no longer be entrusted to inept management. In moving to privatise UTI-II at this stage, therefore, the government may well have created a situation where redemption pressures at UTI-I are compounded by similar pressures at UTI-II as well.

September 12, 2002

RBI sallies into danger zone

Whether banking sector reforms have indeed improved efficiency and stability in Indian banking is a central issue for academics and policy-makers alike. The RBI had first explored this theme in its *Report on Currency and Finance (1999-2000)*. It revisits this theme in the latest *Report* (2001-02)—and attempts something even braver. It sallies forth into what some might regard as dangerous terrain for a central bank: the relationship between ownership and efficiency in banking.

To start with the first theme, improvement in efficiency and stability. Competition, the prerequisite for efficiency, has undoubtedly increased. One commonly used measure for judging the degree of competition is the share of the top five banks in assets. In India, this ratio declined from 51.7 per cent in 1991-92 to 43.5 per cent in 2001-02. The concentration ratio is lower in India than in much of Asia and Latin America (and, while the *Report* does not mention this, in many industrial economies).

Improvement in efficiency in the banking system is most commonly measured by whether the ratio of net interest income to assets (spread) declines over time. For scheduled banks as a whole, the ratio does show a decline over the post-reform period. However, in the case of Public Sector Banks (PSBs), the ratio in 2001-02 was at the same level as in 1992-95. It is the other categories of banks that have suffered from competition—good for the system, good for PSBs, bad for the other banks.

Another key ratio, return on assets, is equally cheering. Profitability in Indian banking as a whole as well for PSBs is higher than in East Asian and advanced economies. This point is yet to be grasped by those who are forever wailing about the lack of profit orientation in the PSB—dominated banking system.

The *Report* says that improvement in efficiency in Indian banking is also borne out by the decline in real lending rates. However, there is no uniform trend in the period since 1992-93. Moreover, the figures mentioned in the *Report* are at variance with those cited by Deputy Governor, Rakesh Mohan, in his address at the Bank Economists' Conference last year. The *Report* shows the real lending rate declining from 8.1 per cent in 1992– to 7.6 per cent in 2001-02. Dr Mohan has a table showing the real lending rate rising from 5.9 per cent to 12.1 per cent in the same period.

As for stability, the Report is heartened by the improvements in capital adequacy and non-performing asset levels. But the greater accomplishment surely is that there has been no systemic crisis more than a decade after liberalization.

Turn now to the juicier bit in the chapter on the financial sector—the relationship between ownership and efficiency. The *Report* presents the results of two comparisons: between five PSBs that have divested minority equity stakes and five wholly government–owned banks; and between the above two categories and old private sector banks. The parameters used are operating expenses, spread, net profit, non-performing assets and capital adequacy.

Broadly, the report finds that old private banks performed better than divested PSBs, which, in turn, performed better than wholly government–owned PSBs. The conclusion rests on particular ratios being higher or lower for private banks compared to the other two categories. This is unsatisfying because the important research question is whether the differences are *statistically significant*. The writer's own research suggests that private sector performance is not significantly superior across all parameters. (*Deregulation and performance of Public Sector Banks, EPW, February 5, 2002*).

More importantly, as the *Report* acknowledges, there is a trend towards convergence in performance. Divested PSBs are catching up with old Private Sector Banks and wholly-owned PSBs are catching up with divested PSBs. It is a fair bet that, given the advantages of scale, it is only a matter of time before PSBs actually forge ahead. The very fact that there are no takers for most old Private Sector Banks should be conveying something to the RBI. To contend, as the *Report* does, that "ownership did impinge on the efficiency of banks" is facile, to say the least.

The *Report* confirms what some of us have been saying for long: improvement in efficiency in Indian banking has gone hand in hand with stability. Government ownership has had a great deal to do with this achievement. The performance of PSBs has begun to approach that of Private Sector Banks. The RBI, which can legitimately claim credit for these achievements, should be drawing the conclusion that the case for privatization of PSBs in general is rather weak. Regrettably, it is silent on the policy implications of its analysis. Having found the courage to venture into dangerous terrain, it seems to have lost its nerve after getting there.

Banks as givers, not takers

India's nationalised banks are in embarrassingly good shape today, embarrassing because they have begun to invite the attention of their lord and master, the government of India.

The government thinks the banks can spare it funds it could use in its present fiscal condition. The banks are reluctant to go along. The government can, of course, get the banks to do its bidding but it would be wise not to attempt anything that might derail one of the outstanding successes of the reform era.

This year's budget mooted the idea of a buyback of government debt from banks at a discount to the market value. The idea does not seem to have made much headway so far. Now the government has hit upon another plan for tapping the banking sector for funds: it wants banks retiring some of the government's equity to do so at the market price, not at the book value with some adjustments.

In the post-reform period, the government has provided Rs 22,516 crore as recapitalisation support to nationalised banks. Of this, banks had returned Rs 867 crore up to 2002. There have been further repayments since and several banks have announced plans to return government equity this year, including some that have returned equity in the past. The amounts returned may be low in relation to the capital provided by the government. But it is the underlying trend that is important—contrary to what critics of nationalised banks had predicted, banks are today givers, not takers, of capital in relation to government.

The fly in the ointment is the price that banks are willing to pay for government equity. The banks are paying the government the book value of equity plus interest earned on recapitalisation bonds minus dividends paid by the banks to government in the intervening years. In effect, capital provided by the government is being valued as debt, not equity.

The banks think this is fair enough. After all, they were constrained to invest the funds in recapitalisation bonds issued for the purpose. The government, for its part, could argue that it was the capital it provided that enabled the banks to be in business in the first place, so it has a legitimate claim on surpluses banks have since generated.

To see whether banks are in the right, recall why firms choose to buy back equity. They typically do so for two reasons. One, they do not have sufficiently profitable avenues for some of the equity lying with them. Two, they believe their shares are undervalued and seek to signal their perception to the market by offering a buyback at a price higher than the ruling market price. In the present case, banks would like to get their shares to appreciate but this has nothing to do with the shares being undervalued.

When a buyback is effected at the market price, the share price remains unaffected. However, when it is effected at a price below the market price, as is true of banks returning government capital, the price of the share will rise after the buyback. Bank management would love this—the share price rises through adroit financial engineering. Trouble is, this benefits shareholders who have not participated in the buyback, namely, retail and institutional shareholders, but hurts the government. If the government were to accept this principle for its entire equity holding, it would end up being a big loser.

At the same time, it does not make sense for banks to buy back government equity at the market price merely to satisfy the government's appetite for funds. As capital would be significantly dented, banks would be obliged to raise fresh equity from the public. This would likely have to be offered at a discount to the market price in order to attract investors. It would also entail transaction costs for banks.

The best way for government to realise a fair value for its capital without imposing costs on banks would be for it to sell its equity directly to the public. There is some ambiguity as to whether the present statutes permit the government to do so. If not, the Banking Companies (Amendment) Bill should facilitate such disinvestment. Unfortunately, the Bill has got bogged down in parliament because political parties and labour suspect it is intended to pave the way for privatisation.

The government must move to allay such apprehensions by making amendments to the Bill as required. The banking sector is a great success story for disinvestment, the sale of equity to the public, as distinct from strategic sale and the implied transfer of control to private hands. The government is well placed, therefore, to assure the nation that it has no intention of departing from a winning formula in the foreseeable future.

June 5, 2003

Mergers and Universal Banking

Not by size alone

Bankers appear bemused by the suggestion reportedly mooted by the Finance Ministry to merge the two leading financial institutions, IDBI and ICICI, in order to create a financial entity that would pack greater punch than either can individually. At a recent seminar, I buttonholed a senior executive from one of the FIs to see if he had an explanation. He responded by grabbing my copy of the Economic Times to seek enlightenment himself.

Part of the inspiration for such a move seems to have come from the wave of consolidation going on in the financial sector elsewhere. It would be wrong to conclude, however, that size is the overriding consideration in all cases. Some are the result of banks wanting a presence in investment banking or fund management. Others have happened because a bank failed to perform and became a sitting duck for a predator. The outcome is a financial giant but gigantism is not the driving force in such cases.

The empirical evidence on the correlation between size and profitability in banking is pretty weak. The literature mentions a U-shaped curve: it appears that profitability increases upto a certain size and starts declining subsequently. This accords with commonsense: with increasing scale come cost economies first and diseconomies associated with managing a large organization later.

The problem with the size argument, however, is that it cannot be operationalized. What is the right size for a given firm ? In manufacturing, there is often a ready answer because technology determines the viable scale of operations. For a bank, the answer would depend on a host of other factors, such as the composition of liabilities, the credit-deposit ratio, the quality of assets, and, not least, fee income as distinct from fund-based income.

Coming back to the proposed merger of IDBI and ICICI. One of the arguments for the merger of SCICI with ICICI was that the former's borrowing costs tended to be higher, without any compensating benefits on the lending side. Will the proposed merger lead to lower cost of borrowing?

Another argument for the SCICI–ICICI merger was that SCICI lacked the capacity to fund projects by itself, so why let it carry on as a separate entity? Now, IDBI and ICICI have increased the proportion of funding they do on their own, but if we accept that at least one-third of their funds would go towards infrastructure, and another one-third towards consortium lending for industry, they can hope to fund on their own only the remaining one-third. Far better, then, to have a single window for industrial borrowers.

Snag one: we may not have meaningful competition for long-term funds. While banks have entered this area, they cannot match the volumes of a combined IDBI-ICICI or their skills in project appraisal. Corporate managers do say they gain by playing off IDBI against ICICI.

Snag two: a single window must provide not only long-term funds but also working capital, and here FIs are at a disadvantage because they lack retail access. ICICI is trying to create one, but it's hard to beat the branch networks the banks established long ago. ICICI could merge with ICICI Bank (and IDBI likewise with IDBI Bank), and both could take over one of the troubled banks down the road.

Or, if you want real firepower, let a big bank–say, SBI–merge with IDBI or ICICI. Then you have an entity that can independently fund large projects and provide both short-term and long-term funds. Merging ICICI with any of the nationalized banks could create problems because of ICICI's superior pay scales, so we can, perhaps, start by merging IDBI with a bank, while ICICI could work out a strategic alliance until bank pay scales move closer to its own.

It's important, though, that the concerned players first attain higher levels of efficiency and effectiveness before attempting mergers. Their current returns to equity suggest they have some distance to go in this respect. The better performers should be able to pick off lesser firms by using higher price multiples founded on superior performance. And they should be able to justify the merger to their own shareholders and to those of the firm they wish to merge with. A gunshot wedding contrived by the Ministry would be the worst way to go about it.

February 19, 2001

Adrift in Blunderland

Heads of banks and financial institutions (FIs) have been vocal lately on the subject of tightening laws to enforce loan recovery; they also insist that rationalization of the workforce is critical to any restructuring in the banking sector.

Fair enough; and the wish-list can be easily stretched. It would be interesting to know, however, what management at banks and FIs are doing about the one area that's within their control and that holds the key to a bank's viability not only here but also internationally: credit management. A modest improvement in this area will do more for Indian Banks than all the effort they might expend on loan recovery or any savings they could effect through trimming their workforce.

The Basle requirement of capital adequacy is no solution to credit risk; it is, arguably, part of the problem. Because they have met the mechanistic requirement of eight per cent, banks can be lulled into thinking they are impervious to collapse. The stark truth is that when a bank fails, the drop in asset value is so steep as to make capital of eight per cent appear quite irrelevant. More importantly, because the Basle rules do not distinguish between different categories of commercial borrower, they can have the perverse effect of biasing banks towards riskier borrowers: for a given amount of capital set aside, banks can earn better returns through higher interest rates.

Nor is improved credit management merely a matter of eliminating behest lending or mala fide intent in bankers, crucial as these requirements are. Suppose we take these as givens in our situation. How do we go ahead and make the best of a bad job?—this is the issue. There is little to suggest that credit management has received the attention it deserves. It is doubtful that more than half a dozen public sector banks have credible credit management practices, leave alone practices approaching those obtaining at the top international banks. We hear plenty of talk about improved Treasury Management and monitoring of interest rate risk. Let's not forget that these merely constitute icing on the cake; it's credit management that accounts for the cake.

In one respect, perhaps, banks are ahead of the FIs, namely, devolving sanctioning powers down the line. At the financial institutions, sanctioning power is still concentrated in top management. In my salad days at an FI, I found the entire 'project appraisal' exercise quite farcical. The corporate bigwigs would meet the people at the top and clear, broadly, the size of the loan as well as the terms. The file would then go down to the concerned officer for 'appraisal'. This meant making the numbers look attractive enough to justify approval. If the numbers weren't impressive enough, my superior would bellow, "Arre bhai, IRR badao (increase the internal rate of return)". As endless iterations were required and spreadsheets had not come into vogue, appraisal usually meant more brawn than brain.

Things have improved somewhat but not to the point where it's possible to fix responsibility for loans that go sour. In banks, the lowliest officers often get hounded by Vigilance and the CBI when borrowers default. Not to justify such hounding, but at least the underlying principle—of fixing responsibility for sanctions—cannot be faulted. Ever heard of such an inquiry at an FI? It is inconceivable not only because similar vigilance mechanisms do not exist at FIs but because top management, which alone has sanctioning authority, is not going to be ordering inquiries against itself.

At investment banks, entry-level analysts make recommendations. They may be overruled but they are free to express their views. Why should middle managers at financial institutions be denied this freedom? Let them write 'yes' or 'no' on the file; top management can overrule if it deems appropriate. Without this elementary system in place, you simply cannot have accountability. And, absent accountability, credit management will lack substance. We badly need a system in which career progression at banks and FIs is clearly related to returns on portfolios over, say, a five-year period, duly adjusted for non-performing assets.

Heaven knows there are a dozen areas where banks and FIs need to improve. As things stand today, however, there is a simple message that needs to be beamed at them. Cut out the fancy footwork. Focus on basics.

March 19, 1998

RBI sees saffron

In keeping, perhaps, with the temper in the saffron parts of New Delhi, the RBI has expressed itself against conversions—at least for the next five years. Conversions, that is, of Development Financial Institutions (DFIs) into banks.

The RBI's views are contained in a Discussion Paper titled, "Harmonising the role and operations of Development Financial Institutions and Banks". Spread over some 99 pages of text and annexures, the RBI's treatment of the subject is exhaustive and—let me confess—somewhat exhausting. For that very reason, though, the paper could easily end up obscuring the central issues involved.

Nearly a fifth of the text is devoted to surveying the literature on universal banking, the notion of a superstore that offers almost every financial product–from banking through mutual funds to insurance and pension. We already have universal banking: banks and DFIs are into a host of other activities, such as mutual funds, investment banking and custodial services, and are eyeing newer pastures such as insurance. So one has to wonder what the discussion on the merits of universal banking is all about. It only distracts from the core issue: how to resolve the problem caused by the demarcation of roles between banks and DFIs.

This demarcation has occurred within commercial banking as practised elsewhere, and it's not terribly helpful to link this up with the much broader issue of universal banking. It occurred because of the perceived need to subsidise investment in a capital–scarce economy. Liberalization has meant the ending of such subsidies and DFIs' access to cheap finance from RBI. This has forced all concerned to confront the question of how DFIs—and especially the big ones, IDBI, ICICI and IFCI–can continue to be viable.

Since banking is all about borrowing short and lending long, DFIs will need low-cost funds provided by savings and checking deposits. Both the Narasimham Committee-II and the Khan Working Group (KWG) seemed to recognize this and they favoured DFIs converting themselves into banks before long. But, with an eye to viability, they wanted less stringent reserve requirements and priority sector norms to be applied for an interim period.

The RBI is against any privileges for converts to banking. It suggests, instead, that conversions be deferred for another five years, but none of the arguments it puts forward is convincing. The RBI says DFIs are needed as the debt market is not fully developed and DFIs have project appraisal expertise. It also contends that the "predominance of short to medium-term deposits of banks constrain their ability to enlarge long-term commitments on a large scale". But this predominance is entirely an outcome of the regulated era in which banks' exposure to long-term finance was restricted. There is no reason, really, why banks can't raise the requisite funds at the longer end.

In any case, if access to term funds and project finance expertise are the key considerations, banks can acquire both by simply merging with the DFIs. Such mergers make sense from the standpoint of the DFIs too because it's hard to see how they can ever compete with the banks' network of branches by building from scratch. Both Narasimham-II and KWG had viewed mergers of DFIs with banks favourably. The RBI is inclined to wait but it must realise that procrastination carries its attendant dangers.

One of the best things to have happened to commercial banks post-liberalisation is the cleaning up of their balance sheets through recapitalization. The DFIs were not subject to such a clean-up and they have tried to grow their way out of trouble. As a result, their NPAs have mounted. There are few takers in the market today for the NPA figures being put out by some of the DFIs. Letting them be for another five years under conditions in which it's hard to make money on incremental loans could mean an exponential increase in the cost of a future bail-out.

If the RBI hopes the NPA position of DFIs will improve with a turnaround in key sectors of the economy, we can only wish it luck. Or has the RBI come to a more troubling conclusion? Does it believe that the problem is so big that mergers with banks are infeasible without recapitalisation of DFIs by the government on a scale that is hard to contemplate in the present fiscal situation?

February 4, 1999

Tell-tale multiples

Who will guard the guardians? The immortal question posed by the Greeks certainly applies to financial institutions. And it is at the root of the unease among LIC, GIC and UTI at ICICI's move to raise Rs 2000 crore of fresh equity. As reported in the *Economic Times,* the institutions fear that if most of the new equity is raised abroad, their stakes would decline to a point where they would not be able to exercise control over ICICI management.

Ordinarily, this should not matter; after all, management cannot be expected to take capital decisions with an eye to the stakes of particular investors. But, as the Indian institutions see it, the situation is by no means ordinary. Apparently, the GDR holders pledge their shareholding to the present management. As the GDR stake could rise above 40 per cent (while that of LIC, GIC and UTI would fall below the 26 per cent needed to block a special resolution), ICICI management could become a law unto itself and the Indian institutions reduced to impotence.

Still, if foreign shareholders are inclined to place implicit faith in ICICI management, Indian institutions have to live with it. Their fear of losing control cannot be a basis for questioning the decision to raise fresh equity, much less dictate where equity should be raised. There is room, however, for Indian institutions to ask what ICICI intends to do with new capital and where exactly ICICI is headed.

As it is, ICICI would stretch definitions of core competence: apart from term finance, its interests include banking, personal finance, investment banking, mutual funds, custodial services, venture capital, credit rating and real estate. Now it is reportedly eyeing a clutch of unrelated businesses such as commodities trading, courier services, events management, e-commerce, software and printing. As diversification is about sustaining profit growth, it is legitimate to ask whether ICICI's plans are a reflection on the long-term potential of its core business. Or whether they are intended to shore up profit until core business potential can be improved through greater access to retail funds.

ICICI's performance in 1998-99 did little to dispel doubts about the long term. Profit after tax (excluding non-recurring gain) rose by Rs 650 crore (7 per cent) over the previous year. Net interest income rose only by Rs 10 crore and most of the increase in profit came from other sources. One was a Rs 240 crore increase in income from securities arising mainly from increased cash balances during the year and repurchase of foreign currency bonds at steep discounts following the turbulence in international markets. Another was a Rs 144 crore rise in income from commission and fees, largely due to increases in loan processing and application fees. While the latter may be technically non-fund income, it is related to fund-based business, unlike, say, fees for advisory services and may not be sustainable under increased competition.

Interest rate spread fell from the already low 3.24 per cent in 1997-98 to 2.56 per cent (ICICI's spread used to be upwards of 5 per cent until a few years ago). The new element here is a decline in loan yield that the annual report ascribes to a shift in strategic focus to top quality corporates. This means the fall in spread cannot be offset by any significant increase in volumes in future. To increase spread, ICICI must lower borrowing costs but this will take time as the company builds its retail reach. ICICI, perhaps, hopes to boost profits in the interim through new businesses that produce quick returns with low investments.

Convincing the markets about this won't be easy as scepticism about diversified firms now runs deep; what is required is a more credible strategy for the core business. The price-earnings multiples in the sector tell all. For all the aggressive moves it's been making, ICICI trades at a multiple of 4.2—a staggering discount of 77 per cent to the market multiple. (The discount for financial institutions elsewhere is around 15-20 per cent.)

Clearly, the market does not believe the present numbers or it does not see long-term prospects or both. As their businesses converge, ICICI needs to benchmark itself with SBI's multiple, currently a respectable 12.6, not with IDBI's pathetic 1.9. The markets are merely conveying the general perception about the relative viability of financial institutions and banks. ICICI management is entitled to think it knows better but investors may be forgiven their nervousness. Don't forget, the Greeks also had something to say about hubris.

August 5, 1999

Urge to merge

Going by the lusty cheers accorded by the stock market, it is easy to suppose that the two recent mergers among the new private sector banks (HDFC Bank–Times Bank and ICICI Bank–Centurion Bank) constitute terrific strategic coups. Indeed, the mergers have reinforced a theme heard earlier: savvy and nimble as they are, the New Private Sector Banks (NPSBs) are set to leave the Public Sector Banks (PSBs) behind.

Appearances can be deceptive, however. The mergers, in fact, underscore realities that should have a sobering effect on NPSB enthusiasts. Foremost is the fact that NPSB stocks as a class have been a disappointment until the recent merger-driven spurt in prices. Of the nine stocks, three traded below their issue price until December 1999 while one sank below the issue price in 1999. Indeed, over a longish period, only two bank stocks, HDFC Bank and Global Trust Bank, have delivered performance, the latter tending to sag in 1999.

Underlying the lacklustre performance of NPSB stocks is the declining trend in profitability. Net profit as a percentage of total assets declined from 1.73 in 1996-97 to 1.03 in 1998-99. Although this is much higher than the profitability of PSBs (0.57 and 0.42 in the two years respectively), the gap between the NPSBs and the PSBs (and particularly with the upper half of the latter) has been narrowing. There are reasons to believe that this trend will intensify, contrary to popular supposition.

For one thing, NPAs for new banks tend to be understated in the initial years as these start building up only over time. Already, net NPAs at NPSBs have risen from 2.54 per cent in 1996-97 to 2.84 per cent in 1998-99, a period in which net NPAs at PSBs have declined from 3.65 per cent to 3.14 per cent. (So much, incidentally, for the proposition that government ownership is to blame for bad loans at PSBs .) Secondly, the PSBs can be expected to sharpen their focus on profitability in the coming years.

But by far the biggest factor narrowing the differences in profitability between PSBs and NPSBs will be size. Their small size limits NPSBs' access to quality corporate assets (because some of the best quality happens to be among big borrowers) or it renders access possible only through aggressive pricing. But an even bigger limitation of small size is that, lacking reach in distribution, NPSBs cannot match the PSBs' access to low-cost savings deposits.

The fact that NPSBs have the lowest intermediation cost among the different categories of banks (1.74 per cent of assets compared to PSBs' 2.65 per cent and foreign banks' 3.37 per cent) means little by itself. The more crucial factor is that they also happen to have the lowest interest spread (1.98 per cent of assets, compared to PSBs' 2.81 per cent and foreign banks' 3.47 per cent).

If PSBs' spreads are helped by low-cost deposits, the key factor at foreign banks would appear to be retail assets (particularly credit cards), a segment in which foreign banks have built up a formidable lead. Lacking either advantage, NPSBs truly their have their work cut out for them.

So the recent mergers must be seen for what they are: defensive moves dictated by the logic of critical size. (NPSBs account for less than four per cent of scheduled commercial banks' assets.)The same logic suggests that consolidation in Indian banking will initially cause the smaller players, whether among NPSBs or the older private sector banks, to disappear. The men in the public sector are relatively safe compared to the boys and the grandpas in the private sector.

The logic of size should also explain why developments in the banking sector have mocked the Verma committee's vaunted ranking of banks on weakness. Within weeks of the report being published, the SBI Chairman was quoted as saying that he would give SBI's associate banks only about three to four years of independent life before they were taken into the parent's fold. This means that it is State Bank of Patiala, ranked at the top in the Verma committee's five categories, that will lose its raison d'etre and not SBI, which ranked a lowly third. Next, Syndicate Bank, which the committee believed was 'close to distress', made a public issue that was heavily oversubscribed. Clearly, the market is able to appreciate the value of size in a way that seems to have eluded the Verma committee.

January 6, 2000

Defying the pundits

So strong is the impetus towards merger worldwide that there is no greater ignominy in the corporate world, it would seem, than a botched merger plan. Germany's top banks have had ridicule heaped on them following the collapse of merger talks, first between Deutsche Bank and Dresdner Bank four months ago and, recently, between Dresdner and Commerzbank.

But the banks need not be unduly defensive about the setbacks. Much as consolidation is the order of the day, the ongoing bout of mergers has drawn flak in the same month from three impeccable sources.

The Economist (July 22-28) quotes a study on mergers by the consultancy firm, KPMG, that found that half the mergers had destroyed shareholder value while another third had made no difference. This is, of course, not news at all. Other studies, covering different countries, sectors and time periods, have come to similar conclusions. Indeed, it is fair to say that in few respects have managers defied the findings of pundits as resolutely as in the case of mergers; every CEO, no doubt, thinks he can bring it off.

The Economist urges companies to draw the right lessons from previous mergers: success requires a "clear vision" and a "clear strategy". The trouble is that corporate bosses routinely claim these attributes for their merger proposals. And analysts and academics have not distinguished themselves at telling whether the claims are well-founded. They are much better at adducing reasons for success or failure after the event.

Another attack on mergers, one with a distinctly leftist tinge, comes from a rather improbable source, Henry Kaufman. A one-time Oracle of Wall Street, Mr Kaufman made a fortune for his firm, Salomon Brothers, and also for himself by getting interest rate movements right in the seventies. Writing in the *Financial Times* (July 27), Mr Kaufman says that mergers are bad because, far from leading to efficiency, these will create monopolies that will "exact a cost on society as a whole".

Mr Kaufman laments the fact that corporate consolidation has gone largely unchallenged. This is because it is taking place against a background of general prosperity and rising stock prices, with much of the stock being held by ordinary citizens. Mr. Kaufman's reservations have, however, not kept his former employer from going through several mergers and ending up as a constituent of a potential monopolist, Citigroup.

A third line of criticism questions the very logic driving mergers, in effect contradicting the positions of both the Economist and Mr Kaufman. Two academics, Pankaj Ghemawat and Fariborz Ghadar, say that big mergers are driven by the belief that industries will become more concentrated with globalization and the spoils of the market will accrue to a select few ("The dubious logic of global megamergers", *Harvard Business Review*, July-August 2000). So companies have begun to view mergers as a do-or-die proposition. Yet the links between the globalization of an industry and concentration in that industry, the authors contend, are weak.

The authors examined more than 40 years of data on the global market shares of companies in more than 20 industries. They found that, by and large, the trend has been towards decreasing concentration. Moreover, even where concentration has occurred, mergers have not always enhanced shareholder value.

The authors confirm damning verdicts delivered by others. Mergers, they say, are driven by managerial biases—an obsession with top-line growth, the temptation to exploit a high stock price, herd instinct, the whims of the top man and misplaced trust in investment bankers—that lead to large-scale destruction of value.

The truth is that many a merger is an escape for under-performing management. Managers who cannot match their peers' performance under given conditions somehow delude themselves—and others—into believing that there is a simple solution: becoming bigger. They fail because they cannot cope with the greater complexity that merger brings or because, in their eagerness to clinch deals, they overpay for targets. It is no accident that some of the firms with a very good record of digesting mergers or acquisitions—Merrill Lynch of the US, Lloyds TSB of the UK, and Banco Santander of Spain, to cite examples from the financial sector—are ones that were performing at high levels of efficiency even prior to union.

August 3, 2000

A merger, an appointment and a lesson or two

Two unconnected news items of the past fortnight carry a lesson or two about the promise latent in Public Sector Banks—and what it would take for the promise to be fulfilled.

Start with the first item, the proposed merger between UTI Bank and Global Trust Bank(GTB). It was easy, going by accounts in the press, to have got the impression that this was another terrific coup brought off by fleet-footed banks in the private sector. It is nothing of the sort.

In the first place, although UTI Bank falls under the RBI's categorization of New Private Sector Bank, it is far from being in the private sector. UTI was given a banking license in the expectation that its equity stake would quickly fall to under 40 per cent, giving UTI Bank something of the character of a private sector bank. But this has not happened. UTI Bank can hardly be characterized as private sector until UTI ceases to be either the dominant shareholder or in the public sector.

Secondly, it is UTI that will dominate the merged entity. UTI Bank's Managing Director will be Chairman of the merged entity; GTB's high-profile Chairman will oversee an insurance venture that is as yet on the drawing board. So the merger is really a case of a New Public Sector Bank taking control of a New Private Sector Bank.

This must confound many who had set store by the superior performance of Private Sector Banks. Wasn't it supposed to be the other way round, that is, private banks conquering their supposedly lethargic counterparts in the public sector? Many will point to GTB's superior performance on key parameters. But the fact that UTI will be in control post-merger can mean only one of two things.

Either GTB's numbers are not credible. Or GTB is in no position to grow organically. GTB's's share performance will not have electrified the market. The bank's share, priced at Rs 10 in August 1994, touched Rs 70 on listing. It declined subsequently

—steeply at times—and has not risen except for brief spells in 2000. Hardly the sort of performance that would enable a company to raise additional funds required for sustaining growth.

UTI Bank's stock has not dazzled either. But the bank has staying power thanks to its parent. One way or another, public sector banks have the advantages of size. This gives them the capability to overtake new private sector banks over the long haul, no matter that the latter might perform better in the short run.

That is the positive side to Public Sector Banks. The negative side showed up in a news item about the search for a Chairman for IDBI. The search has reportedly narrowed to three candidates: an executive director of IDBI, a senior functionary at SEBI and a former official of UTI who now heads a minor financial institution.

Neither the second nor the third candidate has had commercial banking experience for nearly a decade. None has a track record as a CEO elsewhere. Yet we are asked to accept that the three exhaust the possibilities of talent for the top slot at the second largest financial institution in the country. An institution that needs exceptional leadership if it is get out of its present rut. Clearly, the public sector is yet to get its act right when it comes to the all-important task of filling top positions.

In bureaucratic terms, the selection process in the present case must seem impeccable. The job was advertised. A search committee screened applications. Let us grant that the committee picked the three best candidates.

But winning in today's context is all about transcending bureaucratic processes. Was advertising the IDBI chairmanship the only option? Elsewhere, search committees first define the profile of the ideal candidate. Then they proceed to identify individuals who match the desired profile, using headhunters if necessary. This is because, at the highest level, not many executives are going to submit CVs in response to an advertisement. Ask IBM how they found Lou Gerstner.

True, the compensation package at IDBI is unexciting. But compensation is not necessarily the overriding consideration for achievers and there are always takers for big challenges in the public sector. IDBI's own banking subsidiary was able to get a

Citibank executive with international experience to sign on as CEO. At HDFC Bank, Deepak Parekh is said to have literally talked Citibank's country head in Malaysia into taking the CEO's job on a much lower salary.

It is all a matter of selling a challenge to the right person. Setting up a search committee is good as far as it goes. But, unless such committees can bring themselves to approach their task very differently, public sector banks are unlikely to find the leadership that can unlock their considerable potential.

February 11, 2001

Road to universal banking is strewn with pitfalls

The announcement of ICICI's results for the past year coincided last week with the RBI's circulating a list of parameters that financial institutions must take into account in converting themselves into universal banks.

ICICI's results underline once again that financial institutions cannot be competitive unless they can access short-term funds by converting themselves into universal banks. The RBI's circular indicates that it is unwilling to countenance any special regime for financial institutions that choose to convert themselves into universal banks. The two items together raise the troubling question whether such a conversion is feasible at all without a massive infusion of capital from external sources.

ICICI's profit after tax slumped from Rs 1,206 crore in 2000 to Rs 537 crore in 2001. The company ascribes this to 'accelerated provisions'. It has made provisions of Rs 813 crore on top of what is mandated by RBI norms. But to suggest that the provisioning is in excess of what is required assumes that the company is accurate in its classification of assets into the four categories specified.

In any case, higher provisions are not the only reason ICICI's profit after tax has taken a beating. Even after normal provisions, ICICI's profit from operations increased by a mere Rs 98 crore. Combining profit from operations with income from other sources (which includes one-off capital gains from the sale of a 10 per cent stake in ICICI Bank), profit before tax was up by a meagre Rs 63 crore. This was, of course, washed out by 'accelerated' provisioning.

ICICI's spread is stated to be around 1.8 per cent. This compares unfavourably with the spread of public sector banks of more than three per cent. Fee income has risen sharply but is still a mere six per cent of income from operations. So there is no getting away from the lack of competitiveness in the core business, evident for quite some time now. Moreover, it is not as if ICICI's exposure to various sectors has altered materially. There is no assurance, therefore, that fresh additions to NPAs will not accrue down the road.

ICICI's strategy of focusing on online banking and investment in subsidiaries is still far from paying off. For bankers everywhere, the limitations to online banking have become painfully apparent and ICICI is no exception. The subsidiaries are nowhere near making a meaningful impact on the parent's bottomline. If this is the predicament of the most fleet-footed financial institution, that of IDBI and IFCI can be easily imagined.

The way out, it would seem, would be for the FIs to convert themselves into banks so that they can access cheaper short-term funds. The snag, though, is that they will be then required to conform to CRR, SLR and priority sector requirements. And doing so would negate the gains to FIs from being able to access short-term funds. The FIs have, accordingly, be pleading for some relaxation in these norms (as recommended by the Khan Working Group on harmonisation of banks and financial institutions). In its recent circular, however, the RBI has emphatically set its face against any such relaxation.

The FIs know that salvation lies in becoming banks. The RBI believes the FIs must cleanse themselves of past sins before seeking salvation but it seems unconcerned about spelling out this might happen. Both the Narasimham committee and the Khan group had recommended mergers of banks with FIs. This not does appear feasible: given the present condition of FIs, banks are bound to view the proposition with distaste. FIs are not going to be attractive candidates for merger unless their balance sheets are first cleaned up.

A lacuna in financial sector reform has been that, while the government undertook the cleaning up of banks' balance sheets at the outset, it did not so in the case of FIs. The FIs then sought to grow themselves out of trouble but have only ended up making matters worse for themselves.

The government must know that infusion of capital is a must but it is reluctant to say so because it does not want to face up to the fiscal implications (except in the case of ICICI, which is today privately owned). Letting matters drift, however, only means that the requirement of additional capital will mount inexorably to a point where a government bail-out is inconceivable and a foreign bank will have to step in. Which gives rise to a nagging thought: might this, after all, be the denouncement towards which the government is nudging the FIs?

May 10, 2001

Don't expect miracles when FIs convert to banks

The nation's premier Financial Institutions (FIs) are at the end of their tether but you would not guess it from the statistics published by the RBI.

The RBI's latest *Trend and Progress* shows a capital adequacy ratio of 15.8 for IDBI and 14.6 for ICICI. The FIs should be sitting pretty. Instead, along comes the news that IDBI has sought Rs 3,000 crore by way of recapitalisation funds from the finance ministry. As for ICICI, it has sought to bury its problems in the proposed merger with ICICI Bank.

Maybe these ratios are compatible with the existing accounting norms but would be undermined by the RBI's decision to place NPA norms for FIs on par with those of banks with effect from the current financial year. At present, FIs are permitted an overdue period of 365 days for the principal and 180 days for interest. Under the new norms, an asset will be treated as non-performing if interest or instalment remains overdue for more than 180 days.

Whatever be their motivation for doing so, both the institutions have signaled that the present state of affairs cannot continue. But they have chosen to deal with their problems in different ways. IDBI, it appears, would like to write off a chunk of its NPAs, supported by an infusion of capital from the government, before converting itself into a bank. This is indeed the right thing to do.

However, ICICI, which is privately owned, cannot look to the government for support, nor can it hope to raise capital on its own right now. Besides, ICICI probably reckons that it has a stronger banking franchise, one that is strong enough to take care of its parent's problems over three to five years.

IDBI's problems will evoke the familiar litany about the evils of government ownership and behest lending, never mind that a private institution is in the same boat. The fault lies elsewhere-in the government's failure to clean up the FIs' balance sheets even earlier when banks were being helped out. As a result, the FIs were pushed towards growing their way out of trouble. This has inevitably meant more NPAs and a bigger recapitalisation bill.

All hopes are pinned now on the conversion of FIs into banks. This is irritatingly characterised as a move towards 'universal banking', which, truly speaking, is about combining commercial banking with investment banking. There is no call for retaining the distinction between short-term and long-term lending. But the notion that long-term lending will somehow become more viable through the proposed conversion must be viewed with scepticism.

In the first place, it is not the narrowing of spreads on long-term lending that is at the root of the FIs' problems but the overhang of bad debts. Going by Appendix Table IV.5 in *Trend and Progress*, the spread plus other income less other expenses works out to 1.98 per cent of total assets for ICICI and 1.03 for IDBI. The comparable figure for public sector banks (Appendix Table II.5(B)) is 1.34. IDBI may have a little catching up to do but ICICI is much better placed as it is.

However, ICICI's provisions and contingencies, at 1.25 per cent, were the highest of the lot. Subtracting from the figure of 1.98 per cent above yields a net profit to asset ratio of 0.73 per cent. For PSBs, the figures were 0.92 and 0.42 for provisions and profitability, respectively. The comparable figures for IDBI were 0.06 and 0.96. IDBI has clearly under-provided and hence its net NPAs as a proportion of advances is way above those of PSBs. This may shoot up further—as also that of ICICI—consequent to the new NPA norms.

Secondly, while FIs can, no doubt, access cheaper funds by converting into banks, these funds cannot be entirely deployed for long-term purposes without incurring major interest rate risk. So, when FIs talk about becoming more viable by becoming banks, they cannot mean that long-term lending is going to become dramatically more profitable. They mean that they are going to take on banks in the latter's turf, namely, short-term loans and fee income. It is not clear why the FIs should prevail.

This points to two dangers with FIs converting to banks. *One*, without adequate recapitalisation, they end up posing serious systemic risks as takers of public deposits. *Two*, again for want of enough capital, they gradually attenuate their long-term lending role in favour of the cosy spreads provided by risk-free securities. Given the capital market's inability to provide project finance, this has its own implications for industrial growth.

In his recent speech at the WEF-CII summit, the finance minister underlined the problem posed by under-capitalised banks. If he has a strategy for addressing it, he is keeping it secret.

December 6, 2001

Term finance key to IDBI revival

Finance minister, Jaswant Singh, showed commendable courage in grasping the nettle of UTI. He must now act boldly in respect of yet another important institution that needs to be resuscitated, IDBI. The nation's legislators can help him.

The IDBI Bill, 2002, is pending before a Standing Committee of Parliament. The Bill was, in fact, approved by a narrow majority in the Lok Sabha. But the Speaker thought fit to refer the Bill to a Standing Committee so that its implications could be debated thoroughly. This is just as well for, with a little help, IDBI can continue to play a vital role in the provision of long-term finance.

The IDBI Bill provides for IDBI to convert itself into a bank without its having to apply for a banking license. It also seeks to corporatise IDBI. There are three issues on which clarity is required: the extent of recapitalisation to be provided, merger of IDBI with its banking subsidiary, and any special dispensation that the converted entity might need.

In order to be viable, the converted entity must be adequately recapitalised. The Standing Committee must, therefore, ask the government to disclose its recapitalisation plan for IDBI. Critics will scream 'bailout' but it must be understood that such recapitalisation is necessary in the transition to deregulation.

Moreover, we have seen that recapitalisation has worked in the case of Public Sector Banks (PSBs). The notion that government ownership is inconsistent with commercial viability, and, therefore, recapitalisation is to be avoided has taken a battering. Unfortunately, recapitalisation has been unduly delayed in the case of IDBI and it has resulted in a heftier bill than would have been required a few years ago.

The second issue that needs to be sorted out is the possibility of merger of IDBI with a bank. As no PSB is interested, the only option open to IDBI is merger with its subsidiary, IDBI Bank. Merger would provide IDBI with ready access to a 97-branch network and systems that have been stabilised. But the comparison with ICICI is not entirely apt. IDBI Bank is only a tenth the size of IDBI whereas ICICI Bank was about a third the size of ICICI at the time of merger. Further, a lot of preparatory work had preceded the merger in the case of ICICI.

Not least, IDBI Bank's top management is opposed to a merger. It would prefer IDBI to sell its stake in the bank to an international investor even if it means IDBI Bank is stripped of the brand name. IDBI is said to be seeking permission to retain a 49 per cent stake in its subsidiary for the next two or three years and would like to take a decision on merger thereafter.

This is a recipe for trouble. IDBI Bank management cannot be expected to put its best foot forward in the knowledge that if it continues to do well, it cannot avoid its parent's embrace in three years' time. The chances are that key personnel will either leave or will underperform, leading to a depreciation in IDBI's equity stake in IDBI Bank.

IDBI management must, therefore, make up its mind. It must either announce a timetable for merger and deal with the departures of key personnel that would result. Or it must exit IDBI Bank right away and use the cash to develop its own branch network as quickly as possible. Dithering on the merger decision is not on.

The IDBI Bill proposes to exempt the converted entity from SLR requirements for a five-year period. While the Bill makes no mention of this, there have been media reports to the effect that the converted entity will be allowed access to retail deposits but will not be allowed to make retail loans. As retail lending is a big area of opportunity for banks, it would be undesirable to bar the converted entity from this area for as long as five years. If the intention is to offset in some way the benefit of the SLR exemption, then it is preferable to dilute the provision for exemption (say, allow a 90 per cent exemption).

As a late entrant to a competitive field, IDBI cannot hope to replicate what other banks are doing today, which is focus on working capital and retail loans. These may form part of its product-mix but it will necessarily have to concentrate on the area where it has strengths, namely, term finance. .

There is concern today over the vacuum in term 'finance'. It would be in the fitness of things, therefore, if the dynamics of the market were to contrive the existence of an institution that specialises in term finance. Unlike in the past, the viability of the specialist would rest, not on concessional funding, but on access to cheaper funds at the short end. IDBI has a rocky road ahead but, given a clean slate and the right leadership, it has the potential to last the distance.

January 30, 2003

Regulation

RBI Nominee Directors

As it proceeds with deregulation of the banking sector, the RBI needs to review the role of its nominee directors who sit on the boards of private sector banks. Such a review is needed because there may be an inherent contradiction between the RBI's primary objective in nominating such directors, which is monitoring risk and compliance at such banks, and the nominee director's responsibility, as a Board member, to ensure performance on the part of the private bank concerned.

The RBI nominates directors to the boards of nationalised banks as well as private sector banks by virtue of certain enabling provisions in the Banking Regulations Act. Where nationalised banks are concerned, it may have a case for being present on the Board as the representative of the principal owner, the Government of India. This is not true of private sector banks, however, as the RBI has no ownership stake in these banks.

The RBI is present on the boards of private sector banks purely in its capacity as a regulator. Its objectives would be two fold: to ensure compliance with the regulatory framework; and to monitor risk. Thus, the role of RBI nominee-directors would encompass such things as prudential exposure limits for industries and individual companies, reasonableness of large loan sanctions and of deposit and lending rates, and compliance with various RBI guidelines such as those for priority lending. Does RBI really need to have its nominees on private sector banks' boards in order to do its job as regulator?

There is, in the first place, the problem that all non-executive directors face of the time they can devote to scrutiny of papers put up to the Board. It is a moot question, as to what extent the RBI's nominee directors (mostly full-time senior managers of RBI) can stall dubious decisions on the part of a determined management. Further, as deregulation proceeds apace, the RBI also needs to ask itself whether alternative mechanisms for supervision cannot be established short of its foisting nominees on the boards of private banks.

In the case of foreign banks, the RBI does not have nominees on the board. It requires an India Advisory Board and a Management Committee to be constituted, and has stipulated detailed requirements as to what matters each should consider, and also what should be reported to the RBI. Notwithstanding the securities scam, the RBI is apparently satisfied with the quality of monitoring in this system.

Moreover, the newer private sector banks that have sprung up after the recent re-opening of the banking sector to the private sector do not have RBI nominees on their boards. In their case, the RBI seems to have taken the view that the minimal capital requirement of Rs 100 crore is enough of a safety cushion. In the case of several banks, the RBI is reported to have already put in place a system of 'offsite inspection'. With a little refinement, such a system should be adequate to meet the monitoring requirements of RBI in the case of private sector banks as well.

One idea that is said to be doing the rounds at RBI is to identify the weaker banks in the private sector and to confine nominee directors to such banks. This is, perhaps, necessary as part of a phasing-out process, if only to allay concerns about the possible consequences of a wholesale withdrawal. But, on a long-term view, the RBI must face up to the contradictions entailed in a regulatory authority that does not have any ownership interest being represented on the board.

The RBI's nominee-director would have a natural bias towards risk aversion for risk minimisation is the regulator's objective. But performance on the part of any financial institution calls for an appetite for risk. As a member of the Board, the RBI nominee-director cannot escape accountability for performance even though the RBI, lacking an ownership stake, has no particular interest in the bank's performance. Herein lies the contradiction.

This contradiction could prove especially awkward in publicly quoted private sector banks, for RBI nominee-directors could end up being exposed to shareholders' ire in these days of heightened interest in corporate governance. But, in principle, the RBI would be accountable in non-listed private sector banks as well. If there is serious underperformance, the RBI could end up getting tainted by association and having its image and credibility undermined in the process. Exiting from private sector banks and evolving alternative supervisory mechanisms is the best solution under the circumstances.

May 10, 1997

Logic of deregulation

In the wake of the CRB failure, investors, the media and some politicians are baying for the regulators' blood. Even as the investigators try to unravel the CRB affair, we need a few cool heads in government to ensure that we don't get another dose of mindless over-regulation.

In a competitive economy, enterprises will go bust with the best of intentions. In a deregulated financial sector, finance companies will fail even with the most competent and honest people at the top. These are facts of life that people need to get used to as we move from decades of controls towards a market-oriented economy. The logic of deregulation is that, while individual firms fail, the economy performs in the aggregate.

Hundreds of enterprises go to the wall in the US but the American economy continues to perform strongly. Despite the fiasco over loans to Latin America and the colossal failures of savings and loans companies, the American financial sector is vibrant. It is almost as if failures are needed because it is the threat of failure that drives firms—and thereby the economy as a whole—to greater heights of performance.

I'm not trying to gloss over any lapses on the part of regulators in this instance. Yes, the RBI was negligent in conferring respectability on the CRB group by granting it an 'in principle' banking license. SEBI might have helped minimize the damage if it had shared its inspection report with the investing public. And CARE, the rating agency, has not exactly covered itself with glory. But my point is: even with the best of supervision and in the absence of fraud, deregulation implies that quite a few firms will go under. For investors to think otherwise and to expect the regulatory authorities to organize a bailout every time they burn their fingers is to delude themselves.

Deregulation in the financial sector has meant that the limits are off both on borrowing rates and lending rates. Moreover, NBFCs are free to deploy funds virtually as they please so long as they declare their investment intentions upfront to the RBI.

There is nothing to deter an NBFC from raising funds at, say, 24 per cent and deploying all of these in the stock market. If investors want to lend money to such NBFCs, they are welcome to do so, but let them walk into NBFCs with their eyes open.

Don't think that only NBFCs that speculate in the stock market can get into trouble. Even if an NBFC were to engage in pure corporate lending, there would be pitfalls galore. The problem arises from what economists call the 'adverse selection' problem. Quite simply, this means that the wrong sort of clients select themselves.

Higher borrowing rates arising from deregulation translate into higher lending rates. And, in a context of high lending rates, you are bound to have 'adverse selection': you will end up with quite a few of the wrong sort of borrowers. This is because the better class of borrowers will find enough firms willing to lend at a lower rate or they can access the capital market directly. It is the less creditworthy borrowers that will constitute the portfolio of NBFCs that have high lending rates. Quite a few of these borrowers will fail, carrying the NBFCs down with them.

If adverse selection is inevitable in a deregulated environment, with the attendant risk of failures, why deregulate? For this reason: while some finance firms will fail, quite a few will get their portfolios right in the aggregate. They will locate and channel funds to those dynamic enterprises that are capable of powering economic growth. And the whole presumption underlying deregulation is that the impact of the success stories in the economy will outweigh that of the failures.

We have a serious problem with financial failure only when this is the result of mala fide investment decisions. But the answer to this is not to clamp down on deregulation but to come down hard on individuals who profit from mala fide decisions. This is a matter that falls within the ambit of law enforcement, not financial regulation. The experience worldwide shows that for the economy as a whole deregulation works, but that this needs to be backed by stringent law enforcement. We need to take law enforcement a little more seriously if we are to reap the benefits of deregulation.

June 7, 1997

No case for separation

The Narasimham Committee has recommended a separate watchdog for the banking system in place of the existing Board for Financial Supervision that functions under the aegis of the Reserve Bank of India. It is not clear from reports appearing in the press whether the Committee has outlined the rationale for separating out the supervisory function from the RBI. But this is one reform for which the case must be weaker than for some of the others urged by the Committee.

Both types of central banks are to be found across the globe, those that combine the monetary and supervisory roles and those that concern themselves only with the former. The British tradition, from which our central banking practice is derived, was in favour of combination until the decision of the Blair government last year to transfer bank supervision to the newly created Financial Services Authority. The German tradition, in contrast, has favoured separation of the two roles.

The US is conspicuously different. Supervision is shared by several agencies: the Federal Reserve, the Office of the Comptroller of Currency, the state banking authorities and the Federal Deposit Insurance Corporation. There is little evidence to suggest that any system works uniformly better than the other, so one has to weigh the theoretical arguments and figure out what's best in a particular context.

One argument frequently trotted out against combining the monetary and supervisory roles is that it creates potential for conflict of interest. This may happen because monetary conditions might dictate a rise in interest rates, while supervisory concerns about the stability of the banking system might argue in favour of lower rates. Hence, the supervisory role could impede the pursuit of effective monetary policy.

Conflict could also arise because monetary policy is counter-cyclical whereas supervisory policy tends to aggravate cyclical tendencies. Thus, in a recession, the monetary response would be to lower rates and get banks to lend more, whereas the regulatory requirement of higher capital would tend to hobble lending. If the two roles were vested in one central bank, the supervisors might come under pressure to relax their requirements.

But the conflict-of-interest argument can be easily turned around. You could argue that because financial fragility arising from lax supervision is bound to impact adversely on monetary policy, a central bank that combines the two functions would have greater incentive to take its supervisory role seriously. Equally important, it's the central bank that has to deal with payments risk and systemic risk whenever there is a bank failure. If the central bank has to clean up the mess, it should have the ability to prevent one through supervision.

Besides, central banks have developed a culture of independence, which does make for a degree of insulation from political pressures; a new regulatory authority could easily become a happy hunting ground for vested interests. The besetting sin of regulatory bodies everywhere is that they come to be captured by myriad constituencies, and regulators develop their own agendas, which lead to a significant deviation from economic objectives. It makes sense, therefore, for regulation to be carried out by a central bank that is being judged by its performance on crucial economic parameters.

Much depends on how effective the central bank is in its conduct of monetary policy. With an institution of the stature and credibility of the Bundesbank, you don't need to tag on supervision to ensure effectiveness of monetary policy. The Bank of England has followed in the footsteps of the Bundesbank, but that doesn't mean we must rush into emulation. With London's Big Bang and the blurring of boundaries among the different players in the financial sector, it was thought better to have one supervisory authority watching over the emerging financial conglomerates. Such is hardly the case in India, where deregulation has as yet produced only a whimper.

In the end, you have to ask whether the RBI's supervision is improving, and whether its conduct of monetary policy inspires confidence. The answers to both, I suspect, would be in the affirmative, which explains why the RBI is among the more respected central banks in emerging markets. And it would imply that the case for a separate bank supervisor is less than compelling.

May 14, 1998

Conquest of risk

Blood is being split in the American financial sector—on Wall Street for the most part, but Main Street's not escaping unscathed. The villains are not, as apprehended earlier, inscrutable derivatives or high-tech companies, but two of the usual suspects, emerging markets and fixed-income securities.

Losses caused by these have been large enough to resurrect concerns about commercial bank regulation while calling into question banks' expertise in risk management. These concerns ignore the fundamental nature of banking, and are also blind to the improvements in risk management in recent years.

Investors are by now reconciled to losses through proprietary trading in emerging markets and fixed-income securities. Less easy to stomach is the exposure to these that some of the venerable banks opted to take through loans to riskier intermediaries UBS ran up a huge loss on a loan to the now infamous hedge fund, Long Term Capital Management, and Bank America on a loan to a relatively obscure investment bank, DE Shaw. Investors are wondering what the hell management was up to.

Banks are in the business of 'risk transformation', that is, producing desired returns at a lower level of risk than would be possible for individual depositors. They achieve this through the familiar tool of diversification. In principle, lending within prudential limits to high-risk institutions would be consistent with diversification. The problem is opacity.

On the books, these exposures would show up as commercial loans. In actuality, investors and depositors are being exposed to highly speculative activities. When disaster strikes, people feel cheated. Opacity—the inability of investors and depositors to judge the riskiness of assets held by banks—is one reason why banks trade at a discount to the market multiple. It is also the reason we need deposit insurance as well as bank regulation. If depositors could judge accurately how safe their bank was, they would not need to be reassured through deposit insurance; and if the central bank did not need to insure bank deposits, it would not be constrained to regulate. What can be done to pierce the veil?

Precious little. Banks can be required to disclose the broad composition of their assets, but they cannot possibly disclose the identity of individual borrowers except to regulators without harming their business interests.

This does not mean that banks can get away with disguising highly speculative activities as ordinary commercial loans. The Basle norms for capital adequacy that mandate the same weight to commercial loans, irrespective of their inherent risks, need to be amended to provide a graded system of weights that distinguish between a loan to the US government and a loan to a hedge fund.

The proposal to limit overall bank lending to high-risk intermediaries such as hedge funds also deserves to be pursued. Otherwise, risk-averse depositors have to accept that a portion of their funds will be used one way or another for high-risk activities: else, banks as a class would find it difficult to compete with investment banks and other intermediaries. There is little that national regulators can do about this.

The onus for containing risk thus falls squarely on bank management. When banks run up big losses, questions are inevitably asked about whether the sophisticated models for risk management contribute anything. Such criticism overlooks several facts. *First,* the models deal mainly with market risk; credit risk assessment remains pretty much an art as much as a science. *Second,* the models can only help lower risk to an acceptable level of probability; over a long enough time horizon, a low probability event can become a reality.

Most importantly, it is important to tot up both losses and gains over the entire business cycle before judging a bank's risk management capability" what shows up a loss today is probably what caused gains in previous years. The fact that bank failures in the US are fewer despite increased market volatility does suggest that risk in banking has been contained. If, however, the conquest of risk means immunity from big losses, or a repeal of the business cycle, investors are chasing an elusive will-of-the-wisp.

October 29, 1998

Banking on capital

Merton Miller, one of the gurus of finance, once wrote wistfully about how much national economic welfare would rise when "thousands of no longer needed bank regulators (and hundreds of academic banking economists) find themselves forced at last to seek more socially productive lines of economic activity".

Alas, there is no sign that bank regulators are about to preside over their own liquidation. On the contrary, the new framework for capital adequacy proposed recently by the Basle Committee on Banking Supervision means that regulators will have even more to occupy them in the years to come.

The original Basle Accord of 1988 had proposed a minimum capital requirement only for credit risk. This requirement was later expanded to cover market risk. The new framework envisages regulatory capital for interest rate risk (for banks with higher than average risk) and operational risk as well. More jobs in bank regulation, more fodder for bank economists.

Many of the changes to the original Accord proposed by the Basle Committee are both sensible and overdue. In particular, three major shortcomings in the original Accord have been addressed. The uniform weight of 100 per cent for all loans, which had the perverse effect of pushing banks towards riskier loans that yielded higher returns, will make way for a graded system of weights that reflects the risk of the borrower—sovereign, bank and corporate. The weights are to be based on the ratings of credit rating agencies; the more sophisticated banks will be allowed to use internal ratings of borrowers.

Secondly, the new proposals address banks' resort to financial engineering to mask risk exposure and lower capital requirement—say, by swapping mortgages that carry a risk weight of 50 per cent for government bonds that carry zero weight. This problem will be dealt with through weighting of asset-backed securities, again based on market ratings. As for the *third* problem, banks not getting credit for portfolio diversification, the Basle Committee hints at allowing the use of portfolio models down the road.

Capital requirements will be one of three pillars of the new system, the other two being bank supervision and market discipline. By market discipline, the Committee means fuller disclosure and pressures from market participants on banks to allocate appropriate capital.

But this is viewing market discipline purely from within the narrow framework of capital adequacy. It is well to recognize that regulatory capital is based on a feature of banking that strikes at the very root of market discipline—deposit insurance. Deposit insurance makes regulators uninsured creditors of banks. So regulators behave exactly as creditors in the market do with any borrower: they stipulate capital requirements, practise surveillance and so on.

The crucial difference is that in the market you don't have a one-size-fits-all approach to capital norms; this is an inefficiency that is inherent in regulation. Besides, in the market, the cost of borrowing would reflect the riskiness of the borrower. But deposit insurance premia charged by regulators varies very little with bank risk or not at all (although in the US some moves have been initiated towards variable insurance premia). This is because of another distinctive feature of banking: opacity. It is hard for regulators to take a view on a bank's risk profile and arrive at risk-sensitive premia.

How to deal with deposit insurance? One way is to take it as given and to limit moral hazard through capital adequacy, supplemented by other means that deter excessive risk-taking such as assigning a high charter value for banking and bank closure (although research is less than emphatic about the usefulness of these latter).

The bolder alternative is to have limited deposit insurance. As it shifts some of the onus for monitoring banks from regulators to depositors and investors, the attenuation of deposit insurance is key to subjecting banks to market discipline. How far and how fast this can be done depends on how central the traditional banking functions are to an economy. The less central these functions, the lesser is the risk to the financial system.

In the industrial economies, there has been an erosion in the traditional banking functions. There has been a rise in off-balance sheet items in banking (which don't require deposits), greater access to capital markets for borrowers and the emergence of other liquid instruments (such as money market mutual funds) as substitutes for bank deposits. The time may thus have come to grasp the nettle of deposit insurance. But regulators are the last people to be pushing for this sort of reform. For some more time yet, Prof. Miller's dream must await realisation.

June 24, 1999

On unsure ground

In the decade since it was introduced in 1988, the Basle Accord on capital adequacy for banks has undergone refinement and important changes have been proposed recently, which were commented upon in these columns a fortnight ago.

It has also been extensively researched. Economists have sought to assess its impact on bank behaviour as well as on the macroeconomy. The Bank for International Settlements (BIS) has now come out with an excellent summary of research on the subject (*Capital requirements and bank behaviour: the impact of the Basle Accord*).

Any expectation that the research would provide a clear basis for future policy on regulatory capital is, however, in for disappointment. For it is riddled with ambiguities that are truly humungous. The upshot of the BIS survey could well be to reinforce scepticism about the excessive reliance that has come to be placed on capital adequacy as a tool for ensuring stability in banking.

Take the simplest of questions: did the introduction of minimum capital requirements lead banks to hold higher capital ratios? Research shows that capital ratios in the G-10 countries rose from 9.3 per cent in 1988 to 11.2 per cent in 1996. But it can't tell us whether this was because of the Basle Accord itself or because of greater market discipline brought about by the need for transparency ushered in by the Accord.

The BIS paper cites studies that show the Accord did push weakly capitalized banks in the US and elsewhere to quickly come up to prescribed levels. This overlooks the fact that before the era of deposit insurance (which called forth bank regulation), US banks had much higher capital ratios than they have today. Besides, other financial intermediaries in the US even today boast higher ratios than banks.

How do banks tend to meet capital requirements—by raising capital or by reducing risk-weighted assets? Answer: depends on the stage of the business cycle in an economy and on an individual bank's financial situation. The report says, "Raising new capital or boosting retained earnings may be easier in booms whereas cutting back loan books may be more cost effective in economic troughs." Similarly, a bank that was not doing well might be expected to meet capital norms by cutting back lending.

Research is also unable to conclusively determine whether uniform norms for bank loans have, in fact, pushed banks towards taking higher risks, although there is plenty of anecdotal evidence on this. The one area where the evidence is reasonably clear relates to banks' lowering their capital requirements by resort to means such as securitization of assets. This has rendered comparisons between banks' capital ratios increasingly meaningless.

Another key issue, the impact of capital norms on aggregate output, remains a grey area. In theory, if several banks cut back lending to meet capital norms, there could be a credit crunch that would depress output. However, this has been difficult to establish empirically. Some sectors such as real estate and small business that are dependent on bank finance may have been adversely affected by capital norms for banks, but the impact on aggregate output is unclear.

The bottomline? We are on unsure grounds when it comes to laying down capital norms for banks. We cannot quite tell what their impact on bank behaviour or the macroeconomy would be. Even this might be forgiven if only we knew whether or not capital adequacy has made for greater financial stability but this is an issue, the BIS paper pointedly chooses to steer clear of.

However, we do know from recent experience in East Asia as well as from other experiences that bank capital provides scant insurance against bank failure or banking crises. Banks can conform to capital norms and yet crumble because of concentration of credit. More importantly, whole banking systems can be swept off their feet by macroeconomic volatility, by far the biggest factor underlying banking crises, particularly where such volatility coincides with ill-planned financial liberalization.

Thus, regulatory capital has a pretty small role to play in terms of fostering financial stability. At the micro-level, too, it is only one of several tools that can curb excessive risk-taking. A whole range of incentives and market discipline is needed to keep banks from losing their balance—and their balances. Yet capital adequacy has enjoyed such a high profile that both banks and regulators have tended to behave as though capital is all. It's time to move on.

July 8, 1999

Risk after LTCM

Man bites dog A firm that nearly went bust makes payments to its rescuers. Long Term Capital Management (LTCM), the hedge fund whose controversial $3.6 bn bail-out hit the headlines last year, has repaid $1 bn to the 14 banks that stumped up the cash. The move is, perhaps, partly intended to signal to critics that the bail-out has been a success.

Meanwhile, the financial services industry has been labouring to reassure those contemplating stiffer regulation that it is capable of getting its act together. It has just released a comprehensive report on risk management prepared by the Counterparty Risk Management Policy Group which was set up in the wake of the collapse of LTCM and included leading lights from the rescuing institutions. By spelling out in detail what needs to be done in the realm of risk management—and by implication the gaps that obtain today—the report has the virtue of lifting, in conceptual terms, the veil on the collapse of LTCM.

Several hedge funds were in trouble following the turbulence in international markets last year and institutions with exposures to them were badly singed. LTCM's case was exceptional because its collapse appeared to threaten the stability of the international financial system itself. As the Chairman of the Fed, Alan Greenspan, put it, the failure of LTCM could have " potentially impaired the economies of many nations, including our own."

Most people think the problems posed by LTCM arose because its debt to equity ratio of over 20:1 was inordinately high and that lending to hedge funds must be constrained, if necessary through regulation. The key insight of the report is that this perception is incorrect: leverage at financial institutions, it says, must be judged not in conventional accounting terms but in terms of its impact on market risk and liquidity risk.

Thus, an increase in leverage could mean a decrease in market risk—as when financial institutions manage the markets risks they assume from their customers by taking off-setting positions themselves. By the same token, a decrease in leverage could mean an increase in market risk and this was actually seen at many institutions last year. It's the risk profile of assets that counts. On the other hand, leverage amplifies liquidity risk. The implication is that exogenous prescriptions of debt to equity ratios will be of little avail; what is required is a balancing of the market and liquidity risks produced by leverage.

There is more in this vein. The report outlines an analytical framework for integrating leverage, market risk and liquidity risk; improvements in market practices; and regulatory reporting. If reports could kill, risk in the financial world should soon be dead. It is important, however, to step back and look at the big picture. What does a greater focus on risk management mean for financial institutions?

The trouble with models of risk is that they tend to break down in times of crises. The report sets store by 'stress tests' of models to estimate losses under crisis conditions. But the crux of the matter is: what to do when huge losses are indicated under certain assumptions? The logical thing would be to set aside more capital but how many institutions are in a position to do so? If risk management is taken as seriously as the report recommends, it could well mean that many of today's firms must exit their riskier businesses and that the cost of intermediation rises in the rest.

Secondly, if banks could not bring themselves to ask the most basic questions of LTCM, what is their incentive to monitor counterparty risk as rigorously as the report recommends? Remember that the problem was not the failure of LTCM itself but the possible failure of banks exposed to it that were holding positions similar to those of LTCM. Refining tools of risk management will only take us so far; it is the imperative of imposing a greater degree of market discipline on banks that must be grasped.

Finally, implementation of the report would call for a significant increase in resources committed to risk management. Big players could end up having a mini regulatory agency in-house. Since crises are about nasty surprises, only time can tell how well the elaborate edifice proposed will withstand shocks the next time. But at least those of us who are called upon to counsel students on career opportunities know which direction to point in.

July 22, 1999

Corporatisation is no panacea for Public Sector Banks

The quality of governance at Public Sector Banks (PSBs) is making the RBI top brass uneasy. When bank chairmen and directors are primarily accountable to the government, bank performance cannot measure up to what might be in the corporate governance paradigm where it is the Board that calls the shots. Thus, spake RBI Governor, Bimal Jalan, and Deputy Governor, YV Reddy, earlier this month in their addresses at the NIBM and the Bank Economists' Conference in Kolkata, respectively.

Lest this be construed as an argument for privatisation, the two bankers made clear that they do not think highly of the quality of governance in private banks either. A feature common to private sector banks, Dr Jalan noted, was that there was "little check on the CEO, who is generally also closely linked to the largest owner groups. Boards or auditing systems are not very effective".

Clearly, the men at the helm at RBI believe that improvements in PSBs must be sought within the domain of government ownership, not through a change in ownership itself. The key to such improvements, they suggest, might be corporatisation of banks. This means that banks must be covered by the Companies Act rather than by one or other of the special Acts that apply to banks. The two regulators think this essential if banks are to acquire a genuine board-driven culture.

This sounds self-evident in principle. Yet the case is less straightforward than it seems. One reason is that we are yet to see the emergence of a Board-driven culture in corporate India-that is, managers held to account by Boards. With a few exceptions, we have owner-managed companies with the trappings of a Board culture.

The reason is not far to seek. A Board-driven culture emerges when you have institutional investors holding management accountable and an active market for corporate control. In India, institutional investors have tended to be passive and the market for corporate control remains weak. The most likely outcome, should the government relinquish powers to bank boards, would be what Dr Jalan laments in private sector banks—a CEO who is a law unto himself.

The government can experiment with the governance structure at public sector companies in the hope that the right checks and balances will evolve. But it cannot afford to do so with PSBs, given the bailout costs associated with bank failures. For precisely this reason, Dr Reddy's proposal for creating a holding company, manned by professionals, for all PSBs must remain a non-starter: one shudders to think of what such a company's failure might mean. UTI is a case in point. It enjoyed a large measure of autonomy from government but, in the end, the Board proved utterly ineffective.

Given the present state of governance in general, therefore, the RBI is better off pushing for improvements that are attainable under government control. It could stipulate a desirable composition for bank Boards, including the number of government nominees and independent directors. It could lay down qualifications for independent directors. It might lobby for a more broad-based Appointments Board that will select bank directors in addition to selecting CEOs. All this will require some overdue flexing of muscle on the part of the RBI.

But there is a more fundamental reason why it may make sense to live with inadequacies in bank governance under government ownership. There is room for doubt as to whether the objective of shareholder wealth maximisation, on which corporate governance is founded, is appropriate to banks.

Banks are highly leveraged institutions. Where managerial rewards are linked to shareholder value, as in the Anglo-Saxon governance paradigm, bank managers have more incentive than usual to take on extraordinary risk—in finance jargon, the problem of 'risk-shifting incentives' is exacerbated. The pursuit of efficiency could thus easily be at the expense of stability. Indeed, recent research suggests that bank regulation, which factors in bank capital but not top management compensation, may be ineffective. *(Kose John et al, "A theory of bank regulation and management compensation," Review of Financial Studies,* Spring 2000).

PSBs possess enormous advantages in terms of their scale of operations, depositor confidence and untapped avenues for growth. The question is whether these advantages can be made to offset inefficiencies in governance inevitable under government ownership and to conduce to an appropriate trade-off between efficiency and stability in banking. The RBI's answer thus far has been in the affirmative. Should the RBI's judgement change —and only if it does—we should be contemplating changes in ownership rather than changes in structure under government ownership.

January 31, 2002

Investment Banking

Paper thin Chinese walls

In the deluge of news reports about the failed CRB Group, a small item caught my eye. It was about the SEBI inspection report on CRB Capital Markets. The report is said to have drawn attention to the fact that the securities and mutual fund activities of the Group were located in the same building, and expressed its disapproval of this fact. It was a classic case of potential conflict of interest; or, in the lingo of investment banking, the absence of 'Chinese walls' between the two operations.

Conflicts of interest are a fact of life in investment banking. If not carefully handled, they could work to the detriment of investors and become a serious threat to fairness in the functioning of the market. That is why in the advanced markets of the world, the regulatory authorities come down with a heavy hand at the slightest sign of conflicts of interest. We in India are, unfortunately, still very far from getting serious about this business.

There are several sources of conflicts of interest in investment banking. One that happens to be quite pervasive in India is for analysts, traders and even fund managers to trade on their own accounts without being subject to any discipline whatsoever. As employees of an investment bank are privy to a whole lot of information about recommendations and client orders, this presents a ridiculously simple route to make money that not many can remain untempted to.

In the international markets, investment banks and securities firms have strict rules governing trading by employees on their own accounts. In the first place, such trading has to be done through an account maintained with the firm itself. *Secondly*, there is a certain period before and after a recommendation is made during which such trading is outlawed in the case of stocks that are a part of an analyst's portfolio. *Thirdly*, every trade requires the written approval of a fairly senior person.

Major international investment banks view any contravention of the above procedures as insider trading and deal severely with violations. The employee would be dismissed and the matter reported to the regulatory authorities, which would likely lead to deregistration of the employee.

Very few investment banks and securities firms operating in India (including foreign firms) have instituted such procedures. Could it be that people at the top are insider traders themselves and would not like to be inhibited by such procedures? Many firms probably think that winking at insider trading on the part of their employees is a way of keeping salary and bonus levels low. If SEBI is serious about curbing insider trading, it must insist that all firms registered with it institute such practices. It must also begin the process of registering employees at securities firms, so that the threat of deregistration acts as a deterrent to insider trading.

Yet another form of conflict of interest is between the brokerage and corporate finance arms of an investment bank. Corporate Finance needs business from companies and it would be extremely leery about doing anything that might antagonize management at these companies.

The brokerage arm has no commercial interest in the companies it monitors, its loyalties being to its institutional or retail clients. So the brokerage arm would have no qualms about making a 'Sell' recommendation, but this is bound to be fiercely resisted by the corporate finance arm. The matter would be suitably sorted out, depending on the internal politics of the firm.

Most often, investment banks opt to make a 'Hold' recommendation on paper, while counselling their clients over the phone to sell. A Corporate Finance client cheesed off by a 'Hold' recommendation would be pointed out a few favourable things in the concerned report, and suavely assured that the investment bank tended to be extremely conservative in making recommendations, and that a 'Buy' was pretty rare at the firm. If the brokerage arm were to put a 'Buy' recommendation on a company purely in order to help corporate finance win a mandate, that would be a serious case of conflict of interest. Similarly, for corporate finance to pass on information obtained confidentially from clients is simply not on.

Investment banks' recommendations have been suspected precisely because fund managers are aware of the potential for conflict of interest. 'Independent' brokerages—the ones that did not have any business other than buying and selling securities—

played up their independence to the hilt, and won quite a few points for themselves. But such brokerages have been swallowed up one by one by capital-rich investment banks. It is unclear what the regulatory authorities can do about this form of conflict of interest; it's best that clients of the securities arm keep an eye on the Corporate Finance client list of investment banks whose recommendations they are using.

Perhaps, the most serious form of conflict of interest is that between the securities and asset management arms of a financial firm, which appears to have been a part of the problem at the CRB group. The big investment banks, such as Merrill Lynch and Morgan Stanley, also happen to be big names in asset management. In India, leading players such as SBI Capital Markets have sister firms that are also prominent in asset management. Unlike the two forms of conflicts of interest mentioned above which are entirely in-house affairs, this source of conflict of interest is between two separate legal entities. The imperative to maintain a Chinese wall thus takes on added significance in this context.

The potential for abuse here is truly enormous. An unscrupulous management can easily get its securities arm to make recommendations on stocks held by its asset management arm that are calculated to drive up prices of those stocks and boost the net asset value of the mutual fund. Worse, if it believes that certain stocks are headed southwards, it could dump those stocks on unsuspecting clients of its securities operation by getting its securities arm to make favourable recommendations about these stocks.

Regulatory authorities have sought to contain such conflicts of interest by making certain prescriptions about maintaining a 'Chinese wall' between the asset management and securities arms. The most important one is about ensuring that day-to-day management of the two entities is not in the same hands (this is an almost sure recipe for disaster). Another is maintaining a physical 'arms-length relationship', that is, making sure that the two entities are not housed in the same premises. Yet another is about not using staff from one operation for the other; and so on.

It's anybody's guess to what extent such Chinese walls are maintained in our setting. There's no reason to believe that we are less lax in this respect than in others. One way to find out and to make sure that people fall in line is for SEBI to order an audit of transactions of the two arms on, say, a random basis. If SEBI can select firms for audit based on market intelligence, so much the better. Alternatively, such inspections could be made a regular affair with at least major firms being inspected once every few years. Yes, it could prove tedious for SEBI and for the firms concerned. But in a market such as ours, where abuses are rampant, it's worth going the extra mile to convince people that we are serious about regulation.

June 12, 1997

Too hot to handle

European ambitious in the realm of global investment banking received another setback recently with problems surfacing at Nat West Markets (NWM), the investment banking arm of Nat West Bank—UK's biggest in terms of assets. The parent bank sounded a profit warning after incurring losses on account of mispriced options at its investment banking arm. With institutional shareholders turning on the heat, the bank's top management has indicated that it would be taking a hard look at its earlier strategy of trying to build a global investment bank. This could mean NWM shedding its global ambitions in favour of becoming a niche player.

Nat West's problems follow a series of European failures in investment banking in recent years. Barings was taken over by ING Bank, Kleinwort Benson by Dresdner Bank, Warburg, perhaps Europe's most serious contender at one point, by SBC and Morgan Grenfell by Deutsche Bank. Each investment bank's failure has provided an opportunity for a major commercial bank to further its ambitions to straddle both commercial and investment banking. The fortunes of the merged entities are being watched closely, especially by the big American investment banks whose domination of the global business the Europeans have sought to challenge.

European investment banks came a cropper mainly because they lacked the staying power to build a credible business in the US, home to the largest pool of capital in the world. They needed a US presence in order to win underwriting, mergers and acquisition and related investment-banking business from clients worldwide. Given American investment bank's established relationships with domestic institutional investors, this was bound to be long drawn-out affair.

It also meant having to earn returns on a very high cost base, the result either of expensive acquisitions in the US or of luring people away from American investment banks at fancy salaries. European investment banks' capital proved unequal to the task particularly when the downturns in the US market pinched trading profits.

That's where the big European commercial banks, with their deep pockets, came in. The continental banks faced shrinking margins on their mainstream banking business and many concluded that they need the investment banking business in order to sustain returns to shareholders over the long-term.

They key issue is how long, long term is going to be. For as a recent article in *The Economist* points out, most European banks are still a long way off from making their acquisitions work. BZW earned 8 per cent on its capital, DMG 9 percent, and Barings contribution to its parent's profit was negligible. The journal also mentions that Dresdner Kleinwork Benson's return is only marginally better than DMG's. The only decent performer is SBC Warburg which earned 16.4 percent on equity, but even this performance is put in the shade by Merril's 28 percent return on capital last year.

The problem is not just high upfront cost or expensive contracts for stars. There are the inevitable pains that go with integrating an acquisition with the parent, a problem that is compounded where the two entities belong to different countries. What makes matters worse is the problem of marrying the staid, laid-back culture of a commercial bank with the go-getting, aggressive culture of an investment bank. Banking's prudential culture stems from two things: *one*, the high leveraged nature of banking which increases the prospect of equity being wiped out by a major indiscretion: and, *secondly*, the knowledge that governments cannot allow big banks to fail. These two factors impose an awesome responsibility on bankers.

Investment banks do not risk capital for all their activities, they are not as highly leveraged, and they can (and do) sink without governments batting an eyelid. As a result, there is a gung-ho approach to risk-taking at an investment bank that would be anathema to the typical European commercial bank.

To retain this character in its investment banking arm without upsetting structures, systems and attitudes at the parent is quite a challenge for a commercial bank. Some of America's fleet-footed commercial banks might just bring it off if and when Glass-Steagall is repealed. Small wonder, though, that Europe's stodgy commercial banks are finding investment banking too hot to handle.

July 19, 1997

Salomon's judgement

The merger of Salomon Brothers, Wall Street's legendary bond trading firm, with Smith Barney of the Traveler's Group promises to give fresh impetus to the ongoing process of consolidation in the American financial sector. Salomon evidently judged the merger price of twice its book value irresistible; a year ago, it was trading at close to book value.

The merger propels the combined Salomon Smith Barney into second place in terms of shareholders' funds in the American investment banking league, just behind Morgan Stanley Dean Witter Discover. Merrill Lynch, the thundering herd of Wall Street, is now relegated to third place. But the merger has more to it than size. It combines the global presence and investment banking strengths of Salomon with Smith Barney's nationwide retail network, precisely the logic underlying Morgan Stanley's merger with Dean Witter a few months ago.

There we have the defining characteristics of the present wave of consolidation. Capital is one; global origination is another; and retail distribution in the American market the third.

The ruling wisdom is that consolidation, based on these factors, must inevitably lead to ten or fewer players dominating the global investment banking market. As only the top three investment banks measure up on all the three criteria, this would imply that the rest must make up their minds on whom they would like to marry. There's no dearth of suitors for the other investment banks: the top three American investment banks themselves, the leading European aspirants, and, perhaps most importantly, the leading American commercial banks.

With regulatory barriers between commercial and investment banking in the US coming down in recent years, commercial banks have begun acquiring securities firms lately, but the targets have all been small fry. Only two commercial banks, JP Morgan and Bankers Trust, have investment banking operations that put them in the top ten in the American investment banking league.

It's not easy for the big commercial banks to justify an investment banking acquisition. Banks trade at price-earnings multiples of 14, while investment banks, with their perceived higher risks, rate a multiple of only around 10. But commercial banks in the US, like their counterparts elsewhere, face falling profit margins and earnings growth. Besides, returns to equity at the top investment banks are higher.

Moreover, there is a sense that conventional balance sheet lending needs to be supplemented with equity finance if commercial banks are to get intimate with their clients; such intimacy could be crucial to gaining lucrative advisory business as well. So, American commercial banks are beginning to perceive investment banking as integral to their overall profile.

This could mean that not even the top three investment banks are safe. For, the commercial banks outrank investment banks by a wide margin on both market capitalization and earnings. The top 50 US banks have a market capitalization of around $500 billion, while that of the 20 publicly traded securities firms is only $75 billion. Citicorp's market cap of around $61 billion and Bank America's $51 billion are way ahead of Morgan Stanley's $33 billion and Merrill's $25 billion. A Chase Manhattan takeover of Merrill Lynch is a possibility that tantalizes Wall Street.

Yet, it is possible to get carried away by merger mania and lose sight of basics. The Salomon Smith Barney merger, which brings underwriting, advisory and retail distribution under one roof, is a case of vertical integration. And vertical integration is not without risk; it implies a high cost base that renders a firm vulnerable to a downturn. Why own distribution when you can pay a fee to somebody who does? Similarly, one would think that for commercial banks to diversify into investment banking flies in the face of 'core competence'—a nostrum foreign consultants have been merrily peddling to us here. As for size being everything, it appears that American businesses have not learnt from their own dinosaurs.

If there is a disregard for basics, it is partly because of the feeling that, with consolidation on in right earnest, not many good acquisition prospects will be available down the road. But euphoria could also be a factor. After six years of unabated expansion of the US economy, forgetfulness about business cycles is natural. When the present bout of expansion ends, the wisdom of many of today's mergers will be tested. It has happened before.

October 11, 1997

Pocketful of poses

Rating agencies in the country get panned every time a finance company goes under. Our agencies can draw comfort from the fact that their illustrious counterparts overseas have fared no better, their record in South Korea being a case in point. It isn't just that Moody's and Standard & Poor's failed miserably to hoist danger warnings. They have since done their bit to worsen the crisis by over-reacting after the event.

Fund managers who burnt their fingers by relying on credit ratings are now busy dumping Korean assets because their charters bind them to hold only investment grade assets as determined by the rating agencies. The *Financial Times* suggests that the problem is blind dependence on rating agencies; if only fund managers could think for themselves, they would do better.

Really? The FT's faith in the superior wisdom of fund managers is misplaced if only because the investment banking arms of the major financial conglomerates that also manage funds—such as Merrill Lynch, SBC Warburg and Deutsche Morgan Grenfell—produced research on Asia that hardly set them apart from the rating agencies. The leading investment banks failed equally to anticipate the crisis in East Asia and many were slow to react even after the early warning signs, such as the devaluation of the Thai baht.

And fund managers are not some special breed in the financial sector; most of them start off as investment bankers. Research people at funds are drawn from investment banks or rating agencies or the same pool of graduating MBAs. So, fund managers can be safely presumed to be at least as fallible as rating agencies or investment bankers. They would be particularly fallible in the area in which credit rating agencies have shown themselves wanting: analysis of sovereign risk. The job would likely be left to some greenhorn with little familiarity with distant markets.

Consider: if fund managers have superior expertise, how come they tend to be out-performed year after year by index funds?

And how is it that portfolios selected on the basis of dart throws have produced better returns than fund managers using research?

During my days in investment banking, I used to be amazed at the casualness with which fund managers took investment decisions. I got calls from managers asking about companies after they had bought the stocks; often they had no clue as to what businesses the companies were in. Bond salesmen, responding to requests for Indian debt paper, would rush to me for a snap opinion while keeping their clients on hold over the phone: the mind boggled at the thought that a few million dollars would change hands based on my whim of the moment. A great many fund managers have little or no formal background in Finance; quite a few are from the liberal arts. So much for expertise.

Shorn of its pretensions, fund management is all about diversification. Small investors lack the resources to acquire a set of diversified stocks, so funds that pool their savings do the job for them. By spreading funds across large- and small-cap stocks, sectors and markets, it's possible to achieve reasonable performance.

Mind you, performance in this business means, not achieving spectacular returns, but merely doing as well as the market. As long as you are diversified across basically sound stocks, you don't to have worry much. And assigning weights to stocks and markets is no big deal either: market cap or sales (GDP) would do nicely. Given the herd mentality, the outcomes won't be very different if fund managers make their own assessments, instead of relying on rating agencies.

The larger the fund, the greater the scope for diversification. Besides, there are economies of scale with respect to transaction costs and back office operations. Hence, size is critical. Savings on operational costs can then be passed on to investors and can help a fund outperform rivals. So the real challenge, once you have reasonable performance, is to acquire size. And that has to do with marketing, not financial wizardry.

A seasoned investment banker once said to me about investment banking, "Of course, we need to spend time on research, but, remember, 50 per cent of it is a marketing game". Wise words that would apply even more to fund management.

January 8, 1998

Perils of flying high

In less than a decade, Peregrine went from nothing to Asia's premier independent investment bank to liquidation. Its downfall was caused by its star performer, the fixed income group that created a market for Asian junk bonds. Peregrine had a large chunk of junk bonds on its books. When the region melted and borrowers defaulted, the firm was devastated.

The familiar explanations are being resurrected: the star syndrome at investment banks and weak controls. Where an individual or department is pulling in huge profits, management tends to overlook excesses. Risks pile up, leading to an implosion. But if high flyers seem invariably to have weak controls, does that not suggest that the problem is not controls but the growth policy itself?

The problem is created in the first place because management asks the wrong question: what is the maximum growth we can attain? The right question, as Peter Drucker has pointed out, is: what is the minimum growth we need in order to survive? Too low a growth rate could mean loss of competitiveness. This everybody understands. But too high a growth rate increases risks, operational and financial. This, even if understood, is ignored in practice. Growth becomes a test of machismo—and that's a recipe for disaster.

The over-riding importance of growth policy was brought home to me by an American investment bank I once worked for. The firm's been around for all of sixty years—a period in which several big names arose and disappeared. My firm had made it to the top ten. And it had done so, not through leaps and bounds, but by literally clawing its way up inch by inch. Central to its success was management's philosophy of growing at a pace that was consistent with mastering all the existing businesses. And the test of mastery was return on equity: for years, the firm had the highest return on equity on Wall Street.

Particularly in the financial sector, spectacular growth almost certainly carries within itself the seedbeds of an equally dramatic fall. This is partly because of the highly leveraged nature of the business, and partly because rapid growth diminishes the capacity to track risk. So when a finance firm comes from nowhere and starts making a splash, scepticism is in order. Similarly, in an established firm, if profits start soaring and can't be explained, alarm bells must sound. Had they done so at the foreign banks in 1992, we wouldn't have had a securities scam on our hands.

Growth mania is destructive in other businesses, too: one of the most common causes of sickness in industry is a liquidity crunch arising from runaway growth. In the early stages of a business, high growth is something of a statistical illusion as it's on a low base. When management uses that as a reference rate for the future, the business can get into trouble.

The problem is by no means confined to small businesses. Vaulting ambitions on the part of corporates are an important reason why our primary market is in the doldrums today. Remember the 'mega-projects' of a few years ago? Businessmen, who had grown to a few hundred crores, thought they could leapfrog into the big league with a project several times the size of their existing business. They all came a cropper. Indeed, with the exception of the Ambanis, I can't think of any business group in India that's managed to sustain a high growth rate.

What applies to a firm also applies to the economy as a whole. Sure, we need to grow, and six per cent is better than three, but is eight a better target than six? Answering this would require us to think through what would be required to sustain an eight per cent growth rate. If it is to come from domestic businesses, do they have the skills to manage the requisite growth? If foreign investment is the key, do we have the capacity to absorb $10 billion? Are we in a position to take measures necessary to bring in $10 billion—on issues like full convertibility, exit policy, hostile takeovers? And, most importantly, can we handle the downside risks? When high flyers crash, it's not a pretty sight, you know.

Januray 22, 1998

American century

Salaries in investment banking sound like light years in an astronomy class: the numbers simply don't make sense. They also stand conventional wisdom on its head: rolling stones actually end up gathering impressive quantities of moss.

These thoughts are prompted by the recent defections from the ranks of Deutsche Bank's technology group in the US. The team, which was enticed from Morgan Stanley just two years ago, has now switched loyalties to Credit Suisse First Boston reportedly for a sum of one billion dollars. Its head walks into $250 million. Numbers not to be sniffed at even if they cover three to five year contracts. Deutsche Bank's North American strategy mounted at great expense over the past few years, lies in tatters.

What justifies such compensation figures in investment banking? And how on earth does a firm make money in a market where it has to pay exorbitant premia upfront to get people?

At the top end, executive pay in investment banking in the US is not very different from that in other industries. Investment banking differs only in being rather more egalitarian: a star trader down the line can take home more than his CEO. This is possible because investment banking is genuinely a 'people-driven business' in an era in which all businesses tend to appropriate the cliché. It relies heavily either on an individual's skill (as in the case of a trader using his instincts or a rocket scientist drawing up an elaborate structure for a deal) or on an individual's relationships (as in the case of people in corporate finance or brokerage).

You could argue that the latter holds for banking, too, but there is a difference. In investment banking, the relationship is more deal-centred, whereas in banking there is an ongoing relationship embracing several individuals so that the institutional connection is often stronger than that of any individual. The other difference is that banking is inherently risk-averse and this limits the potential for extraordinary performance and reward.

The differences with manufacturing are even more pronounced. When a business is people driven, it implies that individual performance is easily measured. It also means that start-up costs for a new recruit are non-existent. A trader needs only a terminal in order to become operational from day one, unlike in manufacturing where results show over a longish cycle stretching from product conception to launch and thereafter.

Moreover, given the inter-connectedness of various departments in manufacturing, a manager would have to come to grips with cultural and administrative issues at the new firm in order to perform; this factor is less material in an investment bank where several departments are standalone operations. Finally, the stock option culture is more pervasive at investment banks and this appears to foster greater all-round commitment to performance. The rewards are commensurately high.

For firms like Deutsche Bank that have deep pockets, the strategy for breaking into such a market appeared deceptively simple: lure away the best people and await returns over the long haul. Extraordinary salaries in some cases could be justified by a higher overall profile for the firm and by the potential for generating cross-border deals apart from those in the American market.

The downside is now painfully apparent. Stars can be fickle in their loyalties; besides, integrating them with the more staid parts of the business can prove extremely tricky. This strategy having failed, Deutsche Bank is now thinking of acquiring a whole firm. But that risks a clash of cultures on a bigger scale.

If poaching people didn't help Deutsche Bank, can CSFB succeed by raising the stakes even further? It could because it has had a head start in the American market. For CSFB, acquiring a bunch of stars is not about breaking into the market, it's about vaulting into the ranks of the top five. And it's making the attempt when, like its American counterparts, it's benefiting from the US bull market. The lesson is one that several European firms have learnt the hard way, namely, that an entrenched position in the world's largest pool of funds is critical to global leadership in investment banking.

Deutsche über alles? Nichte, mein freund. At least where investment banking is concerned, we seem headed for yet another American Century.

July 23, 1998

Games they play

When Lehman Brothers downgraded Amazon.com, the firm's analysts drew an angry response from Amazon's CEO. Clients of Lehman Brothers who sold must have been pleased, though, seeing the subsequent plunge in the stock' s price. Nearer home, when L&T's latest results disappointed by a wide margin, it was the analysts' turn to feel aggrieved. Following the steep declines in prices of high-tech IPOs here and abroad, investors cannot be too happy with either the companies or analysts.

Companies, analysts and investors constitute the three corners of the investment triangle. So who is to blame when returns disappoint? Analysts for doing a poor job? Or companies for misleading analysts and investors? Or do companies and analysts collude at the expense of investors?

The performance of analysts has been the subject of considerable research. In his best-selling Random walk down Wall Street, published in the early seventies, Burton Malkiel cited studies that looked at analysts' earnings forecasts and others that evaluated returns generated by fund managers based on analysts' recommendations. Analysts' performance on both counts was disappointing.

Recent research gives analysts more credit, but not an awful lot. One study, cited in *The Economist* (July 22), finds that the contribution of analysts is 'modest at best'. Analysts' predictions, according to the study, are useful only in selected cases—loss-making companies, relatively small firms, high-tech industries.

Another study, reviewed and posted at the Wharton Knowledge Newsletter site (July 4-18), looked at 360,000 recommendations from 269 brokerage houses in the period 1986-96. It found that stocks receiving strong positive recommend-ations from analysts did better than the average stock. This suggests that analysts are indeed capable of picking winners. The study, however, found that the gains would have accrued only to large institutional investors who traded large blocks of shares and reacted instantly to recommendations, not to ordinary investors.

Do companies mislead analysts? Analysts depend on companies for vetting their forecasts, so the 'optimism bias' seen in analysts' forecasts often reflects companies' own optimism about the future. Companies have, however, found that deliberate exaggeration or failure to give out bad news on time does not pay. When results are way below expectations, the company's shares get trashed and it is difficult to regain investors' confidence. Many companies these days find merit in inducing 'pessimism bias' in analysts. When earnings exceed forecasts, stock prices tend to rise smartly.

There is one area, though, where companies are keen to have inflated forecasts and analysts seem ready to oblige—IPOs. Anecdotal evidence on this subject is aplenty but a recent study has documented the phenomenon with some rigour. ("Conflict of interest and the credibility of underwriter analysts recommendations", R Michaely and KL Womack, Review of Financial Studies, Special 1999).

The authors studied 'buy' recommendations for 391 IPOs in the period 1990-91. They compared analysts' recommendations for stocks underwritten by their firms with those for stocks underwritten by competitors. The first group should have fared better given analysts' access to superior information; in fact, it was the second group that did. This does point to bias among analysts in the cases of stocks underwritten by their firms.

We should not be surprised. There are huge rewards to attracting underwriting deals—the authors note that analysts who do so earn bonuses two or four times of those analysts who don't. It is impossible to attract such deals without favourable coverage of the firms concerned. One outcome of investment banking relationships is that 'buy' recommendations outnumber 'sell' by a wide margin, something that has attracted criticism from the SEC Chairman, Arthur Levitt.

As the recent wave of overpriced high-tech IPOs shows, investment bankers have changed little over the past decade. But nor has investor behaviour. Michaely and Womack say that investors have not discounted underwriters' bias sufficiently. If they have not done so after getting their fingers burnt so often, it only confirms that irrationality and herd behaviour are alive and well in the stock market. All too often investors have themselves to blame as much as analysts and companies.

August 17, 2000

Blame investment bankers, not manipulators, for market volatility

Hell hath no fury like Finance Ministry scorned by the market. With the stock market having plummeted in the wake of a 'brilliant' budget, the ministry seems to think this is mostly, if not entirely, the work of 'market manipulators'—in the popular imagination, those greasy bumpkins on Dalal Street who make a living out of speculating on stocks. This is taking too facile a view of the decline in stock prices.

Whether a bear cartel took advantage of inside information in order to hammer down prices is a matter that must await SEBI's ongoing enquiry. But even if this is established, it does not follow that this was the key factor behind the recent crash in prices.

For a market crash that is unrelated to fundamentals to be sustained for long would require a much greater erosion of liquidity than has happened in the present instance. After all, there have been no significant defaults at the stock exchanges, and no institutional investor, domestic or foreign, has suffered as a result.

There is good reason to believe that the declines in the Sensex mirror the battering of ICE stocks in the American market just as the earlier rise mirrored the heady rise in prices in the US market. Between 2000 and 2001 (using March 31 throughout), 90 per cent of the decline in the Sensex was on account of the five ICE stocks in the Sensex. The market capitalisation of the five stocks themselves fell by 65 per cent—an order of magnitude that is consistent with the fall in the Nasdaq; not surprising, as two of the stocks happen to be listed in the US market.

The fall in the five ICE stocks has been modest compared to the rise that took place earlier. Between 1999 and 2000, the same ICE stocks had risen by 335 per cent and accounted for 68 per cent of the rise in market capitalisation in the Sensex. Nearly half the increase in market capitalisation in the five ICE stocks came from the two stocks listed in the US market and that rode the crest of the wave of euphoria in the US.

This does suggest that, whatever the manipulation in select stocks, the movements of the market index cannot be ascribed to such manipulation or indeed to factors peculiar to the Indian context. The rise and fall in the Sensex mostly reflected what observers had come to recognize as the Indian stock market's slavish imitation of trends in the Nasdaq.

Inveterate believers in market efficiency will ascribe the high volatility in prices that we have seen over the past two years to the revision in expectations about the new economy in the United States. As the founding father of modern finance, Merton Miller, pointed out, in the Gordon growth model used for estimating stock prices, even a minor change to the expected growth rate or the risk premium can cause huge swings in stock prices. Miller was loath to view such volatility as necessarily the bursting of a bubble. It was quite possible, he argued, for rational investors to radically revise their views about growth prospects. (*Financial innovations and market volatility*).

Others, such as Robert Shiller of Yale University, are inclined to take a less charitable view of market volatility. Shiller has been highly critical of investment bankers, analysts and also the media for peddling exaggerated hopes about the new economy —hopes that were bound to be dashed to the ground. But this is hardly a new phenomenon. It is really the nature of the beast.

The investment community thrives on feeding the market with hype about future prospects. The surest proof is that analysts' earnings forecasts have been found to err on the optimistic side. It cannot be otherwise, given that the corporate finance arms of the firms they work are hungry for business from firms about whom research reports are written.

The conflict of interest between the underwriting and research arms of investment banking firms has proved quite intractable. There was quite a stir last year when a top investment bank, CSFB, sacked its highly rated bank analyst. Many felt that the analyst had paid the price for having had the temerity to issue 'sell' recommendations on as many as 40 banks. Now that investment banks have major interests in asset management, there is further pressure on analysts to produce cheery reports.

With analysts and fund managers holding forth on television these days, the hype naturally gets magnified.

So, for the swings that we have been subjected to, blame mostly the tribe of investment bankers in the US and their cousins in this country. It is a mercy that the disappointments have been confined to the secondary market this time round and we have been spared the agony of vast funds being sucked into spurious IPOs.

April 12, 2001

America's investment banks under siege from multiple quarters

Arriving in New York last week, the writer got a keener sense of the despondency that has swept the Nasdaq and that has been mirrored in our own market. What started as a trickle of cutbacks and failures in technology companies a few months ago has since grown into an avalanche.

A friend, who owns a restaurant in New Jersey, mentioned with some embarrassment that he was being inundated with resumes from Indian software engineers. Many had tried hard to underplay their computer backgrounds and to emphasise instead their proficiency as waiters.

But the similarity does not end with the collapse in high-tech stocks. As in India, the crash in the market has touched off a furore among investors and drawn the attentions of regulators and law-makers to sharp practices in the financial community. It is interesting that even in the world's most efficient financial market, a sharp erosion in shareholder wealth instantly invites suspicions of market manipulation.

Unlike in India, however, the focus of attention is not the secondary market but the primary or IPO (intial price offerings) market. Seven of Wall Street's top investment banks are being investigated for possible malpractices in the issue of IPOs. The investigation is being carried out by the SEC and the US Attorney.

At the same time, angry investors, assisted by America's trigger-happy law firms, have filed nearly a dozen class action suits against investment banks and the companies they took public. On top of it all, analogous to our own JPC enquiry, Congress will hold hearings into the role played by investment banks during the equity bubble of recent years.

The charge against investment banks is that they struck deals with favoured clients that entailed a quid pro quo: clients would be allocated some of the hottest IPOs and would return the favour in ways that were illegal.

The IPO market in the US has no pretensions to 'fairness' to the small investor as it is understood in India or even in the UK. Investment banks can make allocations of IPOs to applicants as they please; clients who generate trading or other business naturally get precedence.

The 'pro-rata' system that gives the small investor a half-way decent chance of getting an allocation in India does not obtain in the US. Nor are people apologetic about the tilt against the small investor in the allocation process. An academic colleague here put it bluntly, "IPOs are all about raising money for firms; they are not about fairness to the small investor".

IPOs are hot property at any time because they tend to be underpriced—in normal times, around 15-20 per cent below the price they would touch when trading began. At the peak of the Internet bubble, when prices shot up several times the offer price on listing, an IPO allocation guaranteed enormous riches.

As reported in the *Financial Times* (May 7), one of the charges against investment banks is that they allocated IPOs to favoured clients on the understanding that the clients would support the stock in the aftermarket. In effect, after keeping stock prices aloft, favoured clients exited, leaving others with overvalued stock. This is clearly a case of rigging that, if proved, is bound to invite severe penalties.

A less straightforward charge relates to the understanding that investment banks are said to have had with clients that the latter would generate commensurate business for the investment banks or pay higher than usual charges on share transactions. On this, the legal position appears somewhat ambiguous. While it is accepted that clients allocated IPOs would return the favour in sundry ways, explicit agreements to that effect are frowned upon.

Investment banks are moving to contain the fallout of the IPO debacle. Many are said to be conducting their own investigations. Further, in an attempt to tackle what is widely believed to be the root of the problem of hyped-up IPOs—the conflict of interest between the research and corporate finance arms—heads of research at investment banks are putting together a code of conduct for analysts. One principle that is being talked about is analysts' bonus will be tied to the overall fee pool, rather than to individual deals. Presumably, this would mitigate the anxiety to sugar-coat the research report in a given deal.

Will it? Can investment banks bring themselves to actually reward analysts who shoot down deals? Anybody with a nodding acquaintance with investment banking will remain sceptical.

May 24, 2001

No easy answers to conflicts of interest on Wall Street

The US Congress commenced hearings last week on conflicts of interest in investment banking even as the American brokerage industry hastily cobbled together a code of conduct for analysts. The unveiling of the code just two days ahead of the hearings was widely perceived as intended to head off possible moves towards fresh legislation of the industry in Congress.

The first round of hearings into what has been characterized as the stock market bubble of recent years focused on the ultra-bullish recommendations issued by analysts through the bubble years. Among the eight witnesses who testified were the president of the Securities Industry Association (SIA), representatives of firms and individuals from outside the industry. Strangely, however, none of the erstwhile stars of dotcom research from the leading investment banks was examined. Future hearings are expected to address the roles played by institutional investors and the financial media in the stock market boom.

The testimony ran along predictable lines. Critics of the industry argued that analysts had misled investors into taking exposures to dubious stocks and had created a general over-allocation of capital to highly risky companies. Apologists for the industry contended that investment banks had merely responded to investor demand, implying that the banks were not responsible for creating the boom in the first place.

The President of the SIA sought to deflect criticism by drawing Congressmen's attention to the new standards proposed for equity research and that have been endorsed by 14 Wall Street firms. This drew the tart response from the head of the Congressional panel that the code merely represented a 'minimum standard' of behaviour.

The Congressman is dead right. The astonishing thing about the code drawn up by the industry is that the standards to which the industry is now committing itself should have been missing thus far. For instance, the code lays down that analysts should not be required to submit their reports to investment bankers or corporate management for approval. The tacit acknowledgement that such practices have existed is in itself damning.

There are several other recommendations: analysts' pay should be based on the overall performance of their recommendations and not linked to particular deals; recommendations must be 'transparent and consistent'; valuations and risks must be clearly described, with the basis for price targets for a stock being spelt out.

The guidelines also seek to address conflicts of interest by asking for substantial disclosure. Firms acting as investment banking advisors to companies must indicate as much in their research reports—"and in plain English". Analysts should disclose whether they or their family members own shares in companies they cover. Analysts must not be selling stock that they are urging others to buy (which clearly suggests that such inconsistencies are not a rarity in the industry.)

The guidelines are undoubtedly an improvement on the lawlessness that seems to have prevailed all these years—and SEBI should add these to guidelines that obtain in India—but nobody should expect a miraculous transformation.

The trouble is that shoddy research has not cost investment banks anything. On the contrary, demand for research in the US has risen sharply even among retail investors. An important factor has been the shift towards 'defined contribution' pension plans (as distinct from 'defined benefit' plans) at American firms that puts the onus of accumulating savings on employees. This has brought hordes of new investors to the stock market in search of superior returns on savings. Many have burnt their fingers in the recent bubble.

If the industry is serious about improving standards, it must get down to defining 'overall performance'. A major problem with analysts' reports, documented by academic research, is 'optimism bias'. This is largely the result of analysts virtually taking dictation from corporate management or going along with the rest of the herd. (Estimates directories are notable for the narrow range with which most forecasts fall). Are investment banks willing to reward analysts based on the accuracy of their forecasts even if this means shooing away potential investment banking clients? This is the acid test for the industry.

The industry is unlikely to meet this test of its own accord. Legislation is not the answer either. Instead, the trend towards greater disclosure signalled by the guidelines must be given a vigorous push. Here is a suggestion: how about asking that analysts' track record with forecasts be appended to each research report and displayed at the firm's website?

June 21, 2001

INDIAN ECONOMY

Introductory Note

No single event dominates the Indian economic scene during the year so much as the Union budget. The budget thus came in for due coverage in *The Big Picture*. One of the problems with writing about the budget is the barrage of comments that readers are exposed to by the time your column makes it to print. A week after the budget, readers are likely to pass comments on the budget by like the idle wind that one heeds not.

I tried, therefore, to steer clear of specific budget proposals and to focus instead on, well, the big picture. I did not share the alarmist view that we were headed for fiscal collapse. I believed that a growth rate of six per cent or so would render the debt burden sustainable. In this, I was fortified by the experience of several economies including those in Europe that had experienced much higher levels of debt to GDP ratios than ours at some point in time. As the growth rate stayed ahead of the interest rate, the debt to GDP ratio had tended to stabilise at lower levels.

It was a different matter that a high fiscal deficit, driven by a high primary deficit, imposed costs on the economy—the cost of growth forgone as a result of resources being consumed by unproductive expenditure. If the primary deficit could somehow be pared by the means suggested *ad nauseum*—cutting subsidies, downsizing government, raising user chargers, etc.—we could have faster growth.

But that's a trade-off that is best left to the judgement of politicians. As I pointed out in my review of IG Patel's memoirs, in a democracy, politicians have a better sense of what measures are feasible in the economic realm than economists or technocrats. In a vibrant democracy such as ours, they can generally be relied upon to settle for policies that will deliver growth while not disrupting social harmony. With projections for the sustainable growth rate for the Indian economy being nudged upwards recently, the prospect of a fiscal collapse has receded even further and, more importantly, it appears we will grow faster than was thought possible in light of the fiscal drag. It would seem India's political class made the right call in not seeking radical solutions to India's fiscal problem in the nineties.

The policy on administered interest rates also figured quite often in my column. I did not believe that a lowering of administered interest rates would cause a *commensurate* decline in lending rates to firms in the economy. One reason was that banks were inclined to park funds in government securities rather than in loans. Another was that risks associated with all but top-grade borrowers might have increased in the post-reform era and banks would want to price in this enhanced risk. Any attempt to force banks to lower interest rates would merely result in credit being cut off to lower grade borrowers.

As recent RBI data has shown, real interest rates to borrowers have *increased* since the advent of reforms. So much for the hype about interest rates in the Indian economy having at last become competitive with international interest rates.

The ICE sector got its meed of coverage. I applauded the success of IT firms but did not share the view that this was all about freedom from government interference. Government intervention, whether through tax subsidies or through investment in technical education, had been an important contributory factor. At the height of the IT boom in 2000, I cautioned against getting carried away by market valuations of IT firms.

More recently, I had occasion to wonder what the change in relative valuations of IT and other sectors meant as pundits had hailed the rise and rise of IT stocks as heralding the emergence of IT as the engine of growth in the Indian economy. Old economy stocks, including those of banks, are now in the limelight and this has raised the possibility of sectors other than IT contributing significantly to a higher growth rate of the Indian economy.

To this, one must now add the concerns as to what IT—or services-driven growth imply for employment and the welfare of large numbers of people dependent on agriculture and manufacturing. The recent focus on agriculture may been as a repudiation of the proposition that the services sector is a cure-all for India's economic problems.

Interview: TN Srinivasan

TN Srinivasan is a PhD from, and Samuel C Park, Jr Professor of Economics at Yale University. Formerly a Professor, and later Research Professor, at the Indian Statistical Institute, Delhi (1964-1977), he has taught at numerous universities in the US. His research interests include international trade, development, agricultural economics and microeconomic theory.

He recently authored *Reintegrating India with the World Economy* with Suresh D Tendulkar (Washington: Institute for International Economics, 2003) and edited *Trade, Finance and Investment in South Asia* (New Delhi: Social Science Press, 2001). He is also the author of *Developing Countries and the Multilateral Trading System* (Boulder, CO: Westview Press, 1998).

He is a Fellow of the American Philosophical Society, the Econometric Society and the American Academy of Arts and Sciences, and a Foreign Associate of the National Academy of Sciences. He was named Distinguished Fellow of the American Economic Association in 2003.

1. *Assessments of the impact of India's economic reforms have varied over time. Initially, they seemed a big success. Then disenchantment set in. Now optimism is back although many reforms haven't really got a big push. As somebody who has closely monitored the economic reform programme and even evaluated it at one point, what do you make of India's performance over the past decade or so? When it started, did you think that we would do as well as we have done—or were you expecting us to do even better?*

A. India's economic performance has been good but it could be even better. To say that people were impressed by the early success of reforms and then became disenchanted when the reforms seemed to slow down would be an inaccurate characterization. There is no reason to feel disenchanted with what has been achieved. There have been substantial achievements in many sectors: IT, telecom and banking, for instance. I would say I am quite satisfied with India's performance following reforms.

2. *Some people are disappointed that growth has not been even better—that we haven't achieved sustained growth of over 7 per cent—but there are still elements in the economic performance that should have come as a pleasant surprise to them. The most obvious is the turn-around on the external front. Could anybody have expected that foreign exchange reserves would approach the $100 billion mark in a little over a decade?*

A. To focus on one parameter such as forex reserves is an inappropriate way of looking at reforms. It is true of any reform process that things you don't anticipate do happen. For instance, when Taiwan undertook outward-oriented policies in the sixties, the question was asked: where will export growth come from? The answer the policy makers gave was: we don't know, we are creating the right framework for exports to grow. It turned out that all sorts of products came to be exported from Taiwan that nobody could have foreseen. Similarly in Mexico after it entered into NAFTA (North American Free Trade Agreement), trade expanded in commodities which were not previously exported. We must accept that, once you set the framework, producers will decide what to produce and at what price. That there are pleasant surprises is to be expected.

Mind you, India is not alone in accumulating forex reserves, China and Pakistan, to take just two examples, are doing the same. Accumulation of forex reserves is partly a response to the East Asian crisis and it reflects the perception that the global financial architecture today does not give adequate insurance against contagion from financial crises elsewhere. It is also true that if you don't absorb inflows as reserves, the exchange rate would appreciate and RBI acting to prevent it is also an element in forex reserve accumulation.

3. *It is not just the swelling of reserves per se that is a surprise but the manner in which it has happened. I suppose those in charge of reforms in 1991 were thinking of merchandise exports growing faster than in the past. Few could have thought that the significant impact on the Bop would come from services and remittances. Could we say, therefore, that there is an element of unpredictability about how reforms would deliver—the law of unintended consequences working out in a benign form?*

A. Well, money is coming in, it is fungible. You can't ascribe reserves to any particular component of inflows. That is accounting, not a causal analysis.

4. *Until this year's spurt in growth, there was dissatisfaction among many about the slowdown in growth since 1997. This was ascribed to the second generation of reforms not quite acquiring the same momentum because these are politically difficult to implement. However, one could also point to several adverse factors that have held down growth since—the East Asian crisis, the collapse of the technology bubble, a bad monsoon, riots, natural disasters, etc. In the one year that the configuration of factors has been generally favourable, 2003-04, growth is vigorous. Might it be that the 'reform' component in the deceleration in growth since 1997 has been somewhat overstated?*

A. You are right in pointing out that there are cyclical components in the slowdown—whether the cyclical component alone is responsible is not clear. Some would say that this year's growth of 8 per cent too is cyclical in nature, reflecting better agricultural performance in the wake of good monsoons. My own feeling is that fundamental factors are also at work in this year's growth. Broadly, while the cyclical component in the slowdown is there, so too are slower reforms.

5. *Many key reforms relate to industry. Yet, there is evidence that the trend rate of growth of industry in the nineties is not significantly different from that in the eighties. Also, the deceleration in industrial growth in the late-nineties is ascribed to the slowing down of reforms but this begs the question why the substantial reforms initiated earlier could not sustain growth momentum in industry for longer. Do we need to look elsewhere for explanations for the deceleration in industrial growth?*

A. You need to view industrial growth in the eighties and nineties in perspective. In the nineties, both public and private investment have slackened. Infrastructure has not quite taken off- power, for instance. There are particular sectors such as capital goods that have witnessed a slowdown. Overall investment has slowed down and is held up only by household direct investment. Banks are not lending enough and this, too, has hampered investment. So, the deceleration in growth owes to many factors. But there are encouraging signs of late in respect of private investment. One is that businessmen have begun to view China as a market opportunity instead of viewing it as a threat that must be met through anti-dumping measures. As domestic industry becomes more and competitive at home and abroad and businessmen grow confident of meeting foreign competition, private investment will revive.

6. *To carry on in the contrarian vein in which I have been posing questions, the fiscal deficit was the great bugbear of reformers through the nineties. It was supposed to push up interest rates, stoke inflation and lead to an unsustainable level of public debt. It hasn't happened that way—interest rates have declined, inflation isn't a problem. As for the level of public debt, if we can manage even a six per cent growth, it ceases to be such a nightmare given the present level of interest rates. Could we say that fiscal deficit too is an area in which the Indian economy has surprised us?*

A. I am afraid the fiscal deficit remains a problem. Once private investment picks up, then we will begin to see problems that have not surfaced so far—high interest rates, a current account deficit, high inflation etc. India has one of the highest debt to GDP ratios among developing countries—it is higher than in many of the crisis-ridden countries such as Argentina. We have to reckon with hidden elements that could cause the debt to GDP ratio to shoot up even further- contingent liabilities, bad assets in the banking sector, public sector losses and so on.

7. *It appears that many of our macroeconomic problems get masked when we have access to the pool of external savings—if outsiders have confidence enough in the economy to park their funds here in some form or another. This is, perhaps, even truer of China. It would seem that a large economy with good potential can thus get away with flaws in macro-management. The question is: why are savings from abroad coming in now? Is it just that we have made it possible for savings to come in? Or is it that fundamentals have improved? Or is it both?*

A. Our FDI inflows are only marginally higher than in Thailand. We can't take much comfort in portfolio inflows because these are volatile and can leave just as easily as they came in. Our overall investment inflows are really nothing to write home about. Also, we cannot disregard temporary factors that have caused inflows to surge, such as the global economic slowdown, low interest rates etc. Once the global situation changes, we cannot be as sure that the present inflows will continue. There is really no room for complacency when it comes to attracting foreign capital.

8. *Yet another area in which the course of events has confounded experts is the improvement in performance of many public sector enterprises, banks particularly. There was—still is—a belief that the public sector simply cannot deliver commercial results and that ownership change is vital. Yet at least in the case of banks, it is hard to sustain that proposition today. If you accept this, then privatisation in the sense of a transfer of controlling interest to a private group appears less imperative. For many enterprises, we may still be able to realise significant improvements through enterprise reform such as widely dispersed public shareholding? What are your thoughts on this?*

A. Well, you have to remember that there hasn't been that much deregulation in banking, only some increase in competition at the margin. Indian Bank had to be recapitalised thrice! As long as the public sector holds a dominant share of banking assets, the "too big to be allowed to fail" syndrome will persist and make demands on the exchequer. Public ownership of banks must be brought down. More broadly, we haven't had a rethinking of the rationale for enterprises being owned by government. There is no social rationale whatsoever for government being in any activity for which there is an effective private alternative. After all, there are many activities, such as in the social sector, for which there is no realistic alternative to the public sector.

Dissipating public resources away from such needed activities towards these with viable private ones is socially wasteful—this is not adequately grasped as yet. It is true that privatization must go hand in hand with competition and regulation post-privatisation. But, just because we have had disasters in privatisation in, say, Russia it does not follow that we must avoid privatisation. It only means that we must get the mechanisms of privatisation right.

9. *Many of the reforms that reformers were insistent on—labour policy, privatisation, dereservation of small-scale sector, drastic reduction in the fiscal deficit—were seen as a precondition for accelerating growth. Yet, we seem to have reached a point where most people believe that growth could touch seven per cent on the present basis itself. The political backlash to faster reforms could have been destabilising. Does this suggest that the much-maligned democratic process in the country may, in fact, be contributing to growth with stability?*

A. The threat to social stability arising from reforms such as those in the labour market is exaggerated. You only need to look at a paper that PC Mahalanobis wrote for Sankhya decades ago. It was a review of Gunnar Myrdal's *Asian Drama*. He said: "certain welfare measures tend to be implemented in India ahead of economic growth, for example, in labour laws which are probably the most highly protective of labour interests in the narrowest sense, in the whole world. There is practically no link between output and remuneration; hiring and firing are highly restricted. It is extremely difficult to maintain an economic level of productivity or improve productivity . . . the present form of protection of organized labour, which constitutes, including their families, about five or six percent of the whole population, would operate as an obstacle to growth and would also increase inequalities" (*Sankhya: The Indian Journal of Statistics*, series B, vol. 31, parts 3 and 4).

Unfortunately, the Indian Left cannot bring itself to accept what Mahalanobis wrote years ago. You don't protect the majority of workers with labour laws—for example, there is no protection for the self-employed (who are the largest component of India's labour force), or casual labour in agriculture. So the notion that such laws sustain democracy is absurd. And a six per cent growth rate in this century is no big deal: it is the twenty-first century equivalent of the infamous Hindu rate of growth. You need higher and sustained growth to eradicate poverty.

10. *Optimism reigns supreme today especially with reports such as the one produced by Goldman Sachs forecasting that India will emerge as one of the top four economies in the world in the coming years. What, in your opinion, are the two or three elements that could go seriously wrong and undermine this prospect?*

A. My fear is that what happened in 1990-91 could recur—a basic crisis of confidence in the Indian economy. This could be triggered by our fiscal situation, given our debt to GDP ratio. The probability of such a crisis is not low at the moment. Unless basic difficulties in the fisc are addressed, India will not have its put its problems behind.

A second problem could be failure to push through power sector reforms—the pricing issue is not yet resolved, you need firm, reliable and inexpensive power and we are not getting there.

A third source of problems could be the social sector-education and health. The Aids problem, if not tackled, could land us in a sub-Saharan situation. These are some of the issues we need to address if our own, let alone the world's expectations about India, are to be met.

Union Budget

Philosophy of growth

When an economy is vulnerable to sanctions, making it even more so is hardly the appropriate response. Yet that is what critics of the budget seem to be arguing for when they say that not enough has been done to enthuse the foreign investor.

As the current account is the flip side of the capital account, higher foreign inflows must imply a wider current account deficit. The latter can be achieved by slashing import duties but that would mean placing the economy at the mercy of foreign inflows. You can't say that the budget should be factoring in possible sanctions and then criticize the Finance Minister for seeking to reduce the nation's vulnerability.

When the Opposition claims that the budget does not take into account sanctions it implies something different, namely, that the tax estimates are unrealistic. It is, willy-nilly, pleading for a stiffer dose of taxation to make good revenue shortfalls that would result from lower than expected growth.

But you can't hobble the economy with a slew of taxes today in expectation of sanctions of unknown magnitude 12-18 months down the road—not when people expect the government to kick-start the economy. Should sanctions begin to bite and the fiscal deficit threaten to get out of hand, there will obviously be scope for additional levies.

If import duties cannot be raised on grounds of efficiency and if sanctions are also to be provided for right now, then the prescription that follows is a big opening up to foreign inflows and higher taxes on domestic incomes. That strikes me as a prescription straight from the CIA: it would slam the brakes on growth and create conditions for an international bailout. I can see the Americans and the British rubbing their hands in gleeful anticipation.

So the threat of sanctions would justify the FM's move to impose an additional tariff. But is the economic argument unambiguously against it? Of course, tariffs must be lowered to prod Indian industry into restructuring. But if Indian businessmen are to invest in upgradation, they need to be able to forecast returns within a reasonable range of uncertainty. This range has, perhaps, been too wide for comfort since reforms were initiated in 1991.

Going by Chelliah, a businessman would have braced for a peak import tariff of around 25 per cent, say, five years down the road, but he could scarcely have built into his computations rupee depreciation of nearly 130 per cent. It's no use saying that the effective rate of protection has remained the same or gone up for a number for products because you also have to take into account the stupendous increase in the cost of imported equipment. On balance, the rate of return on projects might have worked out in favour of modernisation, *ex post*. In many cases, however, businessmen would have found it difficult to arrive at this conclusion, *ex ante*.

For Indian business to take major decisions on modernisation, you need to stick to a clear schedule for tariff cuts while allowing for creeping depreciation—and no more—of the rupee. Then businessmen can work out how to respond. Some would find it worthwhile to invest, others might decide to get out. This is not the same thing as mechanically chanting, 'lower tariffs increase economic welfare'. If investment is not to suffer while tariffs are falling, the government must ensure that business uncertainty does not go up exponentially.

The BJP asks a valid question: how do we give Indian industry a fighting chance to compete? The answer suggests itself: aim at scaling down tariffs but give pause. This is quite different from asking: how do we arrive at tariff rates comparable to the Asean economies in the shortest possible time? The latter approach confuses ends and means.

In today's world, Swadeshi cannot mean autarky. But it does mean emphasising indigenous sources of growth wherever possible. Sustaining Indian entrepreneurship would be integral to this philosophy. So would stepping up public investment in infrastructure. And, yes, unleashing the potential of the housing sector. Like it or not, Yashwant Sinha has brought to bear on his budget a philosophy of growth that is quite different from that which shaped the six earlier budgets.

June 11, 1998

Reforms sans illusions

At least two assumptions underlying the reforms process, which are crucial to containing the fiscal deficit, have been shown up as being hollow. One is that we can merrily cut tax rates in the expectation that industrial growth will ensure that tax revenues rise relative to GDP. The second, on which the first is based, is that cuts in public investment will be offset by a rise in private investment brought about by a fall in interest rates as government draft on savings diminishes.

Yashwant Sinha has had the courage to recognize the futility of persisting with these illusions. He may say that he has only rationalised tariff rates but the fact remains that the changes are not revenue-neutral. More importantly, he has put the brakes on the trend towards tariff reductions, driven by the urge to catch up with Asean levels.

Similarly, in imposing surcharges on personal income tax, however small, the Finance Minister has shown a willingness to buck the trend. It would be incorrect, therefore, to suggest that Mr Sinha's budget merely extrapolates reforms carried out by his two predecessors. There is an all-important pause in tax reductions without which fiscal imbalances would become unmanageable.

Some would argue that we must not get overly upset about the lack of buoyancy in revenues. Everywhere, politicians have found it easier to cut taxes than to cut expenditure, hence difficulties with the fiscal deficit in the interim are only to be expected.

We have the distinguished example of the United States. There the fiscal deficit ballooned to a record high following President Reagan's steep cuts in tax rates, and it was the terrifying mountain of federal debt that finally got politicians to tackle the expenditure side. Once that was done, the US economy got on to a virtuous spiral of lower interest rates and higher growth, leading eventually to a budgetary surplus. This logic, perhaps, explains the harping on the 'second generation of reforms'—cutting subsidies further, downsizing government, etc.

There are several problems with this prescription. First, to get a meaningful reduction in interest rates, you would require a fairly steep reduction in the fiscal deficit in quick time-say, from last year's 6.5 per cent of GDP (on the old basis) to something like 4 per cent. That's a tall order for the political class.

Secondly, it is possible to exaggerate the potential impact of interest rate cuts in our situation. Assume a decline in interest rates of 2 per cent. At a leverage of 1.5:1 and factoring in expected returns on equity and debt, the weighted average cost of capital would decline from 15.8 per cent to 14.3 per cent—or by 1.5 percentage points. This is the extent to which firms will lower their threshold for approving new projects.

As for the impact on profitability of existing businesses, going by *ICICI's Financial Performance of Companies*, one finds that return on equity rises by 1.6 percentage points. Thus, interest rate cuts in themselves will not have the sort of impact on companies that might boost investment sentiment dramatically.

Interest rate declines have proved so potent in the US because they are perceived as heralding the conquest of that formidable foe of business expectations, inflation. Along with political stability and a strong currency, low interest rates contribute to a stable business outlook which is what revives the animal spirits of businessmen.

Absent these certitudes, interest rate declines are unlikely to evoke a similar response in business here. Then there are the other dampeners peculiar to our context: the ongoing consolidation in business, the lack of confidence in the stock market, uncertainty about the regulatory framework in key sectors, etc.

How to contrive growth when private investment is unresponsive? Given the present structure of the budget, a steep rise in public investment appears impossible when tax revenues in the previous year have been sluggish: the ratio of capital expenditure to GDP has hovered around 3.3 per cent in recent years compared to 5.5 per cent in 1990-91. This is where Mr Sinha makes his second significant departure: he has tried to stimulate growth through other means, such as rural investment and incentives for housing.

As a low-risk strategy, it can't be bettered. If it doesn't work, we are back to the familiar fiscal deficit of 6.5 per cent—and nothing worse. But if it does and the deficit declines, Mr Sinha will be well-placed next year to step up public investment. If relying in public investment appears un-American, ponder this: the longest expansion in the US (lasting 106 months in 1961-69) was driven by government spending.

March 4, 1999

Ponzi gambles work

Nine years of stabilisation policies have led the country nowhere. The fiscal deficit remains untamed, nourishing a lively cottage industry of commentaries expressing 'concern' over its magnitude. More importantly, the larger economic objectives continue to elude. Industrial growth has been below the rate of the eighties, infrastructure languishes and the investment rate has gone into decline since 1998-99.

It requires a heroic disregard for fact to opt for more of the same. Unfortunately, Yashwant Sinha has done just that with his third budget. The Finance Minister's efforts guarantee a sense of déjà vu a year from now.

Given that it has held successive finance ministers in thrall, the central tenet of stabilisation, namely, that the fiscal deficit is unsustainable, calls for examination. Fiscal deficits financed by borrowings cause debt to rise. The rise would be unsustainable if the ratio of debt to GDP kept increasing. A point would come where the government would not be able to raise more debt and would be forced to raise taxes to meet its interest obligations.

Yet, as a paper suggests, the approach to the fiscal deficit must be governed by an appreciation of the probability of such an outcome. (*The deficit gamble—L Ball, DW Elmendorf and NG Mankiw, Journal of Money, Credit and Banking, November 1998*). A low probability of failure makes a Ponzi gamble—raising more debt to pay off interest—well worth taking.

Where the primary budget is balanced (that is, revenues cover non-interest expenses, a condition that holds for India), the debt to GDP ratio rises by a factor of (1+r) divided by (1+g), where r is the interest rate and g the growth in GDP. To assess the likelihood of the US government running a successful Ponzi gamble, the authors examined the behaviour of the above factor over the period 1871-1992.

The factor averaged less than one, which means Ponzi gambles do succeed 'on average'. The probability of the gamble failing since the War was around 15 per cent. Using simulation techniques, the authors estimate the probability of failure in the future to be at worst 20 per cent. The authors conclude: " With a high probability, the government can grow itself out of its debt problem simply by balancing the primary budget in the future".

Applying the approach to Indian growth and interest rates since 1970 (and even using yields on government securities at the upper end of the 1-5 year band), the probability of a Ponzi gamble failing works out to around 18 per cent. This explains why the ratio of government's total liabilities to GDP has actually declined from 65 to 56.6 per cent between 1993-94 and 1998-99 despite the failure to rein in the fiscal deficit. It is hard to make out a case against the existing level of fiscal deficit on grounds of unsustainability.

The argument must rather be that the economy could grow even faster if a high level of fiscal deficit did not crowd out private investment by pushing up interest rates. While the latter belief is widespread, there is little reason to expect that in an open economy a high fiscal deficit must translate into higher nominal interest rates. Indeed, several empirical studies have failed to find such a correlation, not just in the US but in Europe and Japan as well. In our own context, interest rates have declined without the fiscal deficit level falling.

This has not stopped finance ministers in the liberalisation era from trying to pare the fiscal deficit in the hope of a triggering a virtuous cycle of lower interest rates—higher private investment—higher growth—lower fiscal deficit. In the event, the fiscal deficit has ended up higher than targeted as growth projections went awry—and with them expected realisations of tax revenues.

The worrisome outcome is not that the fiscal deficit remains the same but that growth impulses in industry are not strong enough—as signified by the decline in investment. With the inflation rate running low and the BoP under no threat, the time was opportune for a big boost to aggregate demand through a significant increase in public investment. So great is the terror of a higher fiscal deficit, however, that Mr Sinha has let the opportunity pass. The logic of a Ponzi gamble—an increase in public spending can deliver a decline in the fiscal deficit level by pushing up growth—evidently finds less acceptance in liberalised India than in Reaganite America.

March 2, 2000

Budget-making in an era of sound byte judgements

As the finance minister rises to present his fifth successive budget later today, he must know quite well that, in an era of sound byte judgements, it is the immediate reaction to the budget that makes or mars reputations. Budgetary projections may go awry with monotonous regularity but that is of little consequence when it comes to managing perceptions. The cardinal sin is to fall down on a few vital counts on budget day.

One such is the stock market reaction. Finance ministers may profess disdain for Dalal Street but they must all yearn for a rise in the market index if only because of the favourable impact this has on the instant judgements delivered on television. ("The market is certainly upbeat about Mr Sinha's budget".)

The market may have merely retreated after an extraordinary run ahead of the budget but the finance minister cannot escape damnation. Alternatively, the market may gain a couple of hundred points from a miserable level of 3500 but this will not stop the applause. In the spectator sport that is the Union budget, the finance minister will have scored the all-important goal.

The second test that a finance minister must pass relates to the laundry-list called 'second generation reforms'. This comprises items such as disinvestment, cuts in administered interest rates, downsizing government, and hire-and-fire policies. These items have become ends in themselves. The growth rate might falter and tax projections go haywire as they have done this fiscal. No matter. The finance minister has risen in stature because of the last budget's unflinching adherence to 'reforms'.

But there is nothing to beat the tyranny exercised by the fiscal deficit figure. It is vital for the finance minister to peg the fiscal deficit below the previous year's target—or at least below the revised estimate. Not to do so is to offend the current theology about the 'unsustainability' of the fiscal deficit. The basis for this theology is worth examining.

In the early nineties, some computations showed that a fiscal deficit of around five per cent was sustainable, that is, consistent with internal and external stability. Now, the average fiscal deficit in the period 1990-91 to 1998-99 was 5.97 per cent (as per the RBI Annual Report, 2000-01). So, it would seem we were right to have been cowering before the spectre of a 'fiscal crisis' through most of the nineties.

However, in his budget for 1999-00, Mr Sinha argued persuasively that the states' share of small savings should not figure in the central fiscal deficit. The average fiscal deficit for the above period, reworked on this basis, turns out to be five per cent. This would imply that the 'fiscal crisis' of the nineties, if not a fiction, had been exaggerated. Another key measure, the primary deficit, has improved from 4 per cent in 1990-91 to 0.52 per cent in 2000-01. The revenue deficit rose marginally from 3.26 per cent to 3.54 per cent after showing declines in many of the intervening years.

But the key test of sustainability of the fiscal deficit surely is the trend in the overall debt to GDP ratio. This ratio for the centre declined from 55.3 per cent to 1990-91 to 49.4 per cent in 1996-97. It started inching upwards thereafter but, at 53.3 per cent in 2000-01, it is still below the level of 1990-91. The combined ratio for the centre and the states of 64 per cent is not too high by international standards.

The World Bank's World Development Indicators (2001) shows the government debt to GDP ratio for India for 1998 as 49 per cent (which, presumably, excludes states' debt). The comparable figures for select countries were: US (43), Singapore (75), Israel (113), Belgium (114) and Sri Lanka (89). UK and Canada had ratios of 49 and 75 respectively in 1997.

In retrospect, it does appear that estimates of the sustainable fiscal deficit made in the early nineties did not adequately factor in the potential for a higher growth rate in the Indian economy. They could also not have anticipated the dramatic improvement in the external account that followed liberalization.

It is possible, although not certain, that a lower fiscal deficit would conduce to higher growth. But any drastic fiscal correction has redistributive implications that no government can ignore, least of all the present one after its recent electoral debacle.

In any case, the proposition that a fiscal deficit of 4.5–5 per cent is inconsistent with macroeconomic stability is not borne out by the experience of the past decade. A recognition that a fiscal deficit of this order is quite compatible with growth of six per cent might help tone down the hype about a 'fiscal crisis' that is the staple of budget-day punditry.

February 28, 2002

Banking bonus for Jaswant Singh

The Finance Minister's budget speech makes no mention of any allocations for the financial sector. It is not that Jaswant Singh has ignored the sector. But you need to go through volume 2 of the expenditure budget to ascertain the allocations.

It is almost as if the recapitalisation of Public Sector Banks (PSBs) and financial institutions, which seemed such an onerous task until recently, has become a non-issue. One would have thought the finance minister would exult at this development but he seems to be making the point by relegating the issue to the footnotes, as it were.

The budget provides Rs 3,000 crore for UTI. It also provides a total of Rs 2,346 crore as assistance for IFCI and IDBI. As reported in the Economic Times (March 1), even the sum of Rs 2346 crore will not be provided as direct assistance to the two institutions.

Rather, the debt owed by the institutions will be restructured, with banks and other institutions settling for a lower interest rate on high-cost debt.

The lenders are to be compensated through the provision made in the budget. Given the nature of such restructuring in general, it is safe to presume that the lenders will be bearing some portion of the cost themselves. Indeed, this must explain why the allocation in the budget is so low compared to the numbers being bandied about last year.

This is not the only area in which banks are expected to take a hit. The proposal to buy back high-cost government debt from banks will also involve some sacrifice on the part of banks. The idea is to buy back government debt at a premium to book value but at less than the market value since the bonds are highly illiquid. In other words, the banks will take a hit in market value terms.

The sweetener for banks is that the premium can be used for provisioning of NPAs, which means that it can be treated as a tax-deductible expense. But the premium will obviously have to be set at a level where the net impact on banks—of the economic loss they will be incurring on sale of bonds to the government and the gain in reduced taxes—would be negative. Otherwise, it makes no sense for the government to offer the buy-back.

But what is in it for banks? Banks with excess SLR securities and that are using up the current limit of 5 per cent of pre-tax income allowed for provisioning can the use the buy-back offer to pretty up their balance sheets. After all, the present low interest regime is not going to last for ever.

The bottomline is clear enough: banks, far from receiving funds from the government, are now judged to be in a position to spare it some. This is an astonishing transformation for a sector that was seen as a potential drain on the exchequer until very recently. Two years ago, the RBI had estimated the recapitalisation requirement of PSBs (other than the three weak banks) over a five-year period at Rs 10,000 crore. Many had felt that the equity component of this requirement would have to be come substantially from the government. Yet, four PSBs raised Rs 938 crore of equity last year under adverse conditions in the capital market.

Going by historical experience, the minimal cost of recapitalising any banking system would be 5 per cent of GDP. Using the average GDP over the past decade, this works out to Rs 64,000 crore. The government has thus far had to spend less than Rs 30,000 crore on banks and financial institutions put together. The difference represents the saving to the government as a result of the improvement in the health of PSBs.

The macroeconomic implications of this phenomenon must not be minimised. The public debt to GDP ratio has been rising since 1998-99 and is around 70 per cent of GDP at present. By itself, this is not intimidating in relation to levels seen elsewhere. Over long periods of time, the rate of growth of GDP tends to be above the interest rate and this keeps the debt to GDP ratio in check.

What worries investors when public debt reaches the level it has in India is the possibility of a 'hard landing' as a result of an unexpected shock. This could be a surge in oil prices or war. Or, more likely these days, a banking collapse. To the extent that the Indian banking system is judged to be more stable, therefore, economic agents have reason to take an optimistic view of India's fiscal situation.

This must cause Mr Singh's budget to be seen in a more favourable light than is the case. Mr Singh is perceived to have failed at fiscal consolidation because he is likely to end up with the same deficit level that his predecessor had bequeathed him. But the diminished probability of a draft on the exchequer arising from the banking system is a bonus that should, in a world of rational expectations, place Mr Singh at an advantage.

March 13, 2003

Reforms

Steady as she goes

As markets tumble one after another, analysts here and abroad are finding nice things to say about the Indian economy. Carping about our failure to accelerate the growth rate to seven per cent is giving way to relief over the fact that we will manage growth of five per cent plus in this troubled environment.

Commentators have focused on what the problems in Asia, Russia and, possibly, Latin America imply for capital controls and managing the transition to a market-driven economy. But the real significance of the setbacks to growth elsewhere may well lie in what they imply for *sustainable* growth rates.

Sustainability is a concept students of business are familiar with. They know that organizations are most likely to stumble when they overreach themselves. They are aware also of the risk-return tradeoff, the notion that increasing returns go with increasing variability. Economic policy makers, however, seem to operate on the premise that a higher growth target is superior without asking whether it is sustainable in economic and political terms. It's time to question this premise.

In the period 1980-89, India's GDP grew at 5.1 per cent—exactly the same as growth in Asia (excluding India and China) according to the IMF's latest *Economic Outlook*. The period 1990-99 promises to be no different: the IMF projects growth for Asia of 5.4 per cent, a figure that India can certainly expect to match. At least over the last two decades of this century, India will not have been lagging behind Asia sans China.

You could argue that Asia's best performers have done better, and that, unlike India, they had impressive growth rates in the preceding two decades as well. But the Indian economy was bigger than many others', so we are comparing growth rates over different bases.

A stronger argument is that the potential for acceleration in the next decade is, perhaps, greater in India. So, if we were to take stock in 2010 and compare growth rates over 1960-2010, we could have some surprises of the hare-and-tortoise variety. It would be interesting to see how many economies, including China, were able to sustain above-average growth without serious dislocation.

There is the issue of political sustainability as well. Those who are critical of India's record of economic management insist that a faster pace of reforms would easily translate into magical growth figures. It is worth asking, however, why no government since 1991 has measured up to the reformers' expectations (and we have had governments from three political formations in that period) and have opted instead for incremental change regardless of the noises they may have made in their manifestos. If governments of all hues settle for the same approach, surely there's a message the political process is trying to convey ?

Democratic politics is all about holding a balance between conflicting preferences and interests. So the pace of reforms and the resultant rate of growth reflects socially acceptable tradeoffs—between present and future consumption and between the costs to one group versus the benefits to the rest.

Cutting subsidies, for instance, would release resources for productive investment which could lead to higher growth in future. But if governments can't cut subsidies beyond a point, that is democracy's way of conveying that a sufficiently large number of people prefer present consumption to higher growth in future.

So also with closing down unviable enterprises. Political parties, unlike economists, are accountable, and they know that they can ignore such preferences only at the risk of being voted out. Thus, the democratic process ensures that reforms and growth proceed at a pace that is sustainable in political terms.

The reformers ask, in effect, for greater efficiency at the existing rates of savings and investment, without pausing to ask if the quest for greater efficiency is economically and politically sustainable. If we could be just a little patient, a higher savings rate in a few years' time would deliver the higher growth rate that we hanker for without creating the sort of turmoil that other economies are going through. And this higher rate, in turn, would be sustainable. The reformers want to go for broke. Recent events suggest that 'steady as she goes' is a much better slogan to have.

September 4, 1998

Harking back to Avadi!

Two points can be made about the Congress' stance on economic policy at Panchmarhi. One, it's absurd to even attempt to reconcile economic liberalisation with the Avadi Congress resolution. Two, the Panchmarhi declaration could mark recognition on the part of the Congress party that it cannot afford to ignore the issue of political sustainability of reforms.

The Avadi session of 1955, at which the Congress affirmed its commitment to a 'socialistic pattern of society', marked a significant milestone in the evolution of Indian economic policy. At Avadi, the Congress didn't quite spell out what it meant by "socialistic pattern of society". But UN Dhebar, who presided over the Avadi Congress attempted a definition a little later: *The Socialist pattern of Society accepts the thesis that there is class conflict. It also accepts that the proper way of removing that class conflict is that the ownership of the means of production should vest in the Society or there is social control of the means of production. But it differs from Marx in this respect. Marx conceived the use of force for its implementation in the final stage of the struggle. We do not conceive of the use of force in our Socialistic pattern of Society. We wish to achieve Socialism through persuasion or conversion.* (AICC Economic Review, 1 June 1956, quoted in *Indian Economic Thinking* edited by Romesh Thapar).

So, the Avadi resolution was clearly about annexing the commanding heights of the economy for the public sector – no two ways about that. The resolution, as we know, paved the way for the Industrial Policy Resolution of 1956, with its pre-emption of major industries for the public sector, and for T T Krishnamachari's landmark budget of 1957 with its massive mobilisation of resources through tax innovations.

In recent years, Congressmen have been apt to talk about 'Nehruvian socialism', a portmanteau expression that is all things to all men and admits of flexible interpretation. Thus, licensing, public sector dominance and high tariffs are 'Nehruvian socialism' in action; the dismantling of this framework under economic liberalisation is also 'Nehruvian socialism'! What is implied, perhaps, is a commitment to broad egalitarian goals, but then the debate on economic policy is about means, not ends. And when you are talking about means, you have to make up your mind whether you want to retain the Nehruvian framework or jettison it.

It is ridiculous to suggest that the Avadi resolution can some how be squared with Manmohanomics in general. And, in particular, with the ringing declaration of the Congress manifesto in the last elections: *"The Congress believes that it is time to redefine fundamentally the role of the public sector"*.

The Congress change of heart at Panchmarhi has been interpreted as genuflecting in the direction of the Lets parties that have, no doubt, received a timely supply of oxygen in the failure of market-oriented policies in Russia. The Commies are, of course, not against privatisation when it takes place in West Bengal, just as they have no objection to private enterprise when their own kith and king are involved.

But it's possible that the change of heart is not dictated by short-term political compulsions alone. It could mark a recognition by the Congress party that it is politically unwise for it to position itself as ultra reformist, whether in respect of PSU disinvestment or protection of domestic industry. This is welcome because posturing and grandstanding on reforms by the leading opposition party sends wrong signals to investors, about what the government of the day can realistically accomplish.

The BJP in power proves more reformist than in Opposition; the Congress, in Opposition, offers a dilution of the stance on reforms it assumed when in power. This, again, is welcome because it suggests that a genuine consensus on economic policies is emerging that will ensure that reforms are politically sustainable. For political parties, though, there is an unwelcome part to all this: they can't expect to win votes by espousing economic radicalism, whether of the Swadeshi or the globalisation variety.

September 19, 1998

Knowing your onions

As any housewife who knows her onions could tell you, off-season prices of fruits and vegetables can be double the prices in the season even in normal times.

When you have a crop failure, you must expect prices to shoot up even more. And in the case of onions, we're talking about two successive crop failures. So the abnormal rise is no surprise. What has gone unnoticed is that in November 1997 before onion prices commenced their dizzy spiral, these had nearly doubled over their level in 1990-91. Thereby hangs a tale of agricultural policies out of kilter.

In the nineties, prices of food articles have risen faster than the wholesale price index as a whole: the ratio of the index of prices of food articles to the index of all commodities rose from 110 in 1990-91 to 117 in 1997-98.

Over the previous seven years, the ratio had actually declined from its 1983-84 level of 112.5. This is even more true in the case of foodgrains in particular: foodgrain prices relative to all commodities declined sharply from 105.9 in 1983-84 to 97.9 in 1990-91, rising there-after to 109 in 1997-98.

The tax paying middle classes may have been compensated for dearer food by tax cuts, but the plight of the rural and urban poor must be truly nightmarish. The sharp rise in food prices is by no means accidential: as the Economic Survey for 1997-98 makes clear, it's part of a systematic strategy since the early eighties to drive the terms of trade of agricxulture vis-à-vis industry in favour of the former.

In keeping with this strategy, procurement prices have been subject to steep hikes, post liberalisation. Nobody would quarrel with procurement prices as an instrument to sustain technological change and to ensure food security.

But there is a strong case to examine whether governments in the post-liberalisation period have not gone overboard in respect of the prices fixed and in their reliance on higher prices as an engine of agricultural growth.

Procurement price increases are meant to offset increases in input costs. Given the wide variations in costs, it is possible to err on the side of excess in fixing prices if that is what the ruling ideology dictates, while appearing to be technically correct.

Higher prices were supposed to be one of several means to tilt the terms of trade in favour of agriculture. Lowering protection to industry, which constituted an implicit tax on agriculture, rectifying the over-valued exchange rate and easing restrictions on exports were all part of the strategy.

These latter reforms were expected to obviate the magnitude of increases in procurement prices as well as subsidies to agriculture. In reality, not only have procurement prices risen steeply, there has been no attempt to contain subsidies to farmers. At the same time, the rise in procurement prices has meant that subsidies under the Public Distribution System (PDS) have ballooned.

Agricultural growth has slowed down in the nineties, compared to the eighties. And key parameters that contribute to output growth—such as area under irrigation, area under high-yielding varieties, growth in yields—have performed dismally. Clearly, higher prices and improved terms of trade for agriculture have failed to deliver superior growth.

At the same time, given our fixation with the fiscal deficit, the growth in subsidies related to agriculture has crowded out public investment, which all agree, is indispensable to improved growth rate in agriculture.

A high level of fiscal deficit is unsustainable. So is a low fiscal deficit, however glamorous it might look, if it's bought at the expense of public investment in agriculture; as we are seeing now, it kills by stoking inflation in agricultural products down the road.

The irony of it all is that Yashwant Sinha, who made a heroic attempt to reverse the declining trend in investment in agriculture in his budget, is having to face the consquences of benign neglect on the part of his predecessors, and the wrath of the public is being visited on the hapless BJP.

November 2, 1998

When markets vote

The government's volte-face on the insurance sector has caused consternation within the ranks of its own party. Although the BJP President has decided to back the government, his cadres must wonder why a move that will alienate key political constituencies is a priority for a party that has just received a drubbing at the elections.

It's possible that a wider access to the Indian market is a bargaining chip the government is using at the ongoing Talbott-Singh talks on CTBT. A successful resolution and the lifting of sanctions would give the BJP a shot in the arm if elections became due in six months' time. But, sanctions or no, the reality is upon us: even with the opening up that has already taken place, the government of the day is constrained to send out signals that foreign investors are looking for. Allowing buyback of shares was such a signal; the proposed Insurance Bill is another.

Such measures may appear inconsequential in terms of their direct impact on the economy, but they do a great deal for that elusive something that rules the markets, 'sentiment'. Foreign investors, scanning markets across the globe while allocating assets, have a checklist of standard criteria by which they measure progress in economic policies.

This applies not just to equity investors but to lenders as well. Direct investment, portfolio investment and loans are all shaped by the same perceptions—and often come from the same sources—and their cumulative impact on our economy is today quite substantial. No government can afford to ignore these perceptions.

You may say this is not a bad thing because it disciplines wayward politicians and prods them in the direction of badly needed reforms as happened in the industrial economies. The key difference, though, is that in the industrial economies the middle-class was bigger than the poor and it constituted a natural constituency for market-oriented policies.

In an economy such as ours, where the poor are larger in number, there is often a conflict between policies mandated by the international markets and the requirements of political survival. For instance, reducing the fiscal deficit by cutting food subsidies and closing down loss-making PSUs may be applauded by the markets but they could cost parties dearly at the hustings.

Foreign lenders and investors lack a nuanced understanding of the compulsions in particular contexts, or, perhaps, they couldn't care less. Politicians today are not insensitive to the need for reform, but, in a democratic context, they would certainly like to control the timing and pace of reforms. It is the need to balance the conflicting demands of the two constituencies—the international markets and the political bazaar—that yields the much-derided 'Hindu rate of reform.'

Parties in power, saddled with the grim business of running the economy, have leaned towards impressing international investors; parties in the opposition can afford to appeal more to the political market. This explains why the BJP, having talked Swadeshi, has aped and even outshone the Congress in its reformist ardour; and why the Congress, which initiated reforms under pressure from foreign lenders, now swears by the Avadi resolution and is cosying up to the CPM.

But the fact that identical policies haven't quite translated into votes suggests that the two principal protagonists haven't able to control the reform process as well as they would have liked to; the international markets have had the upper hand over the political marketplace. This has happened despite the fact that privatisation has not really gathered steam, and the government retains a modicum of control over economic outcomes through its domination of the industrial and financial sectors.

The international markets will clamour for further liberalization. Before obliging them, political parties must find ways to ensure that they don't lose control over the reform process. They must do so in the interests of survival and also to ensure that liberalization does not get discredited. And the ability to control the process could well turn on what parties intend to make of the public sector, whether they can restructure it into a potent force or whether they believe in its wholesale abandonment.

December 10, 1998

Triumph of Swadeshi

If initial assessments of Tata's Indica are proved right, the battle for the Indian car market will be primarily between two Indian companies, one in the public sector and the other in the private sector; the foreign car makers that dominate the world market may well be relegated to the sidelines.

This is a development of no mean signficance. It challenges the view, fashionable in some quarters today, that our economic policies of the past were hopelessly flawed. It debunks the notion that the public sector is congenitally incapable of being nimble and market-savvy. It reinforces the evidence that Indian companies have it in them to take on MNCs even in consumer businesses. Above all, it must induce people to think again about globalisation and the role for Indian entrepreneurship.

In the car industry, we seem to have succeeded at what other Asian countries did earlier: nurturing domestic companies through protection and then exposing them to competition. The others nurtured *private* companies and insisted that they prove their worth by competing in the export market. Here, we got a public sector company, Maruti Udyog, to team up with a foreign partner and exposed it to domestic competition.

That Maruti's most formidable competitor will likely be an Indian company is no accident either. Telco is emerging as a force in the car industry because it was able to develop design and production capabilities and build distribution in the sheltered market for commercial vehicles.

The end result of protectionism is not just the heart-warming spectacle of two *desi* companies battling it out in the domestic car market. The more important thing from the standpoint of the economy is the promise of sustained market growth—on top of the considerable growth that Maruti has already contrived—because products will be available at prices at which a large volume of demand can be generated. Our experience with the car industry is an outstanding triumph of Swadeshi, defined not as autarky but as calibrated globalization that allows Indian entrepreneurship to blossom without compromising the consumer's interests over the long term.

Some would argue that it doesn't matter if the cat is Indian or foreign as long as it catches mice. Had we allowed foreign companies into the Indian market even earlier, they would have produced the same outcomes. There are several problems with this proposition. *First,* it makes the brave assumption that foreign companies would have been willing to make huge investments at a time when the Indian market looked far less attractive. *Secondly,* unless the companies had been incorporated locally and offered shares to the Indian public—difficult even under today's conditions—profits paid out as dividends would have entirely fled the country.

But, perhaps most importantly, it is doubtful that foreign companies would have latched on to the small car possibility as strongly as Maruti and Telco have done. That's because MNCs tend to offer in an emerging market products that have succeeded elsewhere; designing a car tailored to the Indian market's needs and developing suppliers and nationwide distribution from scratch would not have been their priority.

The small car focus is authentically Indian because it requires a feel for the socio-economic milieu to figure out that it is a winner. Foreign companies lack that feel, which is why HLL, with its vaunted market research, did not wake up to the potential of the low-end of the detergents market until Nirma arrived on the scene.

These arguments haven't entirely lost their validity today. So there remains a case for fostering Indian entrepreneurship in the era of globalization—in the private sector as well as the public sector. This does not mean sacrificing the consumer's interests by over-protecting Indian industry: the WTO regime, in any case, sets limits to such protection.

But it does imply that we need not rush to lower tariffs to levels in the Asean region for all products. It also implies that we don't have to look to MNCs for deliverance: the success of Maruti and Telco suggests that neither the public sector nor family managed business is a lost cause as long as companies can bring themselves to shape up.

January 7, 1999

Judgement on Mr Reform

The importance of South Delhi in the coming Lok Sabha polls should not be minimised, talk of a consensus on reforms nothwithstanding. With Manmohan Singh in the fray and political ideology generally taking a back seat, economic reforms must occupy centre-stage in the constitutency. If reforms and their architect cannot constitute a winning ticket in a corner of urban India, that will set people thinking.

The Congress has done well to ask Dr Singh to go to the people. There is no constitutional bar on somebody staying on in the Rajya Sabha, indefinitely. But Dr Singh is not another MP. He has had and could still have a hand in shaping the nation's destiny as few others have. He will stand taller for obtaining the legitimacy accorded by the popular vote.

A victory for Dr Singh would give an impetus to the 'second generation' of reforms; his defeat would send out a message of caution that political parties would find difficult to ignore. The verdict in South Delhi assumes significance because Manmohan Singh is Mr Reform in the eyes of the public, the man who showed the way and won credibility abroad for the reform process.

Besides, while all major parties have come to embrace important aspects of the reform program, they do not base their appeal on economic ideology the way the Congress does. The BJP, for instance, is best known as a nationalist party that is also reformist. The Congress remains the original party of reforms whose position on reforms has been and is still more radical than that of any other party.

It would make sense for the Congress to stick its neck out and play up Dr Singh's reformist credentials to the hilt quite simply because there is no getting away from these. It must also recognize that Dr Singh does not have any other platform to stand on. His personal integrity may be unimpeachable but he is hardly cast in the crusader's mould. Whether in professing to be a permanent resident of Assam in order to get elected to the Rajya Sabha or in hobnobbing with the likes of Jayalalitha, Dr Singh has shown an appreciation of realpolitik that would flatter his more seasoned colleagues. He has a clean image but he is no position to use clean politics as an electoral plank.

Congressmen should not shy away from the prospect of projecting themselves as radical reformers and Dr Singh as their totem. They have long held that their electoral reverses owe not to their stance on reforms but to their failure to 'sell' reforms to the people.

Why policies that are supposedly in the long-term interests of the majority need to be aggressively marketed at all is a puzzle economists have grappled with in recent years. They are loath to accept that only reformist politicians and their advisors can see where long-term economic interest lies while everybody is hopelessly irrational or myopic and would only favour policies that are unsustainable.

Many of the explanations put forward have to do with the redistributive impact of reforms. The burden of adjustment may fall disproportionately on some segments of the population. Institutional mechanisms for compensating losers may not be strong enough. Where there are glaring inequalities (in both physical and human capital), a democratic polity will not permit governments to pursue efficiency goals as much as they would like to.

So opposition to reforms reflects not lack of marketing savvy in reformers but flaws in the product design itself. Reformers may fail to arrive at a mix of policies that addresses the interests of the greatest number no matter that the broad direction is right.

This is not the Congress' interpretation of things. The party has tended to take the position that reforms were swamped by a variety of other issues. More disingenuously, it has contended that its failure lay in not projecting reforms as a continuation of its socialistic philosophy.

Refuting the view that the party's 1996 defeat was a referendum on its economic policies, Mani Shankar Aiyar wrote in *Rediff On The Net*, "I wish that had been so; I wish the Congress had made it so". Well, the Congress now has the opportunity to make at least Dr Singh's election a referendum on its current menu of reforms and its superior competence in implementing these. If Dr Singh cannot carry South Delhi on reforms, the Congress cannot hope to succeed on this plank anywhere else.

August 19, 1999

Lesson of a lost decade

The nineties have turned out to be pretty much a lost decade for India where infrastructure is concerned. Private investment has disappointed. A World Bank publication made available at a recent conference in New Delhi on "Private participation in Indian infrastructure" organized by the Bank and IDFC estimates that investment in infrastructure declined from 5.4 per cent of GDP in 1991-92 to 4.6 per cent in 1997-98 with public investment declining from 4 per cent of GDP to 3 per cent.

Private investment failed to fill the gap, rising from 1.4 per cent of GDP to only 1.6 per cent over the period. Even private inflows of this order cannot be taken for granted in the future. Much of the investment—in the power sector, for instance—has taken place on a basis (assured returns, guarantees, escrow etc.) that is hard to replicate any further.

Speakers at the conference ascribed the disappointing level of private investment to poorly designed policies. This seems obvious but the proposition contains two fallacies. *One* is the implicit assumption that the right policies are readily contrived. *Another* is the premise that the right policies by themselves can overcome investors' perceptions of risk. This is not true: sector fundamentals and country risk are equally relevant.

A basic mistake, as Montek Ahluwallia pointed out, was to suppose that the private sector would automatically occupy the space vacated by the public sector. Private investors will ultimately do so only when we have created conditions that make investment in the sector viable. This means addressing subsidies and tariffs while also putting in place competitive market structures and regulatory mechanisms. None of this can happen overnight.

Other policy errors abound. There is a general sense that, in the power sector, focusing on generation was not such a great idea. As it is losses in distribution that are undermining viability in the sector, privatisation of distribution ought to have been the priority. The muddle in telecom is partly the work of private investors themselves but it also highlights the difficulties in framing policy for a sector in which technologies change at bewildering speed.

As for road privatization, operational problems in our environment could deter investors even when policies are clear enough. Land acquisition, relocation of utilities, limiting access to toll payers and law and order problems related to toll recovery—all these pose headaches for private investors.

Sorting out issues such as these at the sectoral level is a necessary condition for enticing private investment but it may not be a sufficient condition. There are serious limitations inherent in our situation. *One* is that we are at a stage where we require substantial investments of the greenfield variety.

In power, we need to double capacities in the next ten years. In roads, we require basic networks, not refinements to existing networks.

Private investors, however, prefer acquiring existing systems to making greenfield investments. In Latin America, which has attracted the highest private investment into infrastructure in this decade, most of the investment has gone into existing systems.

Secondly, our long-term debt market is underdeveloped and few Indian businesses have shown themselves equal to the challenge of infrastructure. So domestic private investment in infrastructure will be hard to come by. Private investment in infrastructure may well become synonymous with foreign investment.

This means we are talking about investors who need to worry about country risk in addition to the considerable risks that go with infrastructure. For big flows to materialize, foreign investors' perceptions about India obviously need to improve but, also, perceptions about emerging markets as a class must remain favourable. Given foreign investors' experience thus far, it would be unwise to suppose that this will hold true.

A recent Wharton School study (*"How political risk affects infrastructure investments", WJ Henisz and BA Zelner*) makes the point that, after the initial rush into infrastructure in emerging markets, foreign investors may want to rethink the risks involved. It cites a survey of 7500 MNCs that showed that

84 per cent of operations initiated in emerging in the last three years failed to meet their financial targets. Unconventional losses cost investors $24 billion in 1998 alone.

Until policies have evolved further and risks are perceived to be more manageable, private investors will remain lukewarm towards infrastructure. One lesson of the decade, therefore, is that there is no alternative to increasing public investment in the sector in the near future. The urgent need to make available minimal amenities to the citizenry is an important consideration. But the bigger consideration must be sustaining momentum in an economy in which infrastructure investment remains the engine of growth.

November 25, 1999

From retreat to rout

The government is chasing its ambitious target of $8-10 billion for foreign direct investment (FDI) with all the zeal of a neo-convert. It has liberalized the FDI regime. It has also signalled its willingness to sell significant stakes in PSUs to foreign firms. The moves reflect the recognition that the two objectives—higher FDI and privatisation—are intertwined. But the concern must be whether this combination bodes well for the economy.

FDI is of two types: greenfield investment and mergers and acquisitions (M&As). Meeting the FDI target wholly through higher greenfield flows will not be easy. Greenfield FDI tends to follow on the heels of strong economic performance rather than causing it in the first instance. In the past, strong performance attracted greenfield FDI into China and East Asia. India has yet to produce comparable performance that will cause greenfield FDI to double.

Moreover, eight out of the ten top destinations for FDI in the developing world are part of regional economic blocs, either in Latin America or in East Asia. The absence of any strong affiliation to a regional bloc does put India at a comparative disadvantage as an FDI destination.

In recent years, much of the surge in FDI in developing countries has been of the second type, namely, M&As, including privatisation. The weaker the economic performance, the higher seems to be the share of M&As in FDI. Latin America in the second half of the nineties best exemplifies this phenomenon.

According to UNCTAD's World Investment Report (1998), Latin America recorded the highest increase in FDI ($24 billion) among developing countries between 1995 and 1997, mostly on the back of higher M&As. As a result, the share of M&As in FDI rose sharply from 36 per cent in 1995 to 79 per cent in 1997.

An estimated 45 per cent of FDI in 1997 was accounted for by majority-owned M&As (which involved transfer of voting rights in excess of 50 per cent to foreign firms.) Privatisation constituted 19 per cent of FDI in Latin America and 27 per cent in Brazil, the leader in FDI in the region.

By liberalising the regime for both FDI and privatisation, the government is facilitating FDI through M&As. It seems to have understood the limitations to raising FDI of the greenfield variety. The impact on the economy is hardly the same in the two cases.

Greenfield FDI stimulates growth by augmenting investment. FDI in the form of M&As does so to a much lesser extent and that, too, with a lag whereas the country's need for investment is massive and urgent. True, in principle, the government could use the proceeds of privatisation for raising public investment in infrastructure but to suppose this in the present environment calls for a leap in faith.

It is hard to resist the conclusion that the ambitious target for FDI has less to do with augmenting investment than with giving a big push to privatisation. The indications are that privatisation is becoming central to the government's overall economic strategy. If FDI can serve this objective, splendid.

As appetite in the capital markets is likely to be limited for many PSUs, M&As are one way to put privatisation on a fast track. Besides, privatisation is about raising efficiency. This is also an important reason for luring FDI. At least in theory, the two converge in FDI through the M&A route.

The snag is that the efficiency gains of the FDI-privatisation combination may turn out to be illusory as they have in many countries. For efficiency gains to materialise, one important condition is correct pricing of assets. Yet, for a variety of reasons—fiscal pressures, the neglect of PSUs in the run-up to privatisation, the absence in some cases of stock market benchmarks, etc.—under-pricing of assets is almost inevitable. So the new owners' incentive to raise efficiency will be weak and the economic benefits elusive.

The contrast between Asia and Latin America tells its own tale. In the past, greenfield FDI helped sustain rapid growth in China and much of East Asia. Growth in Latin America, which has relied on M&As to boost FDI in recent years, has been disappointing in comparison. If history is any guide, going down the Latin American route is unlikely to improve India's economic performance. All it will have accomplished is turn the BJP-led government's hitherto halting retreat from *Swadeshi* into a comprehensive rout.

February 17, 2000

Disconcerting divide

Parliament is said to represent the will of the people and government, in the Westminster model, may be expected to reflect the will of parliament. In both instances, there are signs of a disconcerting divide between ruler and constituent in our context.

The divide between the leading political parties and the people has been frequently commented upon. When parties seek the mandate of the people, they lay out certain positions on key economic issues. Then they proceed to act differently, depending on whether they end up in power or in the opposition.

We are now witnessing another divide, *one*, between the government and parliament. *Two*, committees that represent a wide-cross section of parliament have made recommendations that question the government's approach to economic reforms.

The Standing Committee on Finance has asked the government to look beyond downsizing of the government, disinvestment and cuts in subsidies in its attempts to pare the fiscal deficit. It stresses that the focus should be on realising savings through good governance. This would include reining in cost and time overruns in projects, reducing NPAs, containing losses in power distribution and speedy resolution of income-tax and excise duty disputes. The Standing Committee on Industry wants the government to prepare comprehensive financial restructuring packages for public sector units.

The message the MPs are sending out is a familiar one: economic reforms raise issues of equity that cannot be brushed aside. To rely entirely on measures such as cuts in subsidies and disinvestment in order to control the fiscal deficit is to ask some segments of the population to bear too much of the burden of adjustment. But, if these are the perceptions of MPs across the entire political spectrum, we have a puzzle: how come those in government seem unconcerned and want to press ahead?

The answer is that prescriptions for dealing with the costs of structural adjustment will vary depending on the condition of the economy and on whether one is in government or not. In a paper published a few years ago, Harvard's Dani Rodrik pointed out that two approaches to dealing with adjustment costs have been attempted elsewhere. (*Understanding economic policy reform, Journal of Economic Literature, March 1996*).

In Spain, Portugal and Greece, governments forged 'social pacts' with key constituents such as labour and strengthened welfare systems and mechanisms for income redistribution while embarking on economic reform. In contrast, countries such as Poland decided that their fiscal position was too grave to admit of debate and deliberation and went ahead with 'big bang' reforms without much thought for equity.

Governing is the art of the possible. Those in government will want to get on with whatever is immediately achievable—cuts in subsidies, disinvestment—without being hamstrung by issues of equity and good governance. They will do so in the hope that their initiatives will deliver improvement quickly enough and create more winners than losers, making reforms acceptable to the majority. The costs of adjustment may be inequitably distributed but the government may judge these to be acceptable short-run costs.

On the other hand, those in the ruling coalition but outside the government will worry that results will take longer in coming and there would be widespread disaffection in the meantime. Those in the opposition would want to harp on equity in the hope of cashing in on such disaffection. This would explain why the government finds itself at odds with parliamentary committees that include its own MPs apart from those of the opposition. MPs' concern for equity is often seen as opportunistic but the underlying issue—how to distribute the burden of adjustment and over what time frame—cannot be dismissed.

Rodrik indicates that there is no manual that reformist politicians can blindly follow but, in our context, the case for stressing equity and gradualism in reforms is, perhaps, stronger than elsewhere. *One,* the economic situation is hardly so grave as to warrant the sort of shock therapy that Poland was put through. *Two,* the numbers of disaffected could prove too large to be ignored even in the short run. *Three,* we do know that where strong institutions and clarity of goals exist, gradualism can produce impressive results—witness the success the RBI has had with financial deregulation. The government must not ignore the advice of the two parliamentary committees even if it can get away with doing so.

May 25, 2000

Time to shed fixation with interest rates

In a repeat of what transpired last year, the government is preparing the ground for a cut in interest rates across the board. It is said to be contemplating a reduction in interest rates on small savings. This will likely be followed by a cut in the Bank rate after the budget. The government needs to be realistic about what these rate reductions can accomplish—and what they cannot.

Last year's moves towards interest rate reductions turned out to be short-lived.

Volatility in the rupee in July prompted the RBI to reverse the cut in the Bank rate from eight per cent to seven per cent effected earlier. Uncertainties on the external front caused by the rise in oil prices ensured that rates remained unchanged thereafter.

The government must reckon that conditions for a rate reduction are more propitious this time round. Oil prices have retreated from their abnormal levels. Interest rates abroad have declined. The fiscal deficit for last year is in line with the target. Most importantly, inflows of $5.8 billion through the Indian Millennium Bonds scheme have led to a huge increase in liquidity.

A cut in small savings rates will reduce the burden on the budgets of the central as well as state governments. Moreover, as state governments have tended to rely heavily on such savings to tide over their precarious financial condition, reducing flows into such schemes is not such a bad thing at this point.

But these are not the only objectives the government has in mind. The government believes that declines in bank deposit rates will follow those on small savings as the two compete with each other. This, in turn, will push lending rates lower and stimulate industrial growth. The government thus expects the cut in the Bank rate that will follow the budget to signal a secular reduction in interest rates. This is expecting too much.

The RBI's annual report (1999-2000) makes clear why. As at

end-March 1999, about 73 per cent of deposits were of maturity of 364 days or more. The effective rate of interest on such deposits is 11 per cent even while the interest rate on fresh deposits is 8-9.5 per cent. Add to this banks' intermediation costs of 2.5-3 per cent of total assets and it is not hard to figure out why banks cannot afford to lower lending rates even if deposit rates decline.

A further complication is that, while deposits carry fixed rates for the most part, working capital loans are at floating rates. So every time banks lower lending rates, the pressure on operating margins is enormous.

A more serious constraint is that few banks are comfortably placed in respect of capital adequacy norms. Hence, incremental funds in the banking system find their way into government securities instead of translating into loans and this again limits the scope for reducing lending rates.

Nor will the direct flow of funds to firms increase as rates on savings instruments drift lower. A reduction in interest rates on bank deposits should cause investors to switch to riskier instruments such as equities. But, thanks to investors' lack of confidence in equity markets, this has not happened except in episodic bursts.

As for declines in interest rates on small savings, this will probably cause investors to switch either to bank deposits or out of financial assets altogether. The decline in savings in financial assets from 10.8 per cent in 1998-99 to 10.6 per cent in 1999-2000 suggests the latter is already happening.

For advocates of a lower interest rate regime, the increase in liquidity brought about by IMD bonds has created a piquant situation. Not only will industry not benefit, there is every prospect that lower rates on securities will increase the government's appetite for market borrowing. As an analysis by the EPW Research Foundation points out, this has happened twice before consequent to large increases in liquidity (EPW, November 18, 1999).

In 1998-99, when the Resurgent India Bonds were issued, the central government's net market borrowings shot up from Rs 32,449 crore in 1997-98 to Rs 68,988 crore the next year. Earlier, after the India Development Bonds were issued in 1992-92, market borrowings rose dramatically to Rs 28,537 crore in 1993-94 from Rs 7510 crore in 1991-92 and Rs 3676 crore in 1992-93 (that is, after the government ceased to be bound by IMF conditionalities).

The whole problem with increased government borrowings is that these have been used merely to postpone hard decisions on both the revenue and expenditure sides. The government needs to act differently now. It must take advantage of cheaper borrowings to step up capital expenditure sharply while not letting up on efforts to boost tax revenues. It is time to shed the fixation with lowering rates to industry as holding the key to a broad-based industrial revival.

February 15, 2001

Excessive reliance on private investment is a high-risk strategy

The strategy was brilliant, unfortunately the underlying assumptions did not hold. It is doubtful that any CEO could get away with an explanation of that sort.

The finance minister is being treated rather more indulgently. Even as the assumptions in the latest budget begin to look shaky, Mr Sinha is being portrayed as a heroic figure undermined by perverse forces in the world at large.

If only the political situation had not turned adverse; if only the Nasdaq had not plummeted; and if only the privatisation of Balco had not kicked up such a storm, the finance minister would have been well placed to achieve the twin objectives of a lower fiscal deficit and a modest acceleration in growth.

Yet, the essence of good strategy surely is that it is built on assumptions that have a fair chance of holding. Given the instability in Indian politics in recent years and the shocks that emanate from abroad with disconcerting frequency, it is wise not to minimise risks on these counts. But the more salient point is that the finance minister's approach carried high risks even otherwise. The turbulence in the environment has only made things worse.

The strategy for containing the fiscal deficit to GDP ratio rests considerably on spurring growth through lower interest rates. The hope is that a reduction in lower interest rates will cause private investment to rise sharply. This ignores the fact that the evidence on such a correlation is pretty weak through the nineties. Private corporate investment, in particular, has been quite unresponsive to interest rate declines.

One oft-cited reason for this is the uncertainties that businessmen have faced in respect of exchange rates, foreign competition, takeover threats etc. Even if the picture is a little clearer today, cheaper borrowings alone cannot stimulate capital expenditure. Businesses need to be able to raise commensurate equity. Thanks to the lack of confidence in the capital market, not many businesses could have hoped to do so even in normal conditions. With equities having been battered since, the prospects for raising equity have receded even further.

That is the situation with regard to domestic private investment. An unstated premise in the budget is that foreign direct investment (FDI), too, will rise. This is implicit in the target of Rs 12,000 crore for privatisation. It would be naïve to suppose that a big chunk of this can at all come from domestic sources. Major privatisation initiatives in emerging markets have invariably been driven largely by FDI. This too entails risks.

As the Balco case has shown, privatisation by itself is going to be a contentious affair. When privatisation is allied to transfer of control to foreign hands on a large scale, the stink this will cause can well be imagined. Yet, the budget tacitly assumes that the sale to foreign firms of a large number of the 27 PSUs marked for privatisation will go through in a year's time.

If private investment, domestic and foreign, does not rise as expected, real growth will end up below the 6.5 per cent that North Block has in mind. Nominal growth of around 13 per cent could still be achieved through an inflation rate of around 7 per cent and the budget's fiscal deficit to GDP target met. But an inflation rate of this order could spell the end of the regime of lower interest rates and, besides, growth will have ended up at the same level as in the previous year—or even lower.

Any growth strategy that is premised overwhelmingly on private investment and minimises the role of autonomous public investment is thus a high-risk strategy. A host of factors—political instability, adverse international conditions, delays in privatisation-could throw projections out of kilter. On the other hand, if the experience in the initial years of reforms is anything to go by, relatively higher levels of government capital expenditure stand a better chance of delivering growth and, in consequence, a lower fiscal deficit to GDP ratio.

Central capital expenditure since 1995-96 has been nearly one per cent of GDP below that in the first four years of reforms. Nevertheless, overall growth ended up at above 6 per cent (except in 1997-9). This was largely because acceleration in the services sector offset deceleration in industry. Some of the acceleration in services, we now know, has been illusory, stemming as it did from the Pay Commission awards. The prospects now are of a further deceleration in services as the US economy slows down. It will be more difficult to sustain growth rate of over 6 per cent without an acceleration in industry. To expect that acceleration to come entirely from private investment is to risk derailing growth.

March 29, 2001

No great paradox in the Indian polity, Mr Khilnani

Last week's hugely successful strike in the public sector, coinciding with pressure from the BJP on the finance minister to soften his recent tax proposals, has evoked the all too familiar refrain about the danger of 'reforms' going into reverse gear. This danger is seen to be especially great where an unwieldy coalition is seen to be battling for political survival.

Writing in the *Financial Times* (April 15), Sunil Khilnani resurrects this argument in light of the recent events in Gujarat. Khilnani is professor of politics at Birbeck College, London, and author of "The idea of India", an incisive analysis of the attempt on the part of the Indian elite to breathe life into the political construct called India.

Khilnani suggests that coalition politics ought to be welcome because the alternative, one-party dominance, could well be a 'recipe for disaster' when that party happens to be one that is committed to the ideology of Hindutva. Such a party "would recreate—magnified many times over—the same mayhem Gujarat is suffering today". A weak coalition government is a better guarantor of political stability, broadly defined, as it is more capable of looking after India's many religious and cultural identities.

However, coalition governments are bad news for the economy because they "are least likely to formulate and push through the deeper economic reforms that India must accomplish". Herein lies an 'ugly paradox' that has gripped Indians—what is good for the polity is not good for the economy.

The paradox, perhaps, lies elsewhere—in the unwillingness on the part of commentators to accept that the very process that delivers a fractured mandate is capable of showing wisdom in the economic choices it contrives as well. It is odd that Khilnani should espouse the viewpoint he does for, in his book, he talks of how Indian democracy has made for sensible economic policies. Regular elections meant that governments had to avoid sharply inflationary policies; they had averted the recurrence of famine; and they had brought new priorities to the fore.

It is not just the present coalition that has had to tread warily on economic policies. Even the Congress government under Narasimha Rao had slowed down in the second half of its term. The inability of governments in general to usher in rapid economic change is an aspect of democracy. It has to do with differences over the merits of particular policies, uncertainties about outcomes and the costs that policy changes impose on important groups in society.

Take privatisation, for example. For all the talk of 'consensus' on the subject, those ranged on the opposite side today include such stalwarts as Narasimha Rao, Manmohan Singh and Pranab Mukherjee. Even that darling of liberalisers, P Chidambaram, has opposed privatisation of profit-making companies such as Nevyeli Lignite Corporation. Nor is such opposition necessarily a matter of expediency. There is genuine concern that privatisation is unlikely to meet any of the objectives intended—improvement in firm efficiency, increase in social expenditure or reduction in public debt.

Similarly, reservations about hire-and-fire policies reflect politicians' alarm over job losses in a context in which there is no social security net and employment growth has slowed down. Politicians are also alert to the perception that Indian businessmen lack the moral authority to retrench because management is seldom penalised for under-performance or skullduggery.

Other measures impose invidious costs on some groups, given the pampering of other groups. The cuts in interest rates and the withdrawal of tax concessions have drawn a sharp response from the salaried class. This group sees itself as being asked to bear the burden of fiscal rectitude even as tax dodgers thrive and food subsidies climb because of hikes in minimum support prices. Meanwhile, the promised rise in investment expected from a fall in interest rates seems as distant as ever.

The lack of enthusiasm for the 'deeper economic reforms' that Khilnani refers cannot thus be ascribed to coalition politics. It reflects the judgement of a political class accountable to the electorate as to the sacrifices it can extract from present generations in pursuit of uncertain payoffs and the trade-offs between contending interest groups.

Democracy is all about mediating competing claims through the political process. Even as the process has thrown up coalitions as the answer to the divisions in the polity, so also it results in a pace of economic change that best responds to popular aspirations. To exalt the former and to disparage the latter borders on the schizophrenic.

April 25, 2002

TFC needs to revisit debt relief

The Twelfth Finance Commission (TFC), entrusted to the safe hands of C Rangarajan, has commenced its labours with interactions with academics and policy-makers in various cities. The central issues before the Commission are the perennial ones—how much of revenues to transfer from the center to the states and how the transfer is to be shared among the states themselves. Among the other issues the Commission will need to grapple with, debt relief to states must rank high in light of the debt swap scheme announced in the last budget.

Transfers to the states take place through devolution of taxes and grants-in-aid as stipulated by the Finance Commission and grants in other forms such as Plan grants. The former accounts for about 65 per cent of all transfers and the latter 35 per cent. The Eleventh Finance Commission (EFC) had fixed the total transfer to states, comprising all these elements, at 37.5 per cent of the centre's revenues. A key task for the TFC is to decide whether this proportion should go up or not.

An important consideration must be whose finances are in worse shape—the centre's or the states'. Going by absolute levels of indicators such as the fiscal deficit to GDP or the debt to GDP ratios, it would appear that it is the centre's finances that need greater consideration. However, state finances have been deteriorating at a faster pace in the post-reform period. The debt to GDP ratio at the centre worsened by about 4 per cent from 61.4 per cent in 1990-91 to 63.8 per cent in 2001-02. In the same period, the states' debt to GDP ratio worsened by over 30 per cent from 19.4 per cent to 25.6 per cent. This would suggest that any revision in the transfer to states needs to be upwards, not downwards, from the level set by the EFC.

The more contentious issue, as always, is that of redressing 'horizontal imbalances', that is, the differences in revenue bases and cost disabilities among the states. Equity is in some sense the raison d'etere for the Finance Commission. However, in the recent past, the Commission has had to take cognizance of efficiency considerations as well. One issue that has cropped is whether states that are congenitally profligate deserve to be rewarded through higher transfers. A related issue is whether the better-performing states will indefinitely accept declines in their share of transfers in the noble cause of fostering equity.

Many of the higher-income states could argue that the debt burden, which is on account of borrowings to finance Plan expenditure, would be lower if their share in devolution of taxes was higher. However, it is not just the level of borrowings that is killing states. The high interest rates on past loans are an equally important contributory factor. Interest payments by states reflect the high inflation rates of the past whereas their tax revenues have been rising at the lower inflation rates of recent years. This is part of the reason for the relentless increase in the ratio of interest to revenue receipts of states.

It follows that debt reliefs to states will loom larger than before in any restructuring of state finances. The Tenth Finance Commission had evolved a formula that linked debt relief to fiscal performance. The relief during the period 1995-2000 on this basis was estimated at Rs 212 crore. The EFC used the same formula but increased the incentive and estimated that the relief in 2000-05 would work out to Rs 600—700 crore.

These numbers are dwarfed by the relief estimated under the debt swap scheme announced in the last budget. The scheme, under which the centre will substitute securities with a coupon rate of over 13 per cent with lower cost securities over a three-year period ending 2004-05, is estimated to save the states Rs 81,000 in interest and deferred payment over the residual maturity of the loans. Assuming that the saving stretches out over a ten year period, we are talking of annual saving of around Rs 8000 crore or nearly 12 per cent of net interest payments of states in 2002-03. Maharashtra alone could save over Rs 500 crore each year, which is more than the amount budgeted for rural development.

The TFC needs to evolve a new approach to debt reliefs having regard to its terms of reference which require it to 'give weightage' to states' performance in human development and investment climate. Making reliefs conditional on performance in these areas might defeat the underlying objective. Defining what constitutes improvement in 'investment climate' could prove contentious.

A better approach might be to tie debt relief to expenditure on social, physical and financial infrastructure (such as the recapitalisation of state financial corporations). As resources are fungible, tied relief does present problems of implementation. But the alternative of conditional relief is unappealing in a context in which states are groaning under the burden of debt—and, perhaps, infeasible as well.

April 24, 2003

Credit Policy and Interest Rates

Interest rate posers

With the frenetic cuts in interest rates that we have been seeing in recent months, there is talk of a "liquidity overhang". Yet, barely a year ago there were loud protests about a "liquidity crunch". Industry leaders, who were earlier suggesting that the high interest rate regime would drive them out of business, are no longer complaining. Is there cause to celebrate? With interest rates declining, have we ushered in a brave new world in which the aggregate cost of capital will be lower than in the past?

Consider the following:

In April '96, when there was talk of a liquidity crunch, M3 had grown by 15.83 per cent over the previous year. Growth in the year upto April '97 has been only slightly higher at 16.13 per cent, so it's not as if the RBI has loosened the tap a great deal. More importantly, the growth rate of bank credit to the commercial sector has declined from 17.18 per cent to 10.53 per cent. M3 growth has been propped up mainly by higher growth in foreign exchange assets of banks—30.6 per cent compared to 1.82 per cent in the previous year. The figures do point to a slowdown in demand for bank funds that is consistent with the evidence of a deceleration in industrial growth. Viewed in this light, the decline in interest rates affords room for worry, not cheer.

Next, in assessing the impact of the decline in interest rates on industry, it is necessary to look at real interest rates. In March 1995, the prime lending rate was 15 per cent with the inflation rate at 10.2 per cent, giving a real interest rate of 4.8 per cent. For 1996, the figures were: PLR 16.5 per cent, inflation rate 4.4 per cent, real interest rate 12.1 per cent; and for March '97, PLR 14.5 per cent, inflation rate 7.6 per cent, real interest rate of 6.9 per cent. So, real interest rates are lower than in '96, but higher than in '95.

What do lower interest rates spell for industry? It has long been argued that high interest rates undermine competitiveness of Indian industry because our long-term rates have been 17-18 per cent or more while our competitors abroad can access capital at half these rates. This overlooks the fact that it is the aggregate cost of capital that is relevant, not just interest rates.

Gearing ratios in India have tended to be higher—2:1 compared to 1:1 or less elsewhere. Moreover, our corporate tax rates (at 43 per cent or more) have historically been higher than those in many of the advanced economies. As interest cost is tax deductible, it is the post-tax cost of debt that we need to take into account in computing cost of capital; the higher the tax rate, the lower is the post-tax cost of debt. Back-of-the-envelope calculations, assuming appropriate costs of debt (post-tax) and equity in India and abroad, will show that the difference in weighted average cost of capital between India and some of the advanced economies is not as acute as the difference in nominal interest rates would suggest.

Nominal interest rates have declined, but, on a post-tax basis, some of the benefit of the decline will be offset by the lowering of the corporate tax rate to 35 per cent. Moreover, with financial institutions nudging borrowers towards a gearing ratio of 1.5:1, the benefits of leverage will be lower than in the past. As against this, lower interest rates translate into lower expected returns on equity. My calculations indicate that the net effect of all the above may be to leave the weighted average cost of capital unchanged. It may be somewhat premature, therefore, to get carried away by the decline in interest rates.

Finally, there is the issue of how exactly we want to bring about lower interest rates. The trend so far is to lower lending and deposit rates so that spreads are not affected. For banks and financial institutions, this is something of a soft option, as it saves them the trouble of grappling with two other factors that impact on spreads: operational efficiencies and non-performing assets. But, beyond a point, lowering rates to depositors or bond holders is bound to impact adversely on deposit mobilisation and the development of a debt market. We will have reason to celebrate only when banks and FIs can lower lending rates without pushing down returns to depositors or bond-holders.

July 8, 1997

Missing pieces in credit jigsaw

Thus far and no further. Governor Jalan's position on the scope for bank rate reduction could not have been more categorical in the latest credit policy statement. The RBI has pushed the bank rate down from 11 per cent to 6.25 per cent—or by 475 basis points—over the past four and a half years. While this is reflected in declines in call money rates and yields on government securities, the average lending rates of banks have not been adequately responsive to bank rate cuts.

The RBI needs to document this contention in some detail. The Governor has promised that the maximum and minimum interest rates of banks would soon be made available at the RBI website. One hopes the RBI can eventually move towards an online system where interest rates for different grades of borrowers are displayed for all commercial banks.

However, from the standpoint of monitoring lending rate movements, the RBI needs to do better. It must know, for a given bank, the proportions of credit lent out to different grades of borrowers so that it can compute the weighted average lending rate for the bank and for banks as a whole. This is necessary because movements in the prime lending rate (PLR) can be deceptive.

Public sector banks may seek to appease the RBI by dutifully announcing reductions in the PLR consequent to a reduction in the bank rate. But they may, at the same time, lower their internal ratings on borrowers so that borrowers are pushed into lower grades than before. As a result, a decline in PLR may not translate into a lower lending rate for the bank as a whole. In the industrial climate we have had in recent years, it would not be difficult to justify such a lowering of ratings on the basis of objective parameters.

The RBI's annual report for 2001-02 has a chart showing that the spread of the PLR over government securities has increased sharply in the period July 2000—January 2002 (page 48). The spread of the average lending rate, one suspects, has been even higher.

To be sure, banks need to be prodded towards addressing the causes for stickiness in lending rates that the Governor drew attention to. But, in seeking to explain trends in credit, it is also important to ask if banks are being constrained by the suggestion that they contain their spread over the PLR.

While no upper band is expressly stipulated, the RBI has sought to convey off and on, including in the latest credit policy statement, that the spread over the PLR might be "unreasonably high". Yet, in private, bankers are apt to suggest that the lower grades of borrowers are mis-priced in the present scheme of things, meaning the interest rates charged do not compensate for the risks involved.

Prima facie, bankers would have some basis for this belief. As you go down the ladder of Crisil's bond ratings, the default probability rises sharply from 2.1 per cent for an AA bond (which is the third rating) to 7.9 per cent for a BBB bond. It then jumps to 36.7 per cent for a BB bond. If the RBI believes that the entire range of borrowers can be accommodated within a band of four per cent over the PLR, then it should be able to demonstrate this using a loan pricing model. Otherwise, bankers must be allowed to trust their instincts and price risk as they deem fit; one would hope that in a competitive market, they cannot get away with arbitrarily high lending rates.

The danger in setting artificial price bands is that banks will simply cut out high-risk borrowers, mostly small and medium units, to the detriment of the economy. They have every motivation to do so where investment in government securities and retail lending are enormously attractive and many banks are operating close to the mandatory capital adequacy ratio.

True, the RBI has sought to rein in banks' appetite for trading by mandating an investment fluctuation reserve into which five per cent of the value of investments must be set aside over a five-year period. But very few banks are as yet even near the one per cent mark.

It could well be, therefore, that banks have responded to reductions in bank rates in three ways. They are willing to offer a lower PLR or even sub-PLR rates to top grade borrowers in the knowledge that fee income still makes the overall relationship worthwhile. Other borrowers find themselves downgraded and hence would not benefit much from a softer rate regime.

Borrowers at the lower end of the scale find themselves unable to access credit.

In such a scenario, bank rate reductions would not be accompanied by an acceleration in credit. However smug banks might feel at the moment, the RBI must worry as to whether such a situation is sustainable for long.

November 7, 2002

When the RBI plays Big Brother

The RBI's monetary stance for quite some time now—and reiterated in the latest credit policy statement—has been towards pushing interest rates down. A natural question to ask, in evaluating this stance, is: how far has the RBI been successful in meeting its objective? A more troubling question, given the level of detail in the RBI's recent pronouncements, is whether the RBI might not be going overboard in managing interest rates in the banking system.

What do we know of the behaviour of interest rates in recent years? There is a general belief that interest rates in the Indian economy have been coming down and are, for the first time, competitive with international rates. Indeed, there's been much hand-wringing over the failure of investment to respond to interest rate declines.

Data on real interest rates tell a different story. The table shows two sets of real interest rates, one used by deputy governor Rakesh Mohan in his address to the Bank Economists' Conference in December, 2002, and another that figures in the *Report on Currency and Finance*, 2001-02 (hereafter "*Report*"). Both show that real interest rates to borrowers and depositors have actually increased in the second half of the past decade.

The differences in the two sets of figures are the result of differing methodologies. In Dr Mohan's address, real interest rates have been computed by deducting the average rate of WPI inflation for manufacturing from the weighted average lending rate of scheduled commercial banks (SCBs). The *Report* uses the average lending rate of SBI and the chain index of WPI for all commodities. (To make the figures comparable, the Report might want to use the weighted average lending rate for banks instead of the SBI rate.)

It is fair to suggest that Dr. Mohan's figures give us a better idea of what is happening to industrial borrowers. The real interest rate has virtually doubled in the recent period. The RBI's success in lowering nominal rates has been nullified by the steep decline in the prices in the manufacturing sector.

When it comes to depositors, it would appear that the *Report*'s numbers, which use the WPI for all commodities and not just for the inflation rate for industrial workers, are more accurate although the results run counter to general perception. Depositors never had it so good! Their real rate of return went up from under 1 per cent to 5.6 per cent in the second half of the past decade. The data thus turns on its head the conventional wisdom that policy has favoured borrowers at the expense of savers.

Where borrowers are concerned, the RBI seems to think that banks' spreads over the PLR are the villain of the piece. The recent credit policy statement notes with satisfaction that, consequent to the RBIs promptings in the April 2002 credit policy statement, banks have moved to reduce their spreads. The number of public sector banks, whose maximum spread is under 4 per cent, has gone up from 2 to 15. The central bank has now indicated that the next bastion to be stormed would be the benchmark PLR itself. It has laid down the method of computation of the PLR and served notice that it will 'review' the determination of PLRs by banks come September.

Table: Real interest rates: up, not down

(all figure in per cent)

	1990-91 Mohan	*1995-96 RBI*	*1996-97 Mohan*	*2001-02 RBI*
Borrower	6.5	6	12.5	7.6
Depositor	–0.3	0.95	1.9	5.62

Source: Rakesh Mohan (2002); Report on Currency and Finance (2001-02)

While the method itself is unexceptionable, it must not be presumed that the use of this method, with Big Brother watching, would result in lower PLRs . The RBI needs to take a close look at the data on bank interest rates it has posted at its own website. HDFC Bank has among the lowest cost of funds among Indian banks and exposures only to high quality corporates. Unlike Public Sector Banks (PSBs), it has a sophisticated system for measuring customer profitability that allows fee income to be factored into calculations of the bank's return on equity for a given customer. This would potentially allow the bank to offer a lower spread to a corporate that generates substantial fee income.

Yet, HDFC Bank has one of the highest bands for the PLR for the quarter October–December 2002: 12.5-15.50 per cent, with a spread for demand loans of 3 per cent over the lower end. SBI's band was 10.25-11.25 per cent, with a maximum spread of 2.6 per cent over the lower end. Several PSBs had lower PLRs and spreads than HDFC Bank.

So what does the RBI propose to do? Is it going to advise one

Ice Sector

One-swallow summer

In the stock market, nothing exceeds like success. So it is hardly surprising that a high growth rate in the Indian IT sector has stretched valuations of IT stocks. Like many an earlier bout of irrational exuberance, this one is bound to meet its nemesis.

One could leave it at that except that commentators are apt to draw broad conclusions from the dizzying rise of IT stocks. In his popular column in *the Times of India* (Swaminomics, January 9), Swaminathan Aiyar sees the IT success stories as proof that Indian companies can take on MNCs. Mr Aiyar also argues that these successes vindicate economic liberalization. Socialists who had the 'gall' to substitute their decisions for 'economic freedom' have been proved wrong. It is worth examining these propositions closely.

Firms such as Infosys and Wipro have drawn abreast of Hindustan Lever in terms of market capitalization. To Mr Aiyar, this is proof that liberalization can throw up Indian companies capable of competing with MNCs. There is a serious problem with using current valuations of IT stocks in making comparisons (price-earnings multiples of Infosys and Wipro are over 200 compared to HLL's 60) but suppose we let that pass.

The issue for economic policy is not leadership in market cap of one or two Indian companies. It is the aggregate impact of competition on Indian business. The IT success stories essentially target the international market. There have always been sectors in which Indian firms found niches at the commodity end of the international market. The growing importance of IT in the industrial nations has created such opportunities in the services sector.

However, in sectors that focus on the domestic market, Indian companies are undoubtedly feeling the heat of competition from MNCs even though it is early days on some dimensions of liberalization. (One reason why many listed companies remain in Indian hands is that foreign companies cannot make secondary market acquisitions.) Given that IT companies are still small in terms of sales, it is brave to suggest that the successes in IT can compensate for the potentially adverse impact of a more liberalized regime on Indian firms in a wide range of sectors.

What does the success in IT say about economic freedom? One reason the market caps of IT companies have soared is because socialistic bureaucrats had the gall to exempt export profits from tax. Absent this exemption, the market caps of IT stocks would be lower by upto 40 per cent. In future trade negotiations, this piece of errant socialist behaviour will likely be disciplined by the industrial nations. IT stocks will then come down with a thud.

In 1993, Infosys scraped through with its initial public offer and it must have been under pressure to show results. In that year and in the next, a flood of foreign inflows threatened to cause the rupee to appreciate. The RBI took the anti-market decision to prevent such appreciation (at a steep cost to itself) so that export growth was not adversely affected. Such intervention undoubtedly helped put Infosys (and other IT companies) on the path of high growth where they have stayed ever since.

Past socialist interference continues to benefit IT companies in other ways. They draw upon a huge pool of trained manpower produced by institutions such as the IITs and the IIMs, all of which provided advanced education at enormous subsidies—another grave departure from the philosophy of economic freedom.

Thus, the IT success story, supposedly the result of a hands-off approach on the part of government, turns out to have been based on a combination of private enterprise and favourable state intervention. No great surprise here. This is precisely the recipe that spelt economic success, first in Europe and the US, then in Japan, next in East Asia and, most recently, in China.

Secondly, IT growth vindicates not the entire liberalization package but just two elements in it—the move towards a market-determined exchange rate and easier availability of foreign exchange. The same package, for instance, has failed miserably to deliver in infrastructure.

The test of economic policy is not whether it produces a couple of stock market leaders or high growth in one or two sectors. Policy must produce sustainable growth in the aggregate while meeting a variety of other objectives. Nearly a decade into liberalization, these results are still awaited. One IT swallow, alas, does not an economic summer make.

January 20, 2000

Even as ICE melts, old economy firms may remain in deep freeze

As the Nasdaq soared in 1998 and 1999, so did IT stocks in India and this helped shore up market indices. The 50 per cent decline in the Nasdaq from its peak in March 2000 has sent IT stocks and market indices crashing in other markets, including India.

But the similarities end with the behaviour of stock markets. The impact on the real economy of the IT–led stock market gyrations varies considerably across countries. There is every likelihood that the US economy, having reaped the benefits of the IT bubble, will now coast along at a more sustainable growth rate. In India, however, the macroeconomic effects of the IT boom have been nowhere as benign—and the downside could be rather more painful.

The IMF's *World Economic Outlook* (September 2000) highlights the remarkable similarities in stock markets during the IT boom. (IT is defined broadly to cover the ICE sectors—information, communications and entertainment .) One, there has been a marked bifurcation everywhere in valuations between old and new economy stocks. Two, IT stocks have been more volatile than traditional stocks. Three, IT stock prices internationally have shown higher correlation relative to non-IT stocks.

While the bifurcation in valuations between old and new economy stocks has been underway since the mid-nineties, it has got accentuated in recent years. In August 2000, for which *Outlook* has graphs, the price-earnings multiple for the IT sector in the US was nearly 50 compared to 25 for the non-IT sector. In Asia, the respective multiples were 90 and 30.

The volatility in IT stocks everywhere mirrors that in IT stocks in the US. The IMF's report notes that earnings volatility in the IT sector in the US increased despite stability in aggregate demand growth. This reflects the riskiness inherent in the implementation and diffusion of new technologies and the highly competitive environment in which IT firms operate. As investors in the IT sector tend to be guided by developments in the principal market, the US, prices in IT stocks across countries have tended to be highly correlated.

Turn now to the macroeconomic effects of the IT boom. In the US, the IT sector is credited with bringing about an improvement in productivity in the economy of half to three-quarters of a percentage point in the second half of the nineties. This is the result of increased productivity in the IT sector and capital deepening, that is, investment in IT in other sectors.

With market capitalisation of the IT sector rising to nearly 50 per cent of GDP, the stock market bubble set off a consumer boom that pushed GDP growth in the US to a phenomenal five per cent last year. By general reckoning, this is unsustainable. But, if the economy lands safely, growth this year will still be an impressive three per cent and this could easily be sustained by the underlying breakthrough in productivity.

In India, the macroeconomic effects of the boom in IT stocks have been muted. With a market capitalisation of less than five per cent of GDP, the IT sector of the stock market is too small to make a difference to consumer spending. Nor is the IT sector in the real economy large enough or its links with the rest of the economy strong enough for IT to impact on productivity in the economy.

If the upside is minimal, the downside is worrisome. The bifurcation in valuations has been more pronounced than in the US. In March 2000, the ET Mindex had an average price-earning multiple of 58 compared to a multiple for the Sensex (minus the IT stocks) of 20. The Sensex average disguises the fact that several old economy stocks today trade at a multiple of five or less. Fundamentals apart, investors' infatuation with IT is at least partly to blame for the levels to which these have fallen.

Low valuations hurt firms more in India. This is because firms here are more dependent on external finance relative to internal funds than firms in industrial countries such as the US. In the US, external finance accounts for just around 10 per cent of total funds of companies whereas its share in India is around 60 per cent.

Poor valuations have impaired the ability of several old economy firms here to raise equity. With gearing ratios going up as a result of declines in net worth, firms' access to debt is also diminished. This has happened at a time when firms desperately need to modernise to meet the threat of foreign competition.

Reallocations across portfolios by investors will hopefully cause valuations of old economy firms to improve. But the setbacks over the past two or three years mean that such firms will take a while to come out of the deep freeze assuming the situation is not past repair.

January 4, 2001

The market can deceive

The stock market bubble of the late nineties dealt yet another blow to the efficient market hypothesis—the belief that today's stock market prices accurately reflect the future performance of companies. Taking prices of stocks at face value in times of euphoria is bad enough. Using stock market prices to draw conclusions about underlying economic trends, as pundits in India were doing, can be even worse.

Stock market bubbles last as long as they do because people believe that fundamentals have changed sufficiently to warrant sky-high valuations. Unfortunately, it is hard to prove the optimists wrong until the bubble collapses. The standard way of looking for signs of a bubble is to compare the market price-earnings multiple at any given point with historical levels. Thus, for instance, the market multiple for the United States for the period 1950-99 has been 15. In 1999, this shot up to 32, which was suggestive of a bubble.

However, this conclusion rests on all variables in the Gordon growth formula for stock price valuation not having changed. These are: the projected growth rate in dividends, the risk-free rate of return and the premium over the risk-free rate. The optimists pointed to changes in all of these that would justify higher valuations. Interest rates on government securities had declined. The greater potential for international diversification had led to a fall in the required risk premium. Above all, the new economy had caused the underlying growth rate potential to accelerate. By the time economists got round to tackling the last claim, the bubble had collapsed.

Getting carried away by particular stocks is not such a great sin. The empirical evidence is that markets are reasonably efficient in the case of individual stocks. Not so at the aggregate level. As Paul Samuelson once put it, the stock market is "micro efficient but macro inefficient". This makes generalisations about the economy based on stock prices less forgivable than euphoria about individual stocks. Yet, pundits in India were quick to leap to conclusions about what the surge in IT stock prices meant for the economy. Manufacturing was passé; services, especially IT-based services, were the wave of the future.

As the accompanying table shows, this conclusion was based on a comparison with 2000 when the IT bubble was its peak. Between 1996 and 2000, the share of manufacturing had declined from 72 per cent to 47 per cent; that of services had risen from 18 per cent to 48 per cent. The share of the ICE sector had leapt from 7 per cent to 42 per cent. (The Prowess database includes software in maneufacturing; we include it in services. IT includes hardware but software dominates.)

The numbers for 2003 should bring the pundits down to earth. Manufacturing is in the lead with a share of 58 per cent. Services are down to 30 per cent; the share of the ICE sector has fallen drastically to 15 per cent. Perhaps a comparison between 1996 and 2003 tells the story more accurately. The transition from manufacturing to services is less dramatic than is supposed. Besides, the services story is not just about IT. Banking has grown in importance, its share rising from 1 per cent to 10 per cent.

A few caveats are in order. Some of the decline in IT's market cap is because of competition from foreign software firms that have set up shop in India. These latter are not listed on the exchanges, hence the market cap of the IT sector is understated. As against this, one could argue that market cap of the software

Market capitalisation: sectoral composition

	June 1996 per cent to total Mkt Cap	Feb 2000 per cent to total Mkt Cap	April 2003 per cent to total Mkt Cap
Market cap–BSE	100.0 per cent	100.0 per cent	100.0 per cent
Manufacturing	71.6 per cent	46.9 per cent	58.1 per cent
Services	17.9 per cent	48.4 per cent	29.9 per cent
Others	10.5 per cent	4.7 per cent	12.0 per cent
ICE sector	7.6 per cent	41.6 per cent	14.9 per cent
IT	1.2 per cent	31.8 per cent	11.3 per cent
Recreation	0.1 per cent	5.8 per cent	0.9 per cent
Telecom	6.3 per cent	4.0 per cent	2.7 per cent
Banking	1.1 per cent	3.5 per cent	10.1 per cent

Source: Prowess Database, CMIE

sector is buoyed up by tax concessions that must go one day. Manufacturing's own share is understated because many big foreign firms are not listed.

The larger issue is how far market capitalisation, which relates to listed firms in the corporate sector, can be said to represent trends in the economy at large. We do know that services have overtaken manufacturing in the broader economy whatever today's market cap data might indicate. But services include a large unproductive component of salaries in government. Market cap data, perhaps, better reflect the relative importance of the productive components of various sectors. At any rate, pundits who swear by market cap must acknowledge that news of the demise of manufacturing has been exaggerated.

Does this matter? Yes, because there was a tendency to write off manufacturing in the belief that the IT sector would more than compensate in terms of growth and jobs. Indeed, some politicians, unwilling to face up to the task of reviving industry, had begun to display an escapist disposition towards wooing the IT sector. The sobering message of the post-bubble period is that manufacturing remains relevant and that services is more than IT.

June 19, 2003

Business Environment

Wake-up call for MNCs

MNCs have had their work cut out for them in emerging markets even if you ignored the *Swadeshi* factor. Market volumes that turned out to be considerably lower than projected; hassles with joint venture partners; established products that failed to appeal in the newer markets; issues of expat managers versus locals; the list of woes can be easily extended.

According to C.K.Prahalad and Kenneth Lieberthal, professors at the University of Michigan, the disappointments MNCs have had can be ascribed to an imperialist mind-set ("The end of corporate imperialism", *Harvard Business Review*, July-August 1998). MNCs, they say, have tended to view emerging markets merely as outlets for incremental sales of existing products or of sunset technologies. The notion of emerging markets as sources of product or process innovation or technical and managerial talent is one that few MNCs have embraced whole-heartedly.

More importantly, not many MNCs have thought through the question of what adapting to emerging markets might mean for the way they do business worldwide. For that would mean challenging cherished assumptions about such things as the cost structure, the product portfolio and the composition of top management at MNCs.

Yet, a fundamental change in mind-set is necessary. It is necessary, in the first place, because emerging markets are impossible to ignore. But the more compelling argument for a change in mind-set, the authors suggest, is that it has the potential to impact favourably on MNCs' operations everywhere, not just those in emerging markets.

Take, for example, the question of market volumes. Volumes are often limited by the fact that MNCs tend to introduce products that have done well in their home markets but which are horrendously expensive by emerging market standards. They can do better. Prahalad and Lieberthal argue that if Ford wants to be more than a small, high end-player in India, it must figure out ways to deliver a low-cost alternative. This would require a rethinking of Ford's business model that could have dramatic spin-offs elsewhere.

The logic applies to product development, brand management, packaging and distribution as well. The authors cite the case of a video-CD player launched by Philips that has had phenomenal success in China although it lacks a market in US or Europe. The Chinese are now likely to be major players in introducing the next round of video–CD standards around the world. Thus, innovations made in peripheral markets could be successfully transplanted to a firm's centre, unlike in the past when the centre was seen as the fount of all innovation.

This may already be happening in software: MNCs such as Texas Instruments and Motorola have begun to use India for software-oriented business development. It could happen in other sectors too. If, for instance, Citicorp can make a success of its experiment with developing a business model for the mass market in India, it may have found a way to serve average Chinese people as well as inner-city residents in New York.

Here, then, is a timely wake-up call for MNCs whose emerging market strategy has been one of muddling through. The authors' central message to MNCs is simple enough: please take emerging markets more seriously. But there is one key question the authors don't tackle head-on: how do MNCs deal with the emotive issue of *Swadeshi* ? They address it tangentially when they ask: how many of today's multinationals are willing to accommodate 30-40 per cent of their top team coming from China, India and Brazil? If the authors imply that a change in top management composition by itself would render *Swadeshi* irrelevant, it's possible to disagree.

The issue of *ownership* cannot be wished away. Having local subsidiaries with public participation is a good idea but it may not entirely eliminate perceptions of MNCs as accountable primarily to shareholders in the industrial economies. For a fundamental transformation in the character of MNCs to come about, dispersion of ownership on a bigger scale is required. As barriers to capital flows are dismantled, such dispersion would take place to some extent on its own as institutions in emerging markets begin to invest in MNCs' holding companies. But for MNCs that want to make the most of emerging market opportunities, part of the challenge surely is to find ways in which they can actively abet this process.

August 6, 1998

Spirit of TTK

The birth centenary of TT Krishnamachari, which falls today, affords an opportunity to recall the services of the greatest economic administrator the country has produced in the post-independence era.

TTK left his impress on several spheres of national endeavour. As a member of the Drafting Committee of the Constituent Assembly, he was one of the architects of the Indian Constitution. As Minister for Commerce and Industry, he erected the policy framework for trade and industry that resulted in the development of a diversified industrial base over the Second and Third Plan periods, and also oversaw the setting up of three giant steel plants.

As Finance Minister (in two spells), he faced up to the challenge of mobilizing resources for a great leap forward on the part of the public sector by widening the tax base. As Minister for Defence and Economic Coordination, he played a key role in gearing the economy towards the war effort and in garnering foreign aid at the time of the 1962 conflict with China.

With his grasp of economic theory, historical perspective and ability to articulate first principles, TTK yielded to none when it came to formulating macroeconomic policy. But his unique strength lay in conceiving institutions and organization necessary for translating policy into enduring results. The number of institutions that owe their existence to him is legion: IDBI and UTI; STC, Export Risk Insurance Corporation and Export Promotion Councils; Commodity Boards ; NCAER; the Border Roads Organization; the Indian Economic Service; the Dandakaranya Development Authority; the list is by no means exhaustive.

This must seem extraordinary for someone who had little formal training as an economist until you remember that TTK had been a successful entrepreneur before entering politics. He had what many policy-makers lack: the businessman's instinctive understanding of what it would take to get investment and production ticking, and a flair for innovation and institution-building. Therein lies the secret of the dynamism TTK was able to impart to economic policy-making.

But TTK also had a quality rare among businessmen: the ability to transcend the narrow interests of the business community in looking at larger national issues. This was a businessman who could declare: " In any elected legislature there can be only one view, that is, the view of the workers, and not the view of the employers. The employer has got the safeguard of money behind him". That must explain something even more extraordinary: how a businessman came to entrusted by Nehru with the task of giving concrete shape to the vision of a socialistic society.

Not that TTK was wedded to doctrinaire socialism. He was a pragmatist who saw a mixed economy, with the State playing the dominant role in propelling industrial development, as an authentic, home-grown response to the ground realities at that time. He insisted that the private sector, including foreign capital, had a legitimate role to play in fostering industrial growth. He set his face against sweeping nationalization of foreign firms, encouraged the setting up of ICICI to promote private investment, and was quick to clear major projects in the private sector such as the expansion of TISCO and the setting up of TELCO.

He did not succumb to pressure to curb the modest imports he had allowed as Commerce Minister, saying that import competition was necessary to safeguard the interests of the consumer. He even went so far as to propose starting industrial units with government capital, which could be sold to private investors down the road, thus anticipating privatization long before it became fashionable. But he did believe that the State in the Indian context must pursue broad egalitarian and welfare goals, and was ready to use fiscal policy for the purpose.

We have come a long way since TTK's days. TTK would, no doubt, have been the first to acknowledge the need to work the mixed economy differently in the changed context. But his basic philosophy—of liberalism in industrial policy combined with a fiscal policy to meet overriding social objectives—remains as valid today. More than his philosophy, however, it's the spirit of TTK—his energy, humanism, innovative flair and capacity for institution-building—that we need to recapture as we fashion our response to the continuing challenges of growth and development.

November 26, 1998

Cope, don't whine

Businessmen are annoyed and angry. As the Sensex tumbled on news of the fall of the Vajpayee government, many went to town about the impact of political instability on the economy. Their lament has been dutifully echoed in the media, and there are suggestions that irresponsible politicians have aborted a putative recovery. This raises the question of the relationship between political instability and economic growth. It also raises the broader question of whether uncertainties in the economic environment today are such as to deter private investment.

It's important to distinguish between political instability and policy uncertainty. In its *World Development Report 1997*, the World Bank highlighted this distinction by citing two examples. Thailand was wracked by coups for many years and this contributed to high political uncertainty. But changes of government did not affect the institutional framework, nor did businessmen fear wide-ranging policy reversals.

In contrast, Peru had a stable government for years but the private sector faced a highly uncertain economic environment because legislation through executive and emergency decrees was all too common there. The Bank concluded that political instability may not be a correct proxy for policy reliability. This is certainly true in our context. Governments have come and gone since 1991 but there's been no policy reversal.

Based on a survey of businessmen covering sixty-nine countries and over 3600 firms, the World Bank found evidence that investment and growth are strongly correlated with an index that captured the credibility of rules. This indicator was composed of five sub-indicators, only one of which stood for political instability. And political instability was not defined in terms of changes of government; rather, this sub-indicator reflected local investors' perceptions as to whether government changes meant far-reaching policy surprises.

The other four sub-indicators were: predictability of rule-making, security of persons and property, predictability of judicial enforcement and corruption. The credibility indicator for

South and South-East Asia was just below that in the high-income industrial countries. Indian businessmen, who fret about political instability, need to pause for a minute and ask whether there really perceive any deterioration in the overall credibility indicator as defined by the Bank.

What about uncertainty in macro-economic variables such as the exchange rate, inflation, the overall level of economic activity, public investment, credit availability, real interest rate etc? In the early stages of reforms, as the emphasis shifts from controls to market forces, one would expect considerable uncertainty about these indicators; the magnitude of rupee depreciation, for instance, could scarcely have been anticipated. But this need not hold true further down the road. There's less uncertainty about the exchange rate today. As for inflation, we have an improvement over even the pre-reform period.

It's true some variables (notably overall economic activity and public investment) are at unsatisfactory levels but the crucial thing is there isn't much uncertainty on the downside. Public investment in the post-reform period has ranged between 3-3.5 per cent of GDP (this has little to do, incidentally, with political instability), and it's hard to see it falling further. Similarly, it requires an overdose of pessimism to see GDP growth sinking below 5 per cent. For the bigger firms, credit availability does not appear to be a problem, and any sharp increase in real interest rates appears improbable. Room for uncertainty is also limited in respect of another key micro-economic variable, tax rates, given the present consensus on reforms.

What all this adds up to is that businessmen can construct a base level scenario, taking into account key economic variables, in the confidence that variations on this are more likely to be on the upside than on the downside. The uncertainty that must really worry businesmen today arises not on account of political or macro-economic factors, but on account of competition, something that they are not accustomed to. There's not much government policy can do about this other than preventing unfair practices.

Dealing with competition and making the most of opportunities in an era of globalisation call for managerial and institutional capabilities that are missing in the older firms. They call for a willingness to invest and expand in the knowledge that non-performance could mean loss of control. Above all, they call for standards of governance that inspire confidence in the markets as well as professional managers. Instead of whining about political instability, businessmen need to examine how far they have gone in adapting their mindsets to the new realities. The fault, dear businessmen, is not in your political stars but in yourselves.

April 29, 1999

Bearable shock

Rising oil prices have always been a problem for oil-importing developing countries such as India but it is important not to lose perspective in viewing the recent surge in prices.

The current price of $30 per barrel looks steep. However, as a chart in the IMF's latest *World Economic Outlook* makes clear, oil prices in real terms are below the levels reached after the crippling shocks of 1973 and 1990 and half the level at the time of the shock of 1980.

This is part of the reason that India's oil imports as a proportion of total imports have shown a declining trend. The ratio was 26 per cent in 1974-75 after the first oil shock and it soared to 41 per cent during the second oil shock in 1980-81. By 1990-91, at the time of the third shock, the ratio had fallen to 22 per cent. The ratio for 2000-2001 will be close to the figure of 26 per cent that obtained at the time of the first oil shock.

This rise is not such a terrifying prospect, first, because the effects on India of the impact of higher oil prices on the world economy at large will be muted. The world economy is in rude good health at the moment. The IMF's *Outlook* projects growth at 4.7 per cent in 2000 and 4.2 per cent in 2001, way above the average growth rates of 3.4 per cent and 3.1 per cent in the eighties and nineties respectively.

Even if oil prices were to stay at around $32 a barrel—or a $5 sustained increase over the IMF's assumed baseline figure of $26.53—the IMF estimates that growth would slow down in 2001 by a mere 0.2 per cent in the major industrial countries and by 0.4 per cent in Asia. As oil shocks go, this one seems pretty bearable.

More importantly, there have been dramatic improvements in recent years in the current account deficit to GDP ratio on other counts (chiefly, the rise in invisibles). If oil prices stay at around $30-32, the current account deficit will rise from one per cent last year to what is regarded as a safe level of 1.5 per cent. This would happen after a whole decade in which the deficit averaged less than 1.5 per cent.

The upshot of all this is that there is no dire threat to BoP that requires the government to curb consumption through savage hikes in prices of oil products. Rather, price hikes are needed in order to contain the cost to the exchequer of subsidies under the administered price mechanism.

There is a clamour from some quarters for passing on the increase in oil prices very substantially to the consumer instead of the government absorbing part of the impact through the issue of oil bonds and reductions in taxes. Given that a rise in administered prices has an immediate impact on the economy, such a course risks seriously derailing growth momentum. The addition to the fiscal deficit, in contrast, will have a lagged effect on the economy (some would add, if at all).

Choosing between the two options requires taking a view on whether oil prices will continue to rule at present levels through 2001. On present indications, this looks unlikely. The rise in oil prices flowed from the recognition all round that the oil exporters had been battered by the collapse in oil prices in 1998 and needed relief.

OPEC decided to cut production in March 1999 in order to get oil prices to rise. It requires a profound ignorance of oil politics to suppose that OPEC, many of whose members are client states of the US, would have acted without the concurrence of the US. But today the situation is different. The rise in oil prices, the IMF estimates, has helped oil producers recoup the losses they suffered over the past two years. So the US is now telling OPEC: enough is enough. OPEC, in turn, has signalled its willingness to return to the $22-28 band. Indeed, oil prices have already come off the recent peak of $37.

Under the circumstances, petroleum minister Ram Naik's move to limit the burden on consumers to one-third of the oil pool deficit is well judged. It will cushion the consumer without derailing growth. The issue of oil bonds will limit the immediate impact on the fisc.

Looking further ahead, the government is unlikely to pass on fully any future fall in world oil prices. This means the subsidy to the consumer could well end up being pruned in the next fiscal. Mr. Naik will thus have taken advantage of the rise in oil prices to put the economy on course towards the elimination of the administered price mechanism scheduled for 2002.

September 28, 2000

Economic policy-making through the eyes of an insider

IG Patel has produced a thoroughly charming memoir (*Glimpses of Indian Economic Policy, An Insider's View, OUP*). This is the story of the evolution of India's economic policies told by an economist who was associated with policy-making over the period 1954 to 1982, with a few breaks in between.

Patel does not attempt any detailed dissection of India's economic policies. Instead, he touches briefly on the considerations that led up to particular policies and the reasons why some policies went awry. He provides vignettes of the principal characters in the drama. He details the interaction between the professional economists in government and the political leadership.

The last is of particular interest because people would want to know from Patel whether economists were able to make a meaningful contribution to economic policy or whether they were mere tools in the hands of a venal or incompetent political leadership. Patel's narrative is by no means unflattering to the political class.

Patel is dismissive of the notion, fashionable today, that the political leadership during the period—and Nehru in particular-led India down a certain path entirely because of its infatuation with socialism. Rather, the principal features of Indian economic policy, he suggests, were largely shaped by history and circumstance.

Patel sees World War II as being an especially important determinant of economic philosophy in the post—War period. Controls and high rates of taxation, felt necessary during the War, continued thereafter—and had the support of the bureaucracy, 'no leftist institution'. The uncertainties of international commerce experienced during the War gave rise to a strong belief in the virtues of self-sufficiency. The sharp rise in prices created a preference for price stability over growth.

Ideology was less important in other respects too. The Bombay Plan, he reminds us, was prepared by industrialists and it anticipated the importance accorded to planned development. The decision to accord a dominant role to the public sector stemmed from the recognition that Indian industry was in no position to undertake large projects.

It will interest die-hard critics of Nehruvian policies to know that "JRD Tata's Air India was not nationalised. He was too happy to hand it over". Fears of a resurgence of foreign domination created an antipathy towards foreign investment. None of this is new but it is useful to be reminded by somebody like Patel because of the tendency these days to believe that the political class let the country down badly until the recent discovery of economic reforms. Mainstream economic opinion was pretty much with the political class.

While Patel treads familiar ground for the most part, he is able to provide the odd twist to accepted lore. Of the Second Five-Year Plan, Patel says that a broad consensus had been reached on crucial features even before Mahalanobis arrived on the scene. In particular, " the ground was being prepared at least for substantial investment in steel and fertilisers and for comparative neglect of organised consumer goods industry". Mahalanobis' contribution was to emphasise investment in investment goods industries.

But the Mahalanobis model, the author says, "was never seriously or consistently implemented in India", thanks to the foreign exchange crisis that emerged. What projects could be taken up came to be dictated by the availability of aid. The result was that the "Second Plan—if it is seen as a Mahalanobis Plan—was still—born". So much for the perception that the Second Plan was the handiwork of a Nehru favourite.

The impression one gets from the book is that the political leadership devised policies in consultation with economists of calibre but with an eye always to the democratic and federal nature of the polity. It is a different matter that these policies were not reversed long after they had outlived their utility.

There was, of course, the odd occasion when a political leader bypassed economists—as when Indira Gandhi decided to nationalise banks and gave Patel 24 hours to prepare the necessary Bill. It could be plausibly argued that, on that occasion, Mrs Gandhi showed superior economic judgement, whatever her political calculations.

Patel persuaded Mrs Gandhi to limit nationalization to 14 banks. A few years later, as RBI governor, he was beseeching Mrs Gandhi to take over another six because of the 'shady goings-on' at these. Mrs Gandhi's instinct about private banks had been right, after all.

Nor should this come as a big surprise. In the very nature of their vocation, politicians in general—and great leaders, certainly—have a better appreciation of the aspirations of people and of what is feasible in the realm of economic policy than professionals whose background and outlook tend to be suffocatingly narrow. For economists and their country cousins in the business press not to recognize this and to keep carping about 'ack of political will' or 'populism', as many are wont to, is sheer hubris.

March 14, 2002

Calculus of a landslide win

The successful prosecution of a war may or may not yield electoral dividends. Indira Gandhi and Margaret Thatcher rode to famous victories in elections after winning a war. But Winston Churchill and George Bush, Sr, got tossed out by voters on the heels of triumphs on the battlefield.

If recent experience in the United States is anything to go by, the conduct of a war against terrorism might be a more enticing proposition for political leaders. George Bush, Jr, has just presided over a Republican annexation of the Congress against the background of an economic record that would normally have meant a certain electoral defeat.

The US stock market has collapsed, the budget deficit has soared and corporate America has been wracked by scandals that have enmeshed the Republican elite. Yet, by focusing steadfastly on the threat to the US from an enemy lurking in the background, Mr Bush has contrived electoral victories in the face of seemingly impossible odds.

Has Narendra Modi successfully replicated Mr Bush's strategy in the recent Gujarat elections? Gujarat's economy has unquestionably faltered in recent years. And, without doubt, Mr Modi's campaign was substantially about the threat of terrorism in a state that is vulnerable on this count. But there are important differences as well.

In matters of foreign policy, the American media is virtually an extension of the political establishment, and it has faithfully plugged the official line on terrorism. The Indian media, especially the English section of it, can hardly be said to have been as indulgent towards Mr Modi. Secondly, given America's brand of Tweedledum—Tweedledee politics, American democracy has long been characterized by voter apathy. India has a higher voter turnout as the electorate does prize the opportunity to vent its anger against incumbents.

So, it would not have been easy for Mr Modi to induce the electorate to overlook fundamental economic problems by invoking a larger threat in the shape of terrorism, much as

Mr Modi's detractors would like to believe this is what happened. But what are the economic realities?

Gujarat's economy has been slowing down since 1997-98. While the compound growth rate of gross state domestic product (GSDP) averaged 11 per cent in 1993-97, it fell steeply to 2.5 per cent in 1998-2001. However, if we take the period 1993-2001 as a whole—and the BJP has been in power for most of this period-, the growth rate of 6.5 per cent would still put Gujarat ahead of the growth rate for India that averaged a healthy 6.2 per cent.

Gujarat's per capita income in 2000-01 was a good 30 per cent above the national average. Moreover, while data on remittances into the state are not available, the existence of a huge Gujarati diaspora does imply that remittances would provide a useful cushion to large numbers of people. This is not a context that would give rise to the sort of disaffection on grounds of economic performance that unseats governments.

There would have been economic hardship and the resultant disaffection had the BJP government pushed ahead with the standard menu of reforms in the state's battered condition: curbing subsidies, increasing user charges, closing down unviable state enterprises, etc.

Not only did the state government not embrace such measures, but, as colleague Ravindra Dholakia notes, it has sought since 1996 to more actively protect the small-scale sector from the impact of liberalization through enhanced subsidies. (*Economic reforms and development strategy in Gujarat, IIMA Working Paper*). These, along with expenditures caused by natural disasters, have pushed up the fiscal deficit to 5.5 per cent of GSDP. But, then, hardly any state is today free from fiscal problems and not many can plead natural disasters in extenuation of their plight.

Mr Modi, like his predecessors, has been accused of being blind to the imperative of reforms. But a man of Mr Modi's shrewd political instincts would know that the best time for reform is when there is an economic upswing. Reformers see growth as contingent on reforms. There is, however, an autonomous component to growth that hinges on the overall domestic and international environment and that can used to time economic policies.

The revival in industrial growth in the country in recent months augurs well for Gujarat. The state's economy is driven by the industrial sector and it tends to outperform or underperform the Indian economy, depending on how well the industrial sector, including exports, is faring. Should the industrial momentum of recent months be sustained.

Mr Modi would be well placed to provide in the economic realm the sort of surprise he has sprung in the political arena.

December 15, 2002

Why optimism is inevitable

The events in Gujarat early last year drew an avalanche of gloomy prognostications about the impact of these on the Indian economy. The poor quality of governance it signified was bound to tell on business sentiment. Foreign investors would be wary of venturing into the country. A distracted central government would not be able to implement badly needed economic policies. And so on.

A year on, the economic pundits must feel as uncomfortable as their political counterparts who forecast a tough fight in the elections in Gujarat and then tied themselves into knots trying to explain away the outcome.

Industrial production was up 5.2 per cent in the period April—October 2002 relative to the same period last year while exports rose by 17.2 per cent. The Sensex is up 20 per cent from its low of October 24, 2002, and 8 per cent from its level at the end of December, 2001.

Two indicators are pointing downwards. Foreign direct investment in the period April-September 2002 was $942 million, down from $1.65 billion in the same period in 2001 but at the same level as in 2000. The only economic indicator that has turned clearly negative in this period is FII flows. There was an outflow of $379 million compared to an inflow of $694 million but this has likely more to do with the battering of the stock market in the US than with the outlook for ours. The Indian economy has shrugged off Gujarat.

We have been here before. The world seemed to coming crashing about our ears following the destruction of the Babri Masjid in 1992 and the riots that rocked the nation's commercial capital of Mumbai. There followed a period of acceleration in economic growth and an unprecedented rush of foreign capital. In the wake of September 11, dire forecasts were made about the effects it would have on the US economy and its potential to halt the trend towards global integration. The doomsayers have been proved wrong.

There is no magic or mystery to these triumphs of experience over gloom. The modern, decentralised economy is capable of enormous resilience in the face of shocks. This was best exemplified during the final stages of the second World War. Much of the savage bombing of Germany, it turned out, had not seriously curtailed Germany's industrial production. It was only the destruction of the highly concentrated ball-bearing factories—ball-bearings are essential for the capital goods that produce weaponry—that ultimately derailed the German war machine.

The inherent resilience of the modern economy, perhaps, explains why there is no precise correlation between social strife or bad governance and economic growth. A classic case in point is Italy whose economic performance defied its unstable politics and the stranglehold of the mafia for decades before the country embarked a cleansing of the polity. Israel has prospered while being in a state of siege throughout its existence.

The US and other industrial economies did not enjoy standards of governance superior to ours at a comparable stage of development—certainly, the problems in the Indian capital market must pale before the excesses America went through. This country itself has been fighting insurgencies in the border states and elsewhere for longer than we would care to remember without these impacting on the trend rate of growth.

Thus, abhorrent as the happenings in Gujarat were, the suggestion that these might cause major economic dislocation constituted a species of wishful thinking on the part of those itching to sock it to the ruling party. More valid were the concerns raised about the sort of polity that awaited us in the years ahead. In particular, Gujarat raised the question whether the inclusivist Indian state would be supplanted by an intolerant and theocratic version.

Here again, history provides room for hope. In the sixties, it seemed that India would be torn apart by linguistic divisions—the expression in vogue was "fissiparous tendencies". The Dravidian movement towards secession, for instance, looked unstoppable and anti-Brahmin sentiment in the then state of Madras was virulent. Today, few doubt the nationalism of the two regional parties, one of which happens to be headed by a Brahmin. In the eighties, it seemed that caste would prove to be

India's nemesis. While caste conflict persists, it no longer appears as threatening. The Shiv Sena rode to power in Maharashtra on a Hindutva plank but its reign in was peaceful.

It seems to be in the nature of Indian democracy to nudge political parties towards moderation and integration when in power, however opportunistic their posturings might be at other times. That and the pressure of world opinion in an era of globalisation make optimism inevitable at the dawn of a new year.

January 2, 2003

Love from a distance

India's professional elite gives the impression today of having mentally seceded from the country. The overriding aspiration of its members is to deposit themselves or their progeny in the west at the earliest opportunity. Having got there, many discover their emotional bonds with their native land. They love to love India but from a safe distance. Do we miss them at all? And how badly do we need the Indian diaspora?

India seems to have got along quite nicely without the talent that has left its shores. From a growth rate of 3.5 per cent up to the seventies when the outflow was still small, we managed a growth rate of 5.5 per cent in the eighties and a little more in the nineties even as the trickle of emigration of the educated elite turned into a flood. All the dire prophecies about the 'brain drain' debilitating the economy have turned out to be unfounded.

This is not surprising when you recognize that the exodus is still quite small in relation to the pool of talent in the country. Much is made, for instance, of the fact that the proportion of IIT graduates going abroad has risen over the years and is currently around 65 per cent. But the odds against getting into an IIT or an IIM are, perhaps, the highest for an institution in their category anywhere in the world: only one out of 80 applicants makes it. For a comparable institution elsewhere, the ratio would be closer to one in 10. This means, of course, that hundreds of students outside the IIT-IIM system, many of whom do not leave the country, represent a quality that is still high by international standards.

The talent that has stayed behind has been good enough to power India's rise to eminence in areas such as software and pharmaceuticals. It has propelled us into the nuclear and missile clubs and promises to take us far in biotechnology. And this very talent now shows signs of making India a force in certain areas of manufacturing as well.

In respect of the 'brain drain', the nation's situation is analogous to that of a large organization from which a few 'stars' depart. A sound organization can take these departures in its stride; if it cannot, that points to infirmities that no 'star' could compensate for.

Just as the contribution of star players in an organisation is circumscribed by the overall capabilities of the organisation—its fundamental sources of competitive advantage—so also at the level of a nation, the best talent can make only a very small difference, not an overwhelming one. Especially so because innovation is today an institutional product, requiring the confluence of a number of favourable factors, not the work of individual geniuses. This must explain why the flight of talent has not kept the country from realising its innate potential; it also suggests that even if the talent had not fled, that would have made little difference to India's economic performance.

The diaspora's contribution towards sustaining a high growth rate in the nineties was mainly in the form of remittances, bank deposits and subscriptions to the Resurgent India Bonds and the India Millennium Deposits schemes. In the period 1991-2002, remittances averaged $6 billion per annum, net inflows into NRI deposits averaged $1 billion and the two bond schemes fetched us around $9.5 billion. These inflows ensured that growth in the years after liberalization was not constrained by balance of payments problems as had happened in the eighties. The heroes in this story were NRIs based in the Gulf, not the professional elite in the west

India's dependence on such inflows has diminished in recent years. The continued boom in software exports has meant a decline in the share of remittances in total invisible receipts from an average of 45 per cent in the nineties to 34 per cent in 2001-02. Thanks to the rise in foreign exchange reserves, NRI deposits are being phased out. Even as the diaspora rediscovers its bonds with its native land, we need its particular contributions of the nineties less than before.

There are hopes that the Indian diaspora will now bring in direct investment of the sort that Chinese emigrants have made in their homeland and that has transformed China over the past two decades. Two points are in order. The Indian diaspora does not boast an entrepreneurial class of a size comparable to China's. Secondly, the Chinese diaspora started investing in China after the country had improved its physical and social infrastructure and attained a growth rate of over 7 per cent by the late seventies.

India's substantive interaction with its own diaspora will likewise follow, not precede, a demonstration of economic strength on India's part. Going by the sentiments expressed at the Pravasi Bharatiya meet in New Delhi, we are still some distance from that denouement.

January 16, 2003

CORPORATE GOVERNANCE

Introductory Note

Few ideas have been so thoroughly flogged in recent years as corporate governance. It has been the subject of innumerable seminars and articles in the popular press. Several committees have probed the subject at length—a Confederation of Indian Industry (CII) committee, the Kumar Mangalam Birla and Narayana Murthy committees constituted by SEBI and the Naresh Chandra committee set up by the government. It is a mantra that is dutifully chanted at every turn. So much so that the very mention of the expression now evokes yawns.

In India, we have seen progress in respect of the forms of governance—periodical disclosures of financial information; the composition of boards including the induction of independent directors, formation of audit; compensation and nomination committees, etc. But, my own sense, reflected in my writings on the subject, has been that we have been missing the wood for the trees. The substance of governance is lacking.

I have focussed on two failures in particular. One is the inability of boards to remove non-performing CEOs. In the family-managed businesses that dominate much of Indian industry, this appears well-nigh impossible even when the financial institutions have the biggest stake. This makes a mockery of corporate governance principles. In the US, it is understood that if earnings decline over successive quarters, the CEO's job is on the line. As I note in one of my columns, CEO tenures are getting shorter and shorter as boards hold them to ever more stringent standards of performance.

The second failure is the unwillingness to relate top management compensation to norms of performance. In this respect, the Indian scene has mirrored some of the unhappy trends in the UK and US where managerial remuneration has risen in the face of declining performance. It is surprising that no committee has found it necessary to make public norms set for top management so that shareholders know whether managers have performed or not and whether they deserve superior compensation.

Neither of these problems can be rectified through the mechanism of the board, however much the independent directors might exercise their independence. This is because the governance problem in India is different from that in the classical Anglo-Saxon paradigm. There, the problem is one of ensuring that management is accountable to shareholders. Here, management is itself the dominant shareholder, so the problem is one of protecting non-management shareholders from the dominant shareholder. Boards can be only of very limited effectiveness in such a situation. They can ask tough questions, blow the whistle. But they cannot act on the basis of their convictions because management commands the votes in shareholders' meetings. The problem is compounded by the fact that institutional activism has been missing in India.

In one respect, *The Big Picture* remained stubbornly contrarian on this subject. It consistently opposed the recommendations of sundry committees to keep institutional nominees out of boards. This reflected my perception that the definition of an independent director as one who does not have a pecuniary relationship is inadequate. An invitation to join a board, especially the board of a prestigious company, is an honour. It can also be financial rewarding with companies now offering stock options and other rewards to independent directors. It is a little too much to expect people to go in and question the very people who have done them the honour.

It is a different matter if you get on to the board as the nominee of a financial institution. Then you are not beholden to the management for your seat. It is easier to question, to probe, to challenge. It is hard to see how there can be effective checks on management without an adversarial element in the composition of the board, whether by giving representation to a financial institution or to workers. Many would see this as cramping the style of management. The answer, in the light of the excesses we have seen in the American corporate world, must be: so be it. But fears on this count are exaggerated. Today, all constituents, including workers recognise that management has to deliver results. Nobody is going to obstruct management for the pleasure of doing so.

The debate on corporate governance rages on. There is a sense, in some of the academic literature today, that it is futile to expect much of corporate governance, that competition is, perhaps, the only meaningful disciplining device. Boards here will have to do far better in future if corporate governance is not to turn out to be the great disenchantment of the present decade.

Interview: N Vaghul

Narayanan Vaghul is currently Chairman of the Board of ICICI Bank Limited which is the second largest bank in India. Mr. Vaghul joined ICICI in 1985 as Chairman and CEO and relinquished his position as CEO in 1996. During his eleven-year tenure as CEO, ICICI came to be transformed from a small-sized long-term credit bank to a large diversified financial conglomerate. In recognition of his pioneering efforts, Mr. Vaghul was named "Business Man of the Year" in 1992 by *Business India* newsmagazine.

Mr. Vaghul serves on the boards of several companies and is also intimately connected with education. He graduated from Madras University and joined the State Bank of India. He later became Chairman of Bank of India, the youngest ever chairman of a state-owned bank.

1. *Several committees that have gone into the subject of corporate governance in India and made recommendations—the CII, the Kumarmangalam Birla committee, the Narayana Murthy Committee. Do you think we have seen substantive progress in respect of corporate governance in Indian companies? If yes, which are the areas of improvement?*

A. Certainly, during the last couple of years an awareness has been built with respect to Corporate governance with the adoption of the recommendations of the various committees. This is indeed a good development in so far as the Indian corporate sector is concerned. The areas which have been more significantly impacted as a result of the recommendations have been the Audit Committee and the Compensation Committee. The mere fact that a charter for the Audit Committee has to be laid down and approved by the board has resulted in a focus on certain key issues, which have considerable significance in the financial statements. The Compensation Committee has also, in quite a few cases has come to grips with the issue of laying down and evaluating clear performance indicators for the purpose of determination of the variable pay component in the compensation package. These have indeed been positive developments.

2. *The Indian context is somewhat different from the classic Anglo-Saxon paradigm where professional managers, with low personal shareholding, are accountable to large institutional shareholders. Here, we have family managed businesses that are the biggest shareholders even if they do not have majority shareholding. Does corporate governance make sense in this context or do we need to rely on the market for corporate control instead? We know, of course, that the market for corporate control is rather weak when it comes to big corporations even in the Anglo-Saxon world.*

A. While, corporate governance, as has been currently thought of would certainly have greater relevance to the corporations of Anglo Saxon model, it would not be correct to say that this would have no relevance to family dominated companies. So long as there is a significant public interest whether it is majority or minority the accountability of the management to a larger body of shareholders continues to remain and in the absence of any other suitable model there is no alternative but to persist with what we are doing at present. One must appreciate that it was the failure of the market mechanism in the post-Enron world that gave rise to greater regulation in the form of stricter rules of corporate governance and in this context it would not be appropriate to leave the family dominated companies alone to be controlled by the market forces. The principles of governance ought to be the same regardless of ownership.

3. *Institutional activism, a key requirement for corporate governance, has been missing here. Do you see signs of change? And is government ownership of large institutions a constraint on activism? There will always be a perception that institutional activism is politically inspired. How do we address this problem?*

A. It seems to me that the constraints that are being talked about with regard to the weaknesses in the institutional mechanism in India have considerably disappeared during the last decade. Two developments have contributed to this. One is the divestment by the government in the institutions themselves leading to greater accountability on the part of these institutions to their own shareholders. Secondly, the grip of the institutional holding on the Indian corporate sector has also weakened with the Indian corporate sectors' foray into the market and the public acquiring greater stake in the companies. Recent events in the public financial institutions in India have only resulted in reinforcing this trend. It will also not be correct to say that institutional action or inaction with regard to the corporate governance issues in the corporate sector has been largely influenced by political forces. There have indeed been a few cases of political activism but it would be unfair to come to any general conclusion based on these stray cases.

4. *Some of us are uneasy with the definition of 'independent' directors. The definition is that these are people with no pecuniary relationship with the company at present or in the recent past. Is this an adequate definition? To put it differently, can directors selected by management ever operate independently?*

A. If one wants to define an independent director properly it has to be done not with reference to any publicly known credentials but with reference to one's behaviour pattern. As it would be well nigh impossible to create a definition with reference to measurable behavioural indicators, a truly independent director can never be appropriately defined. There is no guarantee that the one who answers to all the requirements laid down will truly be independent regardless of the fact by whom he is appointed. We are really looking for a director who is in the position to act in the best interest of the company and its various sections of the shareholders without fear or favour. This is a purely personal characteristic and our success in this area would to a large extend depend on the development of a sufficient number of persons with right attitude. Unfortunately, our weaknesses in this area are only too apparent and at least as of now one has to rest content with the technical fulfilment of this criterion.

5. *There is enormous resistance to institutional nominees being present on boards. Yet, one would imagine that such nominees would bring a degree of independence to the board that management nominees*

would not have. Do you think the objection to institutional nominees is valid?

A. I do not subscribe to the view that the system of institutional nominees should either be done away with or they should be subjected to election by the shareholders. As long as we have a law which enforces contractual obligations, it would be unfair to supercede such obligations by a different piece of legislation. Apart from this legal view, it is my belief that the utility or otherwise of an institutional nominee does not flow from the source of appointment but from the calibre and attitude of the persons so appointed. In other words, the mere fact that a person owes his appointment to the institutions does not ipso facto make him more independent than a person appointed by the management. The key here again is to get the right type of persons.

6. *What about the proposal to let minority shareholders have their nominees? The idea of having workers' nominees was also revived recently. Germany does not seem to have a problem with the latter.*

A. The German system is based on a two—tier board which has no application in the Indian context. I am also not quite sure whether Germany does not have any problem with the workers' representation on the board. In India, we experimented, if I may use the word, with workers' representations in the public sector bank boards, but this has not brought about any significant benefits. While on paper a representation of the minority shareholders looks attractive one has to contend with a host of problems that could arise if such a provision were ever to be incorporated in the law. An alternative could be for the Board to identify certain people who could be elected only by the shareholders without participation by the family management group.

7. *Managerial compensation is emerging as a vexatious issue here as elsewhere. Do you believe that compensation packages should be put to vote and the voting pattern among institutions publicly disclosed? Also, would it be useful to make public the norms used for awarding compensation to top management?*

A. I fully endorse the view that there has to be total transparency with regard to the managerial compensation packages and I am all for voting and full disclosures. It is equally important for the companies to disclose to the shareholders basis on which the remuneration committees/boards have arrived at the fixed pay component and the parameters used for evaluating the variable pay component in the package. I believe that this is a trend which will begin to take place with or without any regulatory requirement because of increasing pressures from the shareholders.

8. *In academic literature today, there is a sense that corporate governance has been a bit of a let-down and that competition alone can get management to perform. Would you agree or do you think that something can still be salvaged in the realm of corporate governance?*

A. If one were to subscribe to this view, he could be legitimately accused of coming to a judgement far too early in the sphere of corporate governance implementation. It has been barely three years since the issue has acquired a degree of attention and various governments are still to come to a total grip with regard to what is right and possible. There is a process of trial and error and attempts to balance the various interest groups in formulation of the various pieces of regulation. It would take some time before this is completed. Also, it is possible that in the initial stages of compliance with the regulations, form will take precedence over substance. Only after the passage of a reasonable time, would we be in a position to pass judgement on the efficacy of the measures. In any case, I am afraid it will be very difficult to argue after the various post-Enron episodes that competition and market forces alone can effectively deal with the situation.

CEOs and Top Management

Exit policy for CEOs

In the family managed businesses that still constitute a big chunk of the Indian corporate sector, CEOs seldom step down even when clearly past their prime. They hang around until carted off by the Grim Reaper, incapacitated by illness or deposed by kith and kin.

Some groups such as Tata have put in place retirement policies for the top brass but the mandatory retirement age for the Chairman (75 in the Tata group) would be considered laughably high in the Anglo-Saxon world. In professionally managed organizations (of which there are not many in the private sector) and also in the public sector, the CEO does depart but this happens routinely after he has attained the retirement age.

These are recipes for non-performance. Corporate governance has come to embrace so many things that it is easy to lose sight of its essence: mechanisms by which suppliers of capital ensure that management provides an adequate return. And the mechanism that is central to meeting this objective is penalising non-performance. This means, above all, removing a CEO who fails to deliver. To put it differently, the tenure of the CEO must be linked to clearly defined norms of performance.

This happens elsewhere, particularly in the country whose corporations dominate the world today, the United States. An article in Fortune magazine ("Why CEOs fail", June 21, 1999) documents how CEO tenures have shrunk in the US. In 1980, 46 per cent of CEOs lasted five years or less on the job; in 1998, this figure had risen to 58 per cent. In 1980, 41 per cent of CEOs lasted 6-10 years; the proportion has since fallen to 23 per cent. Shortened tenures are the result of institutional shareholders setting stiff standards of performance for corporate bosses.

In general, one must expect to find CEO tenures fairly short wherever norms of performance are stringent. This is because it is hard for CEOs to sustain high levels of performance over a very long period in a world in which the business environment is as complex as it is today. Manfred de Vries, professor of human resource management at Insead business school, who has written extensively on leadership, believes the optimum tenure for CEOs is ten years plus or minus two, his own preference being for minus two.

Prof. de Vries suggests there is a life cycle for CEOs with decline being inevitable over time. Decline typically sets in because, after latching on to a winning theme that fits their style and background, CEOs tend to get fixated on this theme and are unwilling to make departures. They lose the openness to ideas and change that mark their early years and the appetite for performance.

There are signs aplenty of decline. There's no change in the product portfolio, the customer base or key personnel. The CEO becomes remote from organisational affairs and starts pursuing glamorous interests. He begins squandering company resources on airplanes, retreats and the like. The organisation starts accumulating excess cash as executives run out of ideas for spending money, or, worse, the CEO goes in for mergers just for kicks.

The best thing, once signs of decline begin to show, would be for the CEO himself to quit gracefully. Alas, such grace is as rare in the corporate world as in Indian politics. The lifestyle is just too good to give up. So it is incumbent on the board to preempt decline in the CEO and the company through a clear exit policy for CEOs. That is what succession planning is all about.

Boards in the US now take succession planning very seriously. A recent round-table on the subject among directors of top corporations in the Harvard Business Review identifies some key elements in succession planning . (*"Changing leaders: the board's role in CEO succession", May-June 1999*). One, identifying potential successors early on and reviewing their performance and abilities at regular intervals; two, making succession planning part of an overall management development programme for the enterprise; three, regular and direct contact between the board and the identified candidates; four, board members discussing succession without the CEO being present. Often the succession process commences at least four years before a CEO leaves. Since most CEOs last less than five years, this means the board starts digging the CEO's grave almost from day one.

Thus an exit policy for CEOs would have two components: systematic evaluation of CEO performance and succession planning. Self-evident as this may sound, these twin principles find no mention in the CII's code on corporate governance. This is only to be expected considering the preponderance of family-managed businesses in CII.

Almost any major document on corporate governance talks of the evaluation of the CEO, his appointment and removal. The OECD's "Principles of Corporate Governance" makes explicit reference to "selecting and.replacing key executives and overseeing succession planning" as a key function of the board. CalPERS, the formidable American pension fund that has been in the forefront of corporate governance, recommends a separate committee of independent directors for CEO evaluation. It lays down the principle that "the independent directors establish performance criteria and compensation incentives for the CEO, and regularly review the CEO's performance against those criteria".

TIAA-CREF, another large American fund manager, also has a section on CEO performance evaluation. The first of the functions of the board listed by Business Roundtable, a CEOs' body in the US, is to "select, regularly evaluate, and, if necessary, replace the chief executive officer....". Absent such a clause, the CII's code on corporate governance lacks substance.

The onus is on institutional shareholders, their nominees on the board and also non-executive directors to prod Indian firms towards framing an exit policy for CEOs. There can be no ambiguity or compromise on what this must mean: the board and the CEO agree on targets in respect of key performance criteria over a stipulated period. Failure to meet the criteria must trigger the CEO's exit. Digging the CEO's grave is a good idea specifying the coffin in which he is to be laid to rest is even better.

September 20, 1999

Toothless governance

Corporate governance may mean several things, but the essence of governance surely is ensuring performance on the part of top management.

In this respect, we have a long way to go. In neither the public nor the private sector do we have clear-cut norms for performance on the basis of which a non-performing CEO can be booted out. In PSUs, limited tenures for CEOs at least keep non-performers from sticking to their jobs. In much of the private sector and particularly in the family-managed business, the removal of a non-performing CEO occurs only in the rarest of rare cases.

How do we measure performance? And, once we have certain measures of performance, can we be confident that these will automatically trigger precipitate action on the part of major non-management shareholders in instance of non-performance?

The recent CII report on governance fails to tackle these questions head on. And the ICICI decision to set up a Nomination Committee to evaluate the performance of the CEO and top management does not provide us the necessary assurance either.

The CII report talks of better disclosures and beefing up the presence of non-executive directors. The report also highlights the role of takeovers in keeping management on its toes (although its recommendations on takeovers appear designed to make these more, not less, difficult).

But if we accept that takeovers, at least of big companies, are going to be difficult in the immediate future, how exactly are we going to use better disclosures and non-executive directors to ensure performance?

The question applies to the ICICI Nomination Committee as well. It is not enough that management is removed when a company turns sick. Nor is it enough for top management to be evaluated on the basis of the '10 per cent rule': show sales or profit growth of over 10 per cent, and you are considered to be doing fine. In an economy, such as ours, where competition is still not intense in most sectors, it does not require managerial genius to pass the 10 per cent rule is not enough to push Indian industry towards higher efficiencies. No, we need more stringent norms of performance.

We could make a start, perhaps, with five key measures of performance suggested by management guru Peter Drucker: market standing, innovation, productivity, liquidity and profitability. I would add another measure: stock performance relative to competition. The annual business plan or budget given to the Board (or the Nomination Committee in the case of ICICI) must indicate clearly what top management expects to achieve in respect of each of these parameters. Once accepted, these targets must form the basis for evaluation.

Drucker also suggests that the Board entrust the work of measuring performance to an independent firm. We could have an independent firm. We could have an independent business audit every three years comparable to the external financial audit. If performance falls short of norms, the Board must not hesitate to fire top management.

Such accountability can, of course, be reinforced with suitable incentives. Renewal of tenure would be an obvious incentive, although for this to be meaningful, we have to ensure that the top management team is young enough for it to have something to look forward to when its tenure ends. Long-term stock options linked to achievement of performance norms could be another incentive, for these help align top management behaviour with sustained performance on the part of the firm. An analyst on my staff once came to me with a bullish report on ITC at the height of its board room problems which ran: Despite top management problems, we expect ITC to post profit growth .... I suggested that he could replace 'despite' with 'because of'.

I wasn't being facetious. In our kind of economy, you don't need top management wizardry—you, perhaps, don't need top management for a fundamentally sound company to have modest profit growth. The challenge to corporate governance is to get top management to measure up to *higher* standards of performance.

May 24, 1997

Succession blues

I wrote recently that a model for family businesses seeking to retain control with a low ownership stake could be the House of Tata under JRD. It must seem ironical, then, that this legacy is being diluted by Ratan Tata with his focus on raising the Tata stake in group companies.

This has been viewed as a response to the threat of hostile takeovers in the liberalized environment. I suspect, however, that it was partly dictated by the need to assert the primacy of the group over professional managers who had reduced their companies to personal fiefdoms.

Some have questioned the decision to pack off managers with a proven track record by contrasting their performance with Mr Tata's own. The comparisons are inapt because you can't compare performance in the cosy, pre-liberalized era with that in a more competitive period; besides, you are not always looking at comparable businesses. But that is beside the point. Mr Tata surely deserves support for making the incontrovertible point that a change of CEO is vital to organizational renewal.

Unfortunately, professional managers are reluctant to bow to this reality. There are companies such as Hindustan Lever, where there is a systematic process of first surfacing people of merit and then narrowing the race to a few outstanding candidates over a fairly long period. But these are distinguished exceptions. By and large, 'succession planning' is pretty much a farce. 'Succession planning' often has more to do with avoiding succession than finding a capable successor.

Not that this reluctance to depart should come as a surprise. The trappings of power—a chauffeur—driven car, first class air travel, five-star accommodation, club membership etc—are certainly a powerful inducement. Many CEOs would be in a position to afford all these even after retirement, but when you have been used to having everything on the house, I suppose it really pinches to reach into your own wallet. Still, I'm not convinced that pecuniary considerations explain all.

The power of patronage—the ability to dish out favours, not least to kith and kin—is an equally powerful motivation. But, above all, it is the prospect of a mental vacuum after retirement that drives corporate bosses to hang on. After years spent clawing up the corporate ladder, many CEOs lack an alternative vocation or even hobbies, and are too spent mentally to develop any.

The problem is particularly acute in India because people are quite old by the time they qualify for the CEO's job (although this is changing slowly). If you are in your late fifties when you get the job, and in your late sixties when it's time to exit, then there is a fairly high probability of panic setting in towards the end: it's rather late in the day to start something, even a hobby. Abroad, CEOs tend to be much younger, and can often look forward to a whole new career when they step down. This, incidentally, is also a strong motivator of CEO performance because a CEO would like to levitate to a leadership position elsewhere when his tenure at one firm ends.

A gimmick greatly favoured here is for the MD to deftly step into the Chairman's job after having made sure that his protégé is made MD. This is justified on grounds of providing 'continuity'. Continuity may be required in a family business because of the brand value associated with the family, but it is the last thing that a professionally managed organization needs.

Over the tenure of a CEO, a company becomes too set in its ways; its businesses are based on assumptions that have been overtaken by changes in the environment; and there are the inevitable 'ego products' of the CEO that nobody dares challenge. The company needs, not continuity, but quite the opposite: somebody who will question basic assumptions and shake up structures and systems. It's hard for the new CEO to do this when his former boss is watching in his new *avataar* as Chairman.

Fixed tenures for CEOs is a good idea. Ten years, a five year term followed by another if the first is satisfactory, should do nicely. Pick a young guy and make sure he leaves after ten years. Any suggestion of 'continuity' deserves a forthright response. Disappear. Make yourself scarce. Get the hell out.

September 13, 1997

Ending the CEO's dictatorship

In the modern corporation, the CEO is monarch of all he surveys, his right there is none to dispute. The major advance in corporate governance in the more developed capital markets has been to ensure that the dictatorship of the CEO is ended at least when he ceases to perform. As long as he is in the saddle, however, the checks on the CEO are feeble at best and non-existent at worst—forget the claims made on behalf of corporate governance.

The United States, where corporate governance is most developed, has been happy to live with this state of affairs in the belief that the all-powerful CEO is central to the success of American corporations. Now, however, the cult of what the New York Times calls the 'imperial chief executive' is under siege. In the wake of the series of scandals in the American corporate world, changes in corporate governance have been proposed that are aimed at curbing the powers of the CEO.

Leading the charge at the moment is the New York Stock Exchange, which issued a set of proposals for reform in early June. The key proposals are: independent directors must form the majority on the board; the audit, nomination and compensation committees must be made up entirely of independent directors; and independent directors must meet without management being present.

The recent scandals involved outright fraud. This is something against which the most independent board cannot provide immunity. Those seeking an overhaul of corporate governance must know this. They must also know that a more independent board can only cramp the CEO's style. Evidently, they want this to happen and are using the current antipathy towards corporate bosses to usher in change.

Social commentators have long fretted about the paradox of democratic societies harbouring an institution as undemocratic as the modern corporation. Their musings made little impression on the financial community. Investors were happy to cheer strong leaders who seemed to be able to deliver superior performance.

The string of collapses in recent months seems to have changed this.

There is a sense in the US today that the dominance that the CEO has hitherto enjoyed exposes the corporation to undue risk and deserves to be checked. Especially so given the size of today's corporations and the speed at which they can unravel once fraud is exposed. If reining in the CEO means losing out on risk-taking, so be it.

In a well-functioning capital market, mechanisms for corporate governance must go hand in hand with an active market for corporate control. It is ironical that even as there has been a trend towards strengthening of the former, there has been a weakening of the latter in the US.

In the eighties, America discovered a potent means for disciplining management, the hostile takeover. This was facilitated by two great financial innovations, junk bonds and leveraged buy-outs. Complacent CEOs found themselves ejected by upstarts with ready access to finance.

Corporate America, however, managed to ensure that the takeover wave was aborted. It did so by lobbying for regulations that stifled hostile takeovers—state laws that restricted takeovers, changes in the tax treatment of junk bonds, regulatory prohibitions on savings and loan associations on investing in junk bonds.

Indeed, there are some who see in the jailing of junk bond king, Michael Milken, the corporate establishment having its revenge on somebody who dared to help shake it up. The ironical outcome is that in the world's leading market economy, regulation as a means of disciplining management has gained ascendancy over market forces.

Here in India, entrenched management has been busy trying to ensure that the market for corporate control does not even emerge in the first place. Industrial groups have focused on increasing their already high stakes in the companies they control even though takeover finance is hard to obtain and foreign companies cannot make secondary market acquisitions of shares.

This makes it vital that the movement towards corporate governance envisaged by the Kumar Mangalam Birla committee is fully realised. SEBI must assess how far companies have complied with the code of governance and publish a status report. It must also ascertain what action has been taken by stock exchanges in instances of non-compliance. Since the market for corporate control will remain stunted in the near future, this is not enough. SEBI must ensure next that we catch up with the trend towards a greater say for independent directors.

July 4, 2002

Hail and farewell: 'Neutron Jack' takes a bow

For the outgoing CEO, there was an outpouring of accolades; his successor faced the inevitable scepticism about his being able to emulate a legend. The handing of the torch at General Electric earlier this month from Jack Welch to Jeffrey Immelt drew media coverage in the US surpassed, perhaps, only by a change of guard at the White House.

This may seem excessive even for a nation whose business is famously said to be business. But then GE under Welch has been no ordinary corporation. It has come to symbolize the ability of corporate America to raise its game to new heights, the capacity of superior management to transform businesses through a relentless focus on shareholder value.

Mr Welch inherited in 1981 a business that was already big by contemporary standards, with revenues of $25 billion and profits of $1.7 billion, and made it even bigger. Last year, GE's revenues were $130 billion and profits $28 billion. Mr Welch's success made him an icon and GE a widely admired company because it flew in the face of two cherished tenets in business management. *One,* big companies cannot deliver exceptional returns to shareholders because their growth possibilities are limited. *Two,* diversified businesses have little to commend them because they cannot allocate capital better than the market.

Mr Welch showed, *first,* that size can co-exist with nimbleness and hence with high growth. *Secondly,* that a conglomerate can compensate for inefficiency in capital allocation by its sheer ability to transfer ideas—another potent source of competitive advantage—across a range of businesses.

The story of how Mr Welch transformed GE has been told and re-told in biographies, in the business press and in several case studies prepared by the Harvard Business School. GE was already a well-run company when Mr Welch took over. Mr Welch's genius lay in grasping that GE's systems, widely believed to be impeccable, had outlived their utility and that nothing short of a demolition job would do.

There is an interesting sidelight to Mr Welch's accession. Mr Welch used to participate in case discussions at Harvard before he became CEO. Students, polled on whether he would get the job, voted 'no'. They thought him too much of a maverick. It is a tribute to GE's succession planning system that the company decided a maverick was what it needed.

Mr Welch's initiatives are today the stuff of corporate legend. First, there was the downsizing that resulted in 100,000 jobs being lost with several layers of management being removed. This earned him the moniker that he despised greatly, 'Neutron' Jack, after the bomb that annihilates people while leaving buildings intact.

Next, there was the sloughing off of businesses in which GE could not be number one or number two and the dictum Mr Welch gave his business unit heads: fix it, close it or sell it. Third, defining the business in the widest possible terms and making acquisitions as required from cash acquired through divestitures. Fourth, the emphasis on training and development that entailed a huge commitment to GE's famed training center. Fifth, the search for superior ideas and best practices and the transfer of these across the 'boundary-less' corporation.

Much of this is straight out of the book. De-layering the organization of knowledge workers and the abandonment of yesterday's businesses were anticipated in Peter Drucker's writings. Defining the business in generic terms was an idea that had taken the management world by storm following Theodore Levitt's famous exposition. And training and benchmarking are commonplaces in management literature. The trick is to make these things happen, to institutionalize practices in ways that produce tangible additions to shareholder wealth. GE under Jack Welch showed that it could actually be done.

It is often the case with messiahs that their central messages get distorted and end up causing more harm than good. It is all too easy for management elsewhere, including in India, to focus on downsizing as the key to improved performance. It is well to remember, however, that Mr Welch viewed downsizing not just as cutting costs; he viewed it as stripping away corporate bureaucracy and enabling the organization to better focus on opportunities on the outside. In a context such as ours, it is the creative, regenerative side to Mr Welch's initiatives that has greater relevance.

In any case, management has the moral right to lay off people only if its own continuance is based solely on superior performance. Family-owned businesses that believe themselves exempt from penalty from failure have this to chew over: Mr Welch chose to step down at the age of 65 even when shareholders would have been happy to have him carry on.

September 27, 2001

Define performance

As rewards to top executives these days go, the ten million pound bonus recently awarded to Chris Gent, the CEO of the telecom company, Vodafone AirTouch, is no great shakes. It certainly pales in comparison with the £348 million in stock options exercised by Walt Disney's boss, Michael Eisner, in 1997. If, nevertheless, the bonus seems egregious to many, it is because it breaks new ground.

Mr. Gent gets his reward not for exceptional results but for a strategic move that could lead to one, namely, the acquisition of his firm's erstwhile rival, Mannessman of Germany. True, the acquisition is seen as a coup for Vodafone but the company's shareholders might have liked to wait for results before showering their CEO with largesse. The past record would certainly justify waiting: the evidence in acquisitions is that, in general, shareholders of acquired firms benefit but not those of the acquiring firm.

It would seem that in the rarefied heights of the boardroom, such rewards are not for the victor alone. Even the vanquished can expect a share of the spoils. So it is that the outgoing chairman of Mannesmann gets an "appreciation reward" of Euro 15.9 million. This is for causing shareholder value to rise through the heroic defence he mounted against Vodafone's bid before the eventual surrender.

As consolidation is the name of the game everywhere, including in India, the Vodafone example will, doubtless bring a gleam into the eyes of many a CEO. But at least CEOs in Britain must not start counting their chickens. The British government is determined to put in place minimal checks on top management's penchant for rewarding itself.

One proposal aired by the British government is to give institutional investors the right to vote on managerial remuneration. Another would require pension funds, among the biggest shareholders, to disclose their policies on socially responsible investment and the exercise of voting rights.

The proposals are a good start but they will not by themselves make a significant difference. In the US, institutional shareholders do vote on options for executives—the giant investor, TIAA/CREF, votes against one in five stock option proposals—but determining what is the right reward for a given level of performance is not easy. So institutions tend to go along with whatever companies claim is 'market practice'.

Secondly, in evaluating rewards for corporate management, institutional investors face conflicts of interest. Investment banks would not like to lose business by annoying corporate bosses. Corporate pension fund managers are often inhibited by the fact that they are on deputation from the parent company.

The key, really, is getting companies to spell out in some detail what performance criteria have been bettered. Even in the US, few companies attempt this. The better managed ones only go so far as staffing remuneration committees wholly with independent directors. One criterion that is used to justify rewards, shareholder returns, is unsatisfactory because all too often it results in top management simply reaping the benefits of a bull market. (It is interesting that the moment there is a downturn in the stock market, companies reprice stock options or shift to other forms of reward.)

Ensuring that companies have explicit performance norms for top management thus constitutes the next frontier in corporate governance. Some years ago, management guru Peter Drucker had proposed five measures of performance for management: market standing, innovation, productivity, liquidity and profitability. (Note the absence of any market-related measure.) He had also proposed that the task of measuring performance be entrusted to an independent firm. The latter sounds Utopian at the moment but the former does provide a basis for evolving sound norms of performance.

All of this applies to India as well. Few terms have been bandied about so much in the country in the liberalisation era as 'world-class'. As base pay for top managers has skyrocketed, companies insist that it is only finding its market-determined level following the removal of statutory limits. This is necessary, they say, for firms to attract talent that can help them become 'world-class'.

One could go along with steep revisions in base pay relative to the limits imposed earlier by government. But additional rewards such as stock options must be based on clearly defined performance benchmarks. The worst prospect for shareholders is that the only thing that is world-class about companies here is compensation for top management.

July 6, 2000

Executive pay under the lens

Greed is good—the infamous slogan of the eighties became corporate America's motto in the roaring nineties. Not only did executive pay soar into the stratosphere but, as we now learn, this became disconnected from corporate performance. A survey by the Financial Times has revealed that top management at the 25 biggest collapses in recent months amassed $3.3 billion in various forms of compensation even as the companies they headed hurtled towards bankruptcy.

What ever happened to the alignment of managerial incentives with shareholder wealth, said to be one of the great achievements of the American financial market? The question is agitating regulators and legislators. It must also weigh heavily on the conscience of academics. For, while the slogan about greed may have been coined by Hollywood, it was underpinned by weighty academic research.

Harvard Business School professor, Michael Jensen, summarises much of this work in his book, Foundations of organizational strategy. One paper, co-authored by Jensen with Kevin Murphy, was particularly influential. Based on empirical evidence, the paper drew important conclusions. *One,* CEO salaries and bonuses in the period 1974-88 were lower in real terms than in the thirties. *Two,* the link between pay and performance, while statistically significant, was weak in magnitude. (On the average, a $1,000 increase in shareholder wealth translated into an increase of a mere $3.25 in CEO wealth). *Three,* CEO stock ownership was ten times greater in the thirties than in the eighties.

The authors argued that, contrary to popular perception, top executives were underpaid. 'Political forces' had kept boards from rewarding executives aggressively for performance. As a result, boards were also reluctant to impose penalties for poor performance. America's executives were being rewarded as bureaucrats are.

In the nineties, corporate America seemed to be responding to these broad messages. Executive pay rose steeply, with a stronger stock component, while at the same time average tenures for CEOs fell to half their eighties' figure of ten years.

So what went wrong? The narrow response to top management malfeasance would be that this has entirely to do with faulty disclosures. Hold CEOs personally responsible for financial statements and tighten audit and all will be well. Alas, the problem will not go away that easily: there are just too many cracks in the corporate governance system.

For stocks and stock options to align managerial incentives with long-term performance, managers must be required to hold these for fairly long periods—say, 8-10 years. Yet, boards have been all too willing to let top managers encash their rewards much earlier.

A more fundamental problem is that the definition of performance is too lax. Rewards are linked to absolute performance of a company's stock, rather than relative performance, which would be a more accurate measure. This has allowed managers to reap huge rewards by simply riding a stock market boom. Thirdly, increasing stock-related rewards for managers could have a significant impact on the bottomline but this is not captured accurately because top management is resistant to accounting norms that would do so.

It follows that managerial rewards can no longer be left to today's closed club: the-you—sit-on my-compensation—committee—I—sit-on-yours syndrome. Compensation committees must include nominees of institutional shareholders and minority shareholders. Following from the German model, there must be worker representatives on boards—it's good to inject some disruption into the cosy atmosphere of boardrooms. The norms used for rewarding top management must be made part of the disclosure requirements.

These principles for improving governance hold for us in India as well, especially since we have a habit of importing western models sans the checks and balances that must go with these. But the more salient point is that, in a market such as ours—overwhelmingly price-driven and with a large pool of low-cost professionals-, the clamour for superior incentives can be overdone. One recalls the dire predictions about the likes of SBI and LIC when the financial sector was thrown open to new entrants. There were some high-profile departures but both SBI and LIC have gone from strength to strength.

There is an issue of compensation in the public sector and it needs to be addressed. But it requires a solution that is anchored in Indian realities. For there is one thing of which you can be certain: if a model is found to be badly flawed in the American context, there is not a hope in hell of its working here.

August 15, 2002

Policy Issues

The siphoning effect

Following the convulsions in East Asia, commentators in the US and Europe were quick to exult at the superiority of the "Anglo-Saxon" model of corporate growth over that driven by "Asian values". The view is now official: a committee of experts set up by the OECD to lay down international standards on corporate governance has urged focus on shareholder value as one of two legs on which governance could profitably rest, the other leg being an independent board.

The combination of a raging bull market in the US and Europe and devastation in East Asia appears to have dispelled lingering reservations about placing the shareholder at the centre of things. This may not be the last word on the subject, but suppose we accept that the Anglo-Saxon model does work. Before we rush headlong into imitation, we need to be clear about the conditions required for the model's success.

One of the early concerns about focusing on shareholder value was that it fostered 'short-termism' in companies: management would only think about the next quarter's profit and its impact on stock price. Management would be reluctant to commit resources to intangibles (such as R&D, staff training etc) or to adopt strategies needed for long-term competitiveness (such as increasing market share through lower prices) because of the likely adverse impact on share price in the short term. Firms in Japan, East Asia and Germany were better placed to take a long view because their principal shareholders happened to be banks that were not interested in booking profit in the next quarter.

It turns out that in an efficient market such as the US some of these concerns are misplaced. Where management is transparent in its dealings and market participants are sophisticated enough to assess a company's ability to generate sustainable competitive advantage, the market is capable of seeing through attempts to boost short-term profit at the expense of long-term performance.

Companies spend a lot of time interacting with analysts, with the CEO himself taking pains to outline his company's strategy. And institutional investors that attract the best products of engineering colleges and business schools certainly have the capability to process information. In the Anglo-Saxon model at its best, asymmetric information, the bane of East Asia, is not a major problem. So, corporate disclosure and sophisticated market players are clearly one important condition for the model to work; on these counts, the Indian market has certainly shown improvement.

The other condition needed for the success of the Anglo-Saxon model is that managers' incentives must be aligned with the firm's long-term success: the market must be able to deal with the "principal—agent" problem. The American market has done so partly by getting boards to enforce accountability, and partly by linking compensation to stock options. Executives will benefit from the options only if the company performs over the long term.

But such measures presuppose that management is precluded from enriching itself by other means. Stock options mean little to a CEO who can siphon off funds by under-invoicing exports or inflating prices of equipment; a performance bonus for a fund manager is a non-starter if he can collect commissions from brokers he deals with (and his fund's non-performance will not cost him his job); a banker lacks the incentive to keep his bank's stock moving up by limiting non-performing assets if his bank balance increases in direct proportion to questionable loans sanctioned by him. Not that these things don't happen in the US, but it's harder to dodge the long arm of the law.

Corruption and weak law enforcement have been major problems in East Asia as much as in India. The 'siphoning effect' would make nonsense of the Anglo-Saxon model in such contexts. And if you believe that this model is central to the market, you can readily see why the market will fail to deliver the goods. The public sector in India and a bank-dominated private sector in East Asia may thus be viewed as pragmatic responses to a situation where there were not only market failures, but the state was incapable of playing its role as law-enforcer. It is the latter ground reality that needs to be tackled before we can institute the Anglo-Saxon model.

April 16, 1998

A trust for FIs ?

The CII wants nominees of Financial Institutions (FIs)—widely defined to include banks, long-term FIs, mutual funds and pension funds—to exit corporate boards. It argues that these nominees have not been able to prevent erosion in net worth in a host of companies anyway; besides, the institutions' objective of maximizing returns might just as well be met through market operations.

India's corporate sector has good reason to be wary of FIs, controlled as these are by the government, but it cannot expect its demand to be taken seriously by anybody acquainted with corporate governance worldwide. He who pays the piper does not necessarily call the tune but would certainly like to be present when the tune is being played. Providers of capital have not sought to exercise control (except in extreme situations) but they have always influenced decision-making at the board level.

This is true not merely of bank-centred economies such as Germany and Japan, but also of capital market-centred economies such as the US and the UK. The difference is that, in the latter, institutions such as pension funds and insurance companies are the dominant shareholders, not the banks, although the banks themselves command voting power in excess of their holdings as they manage many of the institutional funds.

In the industrial economies, the presence of FIs on corporate boards is not entirely a matter of the former demanding a presence in order to safeguard their interests. Companies have thought it in their own interests to accommodate providers of capital, whether equity or debt, on boards. For, apart from helping to strengthen existing commercial relationships, institutional nominees can provide vital information about the financial markets and other firms.

Thus, in asking FIs to stay away from corporate boards, the CII is being rather myopic. It is also displaying scant regard for institutional interests. Institutions cannot always take care of their interests through market operations. Where institutional holding is large, buyers may be hard to find; moreover, large sales could cause share prices to fall steeply resulting in big losses.

Nevertheless, it is important to address the CII's unstated concern about the FIs, which must relate to political interference in FIs' commercial decisions. Some see privatization as the answer, but that could be too big a risk to take where something as fragile and pivotal as the financial sector is concerned. The risk arises because it's unclear whom the privatized entities would be accountable to. Unless, of course, a dominant private owner emerges, but this is hard to envisage as sell-offs to foreigners are unlikely. In any case, full-fledged privatization of the financial sector, including the insurance companies, is politically unthinkable at the moment.

The task of creating politically neutral FIs cannot wait, however. A way out could be to revive G.V.Ramakrishna's idea of a National Shareholding Trust for PSUs but to confine it to key FIs—say, IDBI, LIC, and GIC, to start with—instead of bringing assorted PSUs under a single umbrella. (As these three FIs are dominant owners in other institutions such as IFCI and UTI, government control over the latter too would diminish.) A Trust for select FIs would be easier to manage and would also be more focussed. Government stakes to the extent of fifty one per cent of the FIs' equity could be transferred to the Trust which would be managed by an independent board.

Such a Trust could provide a new basis for institutional monitoring of the private sector. But its advantages go well beyond this. Since many FIs are also holders of PSU stocks and will pick up more, the Trust could fill the monitoring vacuum that will be caused when government ownership in PSUs falls below 50 per cent, making it easier for the government to cross the hitherto dreaded threshold for privatization. Further, creating such a Trust would defuse criticism that divestment merely replaces direct government control of PSUs with control through government–owned FIs. Finally, we can evaluate FIs' performance under the new system of accountability and judge whether and when full privatization of the FIs is warranted.

Institutional monitoring is central to corporate governance. However, such monitoring can carry conviction only when government is kept at arm's length from FIs. As privatization could be difficult to push through and is fraught with risk, creating a Trust for FIs seems an attractive option.

June 10, 1999

Shoot it down

India's business community seems hell-bent on keeping institutional shareholders out of corporate boardrooms. Sometime back the CII had suggested that financial intermediaries of any sort must not have nominees on boards. The SEBI committee on corporate governance headed by Kumarmangalam Birla, which will submit its recommendations shortly, is being a trifle more generous. It is reportedly in favour of letting nominees of banks with loan exposures stay on boards but would deny seats to institutional sharholders. It must not be allowed to have its way.

The case again institutional shareholders' presence on boards in weak. One argument is that they could use their access to information to engage in insider trading. If this argument is accepted, promoters too should be kept out of boards as also employees who own company stocks. The answer to insider trading is not denying institutions their legitimate monitoring role but tackling the problem head on by asking instititions with board nominees to declare their transactions in a given company's shares. Such disclosure, incidentally, is required elsewhere of directors and the information is in the public domain.

The contention that institutional shareholders do not need to be on boards because they can vote with their feet is not valid either. Given their significant stakes in relation to floating stock, institutions may not always be able to exit at will especially because the market for corporate control is as yet underdeveloped. They may have no choice but to lean on management in order to obtain better returns.

Nor is institutional activism wholly contingent on lack of market liquidity. Even in highly liquid markets, activism has increased in recent years as institutions have found that the gains to monitoring exceed those afforded by exit. Another factor underlying increased activism is pension funds' investment strategies that mimic the market index; this makes it impossible for funds to exit from large companies without upsetting the strategy. As insurance companies here begin to adopt such an approach, they too will be constrained to pursue greater activism.

True, shareholder activism in the US generally stops short of institutional shareholders putting their nominees on boards. (The legendary fund manager, Warren Buffett, who has dominated more than one board in his time, is a distinguished exception but so is his highly focused approach to investing). It is impossible, however, to overlook the material differences between our context and that in a sophisticated market like the US.

The law enforcement regime in the US is of a different quality altogether and shareholders' ability to sue directors at the drop of a hat makes a huge difference. In the bigger companies, institutions do not have to reckon with management with large shareholding and hence are better positioned to fight proxy battles. Institutions have been able to ensure that independent directors are present in strength and often constitute the majority of non-executive directors. Further, boards routinely scrutinize the CEO's performance and show the door to laggards. In such a situation, there is little call for institutions to have a presence on boards; shareholder resolutions suffice for their purposes. In all these respects, the Indian reality is sadly different. That is why institutions' option to have nominees on boards must remain wide open.

If financial institutions don't inspire confidence in respect of their own governance, this must be addressed in right earnest. It certainly does not mean that we ask them to abjure their monitoring role. We need more monitoring of management, not less. Particularly as privatization proceeds apace, we badly need to develop a culture in which FIs take seriously the business of enforcing accountability of corporate management.

It is unrealistic to expect the Indian business community to be enthusiastic about such monitoring. SEBI's choice of a businessman as head of a committee asked to devise a code of corporate governance was, therefore, inappropriate; the interests of investors would have been better served had the chairmanship been entrusted to someone more capable of take a non-partisan approach, say, a jurist, a professional manager or an academic.

It is actions such as these that raise doubts about the quality of leadership provided by SEBI in the realm of improving capital market practices and point to a chasm between words and deeds when it comes to investor protection. SEBI must shoot down the proposal to bar institutions from boards if it is not to be perceived as hostage to vested interests in an area of vital concern to investors.

September 16, 1999

Why investor protection is more important than you think

Among the bigger ironies in liberalized India must be this: as the government prepares to vacate vast tracts of business in favour of the private sector, at least domestic business will not find it easy to step in. This is because, barring a few exceptions, few firms or groups are in a position to mobilise large amounts of capital.

Businesses, by and large, do not inspire confidence in investors, whether shareholders or creditors. This is reflected in the virtual collapse of the IPO market and in banks' own wariness about lending. The vote of no-confidence in the stock market, which has been well documented in the SEBI-NCAER survey of investors, has made a mockery of the improvements in the market infrastructure that were intended to broaden and deepen the Indian Financial Markets.

Where promoters vanish with people's savings and where there is no orderly mechanism for meeting creditors' claims in the event of bankruptcy, external finance simply dries up and financial markets remain stunted.

While the link between investor protection and financial market development seems intuitively obvious, recent research on corporate governance has documented this link with some rigour. As a concise survey of this research in a leading journal shows, the degree of investor protection is indeed central to understanding whole patterns of corporate finance in different countries. *("Investor protection and corporate governance", Rafael La Porta, Florencio Lopez-de-Silanes, Andrei Shleifer and Robert Vishny, Journal of Financial Economics, Special Issue on International Corporate Governance, October 2000).*

The authors are among the top academics in economics and finance today (the first three are at Harvard and the fourth at Chicago) and have done pioneering work on corporate governance and on privatisation. Andrei Shleifer was the winner last year of the American Economics Association's prestigious

John Bates Clark medal. The medal is awarded to a leading economist under the age of 40 and is widely regarded as pointing to Nobel prize potential.

Investor protection is seen to matter in three areas: ownership of firms, the development of financial markets and the allocation of real resources. Where investor protection is poor as in India, one might expect to find concentration of control because the benefits of expropriation to insiders can be huge.

The empirical evidence is unambiguous on the subject. In another widely cited paper of theirs, the authors examined ownership concentration in 49 countries using various measures for shareholder rights, creditor rights and law enforcement. Countries with poor investor protection typically exhibited more concentrated control of firms than did countries with good investor protection. Yet another study of 3000 firms from nine East Asian economies and found likewise.

The prediction of the legal approach to corporate finance that investor protection encourages the development of financial markets is also seen to hold true. Countries that protect shareholders have more valuable stock markets, large numbers of securities listed per capita, and a higher rate of IPO activity than do the unprotective countries. Countries that protect creditors better have larger credit markets. What is more, there is evidence that firms in countries with better shareholder protection have higher valuations than firms in other countries.

The effects of investor protection on the real economy follow from its effect on financial markets. An impressive body of literature has developed that links financial development to growth—through higher savings and capital accumulation and through higher efficiency of resource allocation.

In most countries, the authors point out, investor protection requires radical legal and judicial reform. However, as this will necessarily be a long drawn-out affair, tighter regulation of markets and improvements in corporate governance could make an immediate difference.

Both Poland and the Czech Republic have weak judicial systems. But Poland's stock market has developed remarkably as the government there was quick to enact a tough securities law focusing on shareholder protection. The failure to do so in the Czech Republic led to stagnation in the stock market there and it also led to major disasters in privatisation.

Not only is our judicial system ineffective, we have a long way to go in respect of market-based mechanisms for protecting investors. All the four key corporate governance mechanisms—managerial ownership, takeover, monitoring by institutional investors and monitoring by banks—are weak in the Indian context. We need to be clear about which of these mechanisms can be improved offers scope for qualitative improvement and focus on securing the improvement quickly. In the absence of such improvement, efforts at boosting the capital market—or the credit market, for that matter—are foredoomed to failure.

January 18, 2001

A fresh look at governance

In May 1999, the Kumar Mangalam Birla committee on corporate governance submitted its report to SEBI. A little over three years later, the regulator has appointed a committee headed by N R Narayana Murthy to not only take stock of the implementation of the earlier report but to revisit the entire proposition.

If the move evokes cynicism and even apathy, that will not be surprising. So monumental have been the failures of corporate governance in the world's most efficient market, the United States, that the very expression threatens to become a hollow cliché. Even before the recent problems in the US, a wealth of theoretical and empirical work had begun to pose a question mark over the link between corporate governance—whether based on internal controls or on market mechanisms such as takeovers—and firm performance.

One reason corporate governance has been ineffective is that insiders have been able to manipulate things to their advantage—through anti-takeover measures, non-voting shares, limitations on voting rights etc, and by dominating the board itself. The lesson that regulators have drawn from the recent corporate disasters in the US is that if the Anglo-Saxon model of governance is to have any chance of success, a preponderant role for independent directors is a must. Accordingly, in August this year, the New York Stock Exchange approved proposals that mandate that the majority of directors on a board must be independent. Further, it laid down that the nomination and compensation committees must consist entirely of independent directors.

The crucial element here is the selection of independent directors. Who picks them is important. In the Anglo-Saxon model, institutional investors would have a say—perhaps a decisive say—in the selection process because managers in large firms do not have substantial share ownership while institutional investors do. The idea in putting independent directors in a majority, of course, is that a non-performing CEO can be checked and even removed before matters get out of hand.

In India, the situation is very different. In the family-managed business that is the norm, management has substantial shareholding and selects directors. It is not enough, therefore, to define independent directors as those who do not have a material pecuniary relationship with the company in question. As long as directors owe their presence on the board to management, their independence would be questionable. Add to this the fact that institutional activism itself is absent and you can understand why the controlling shareholder is hardly ever removed for non-performance. All the tenets of governance amount to nothing where the ability and the willingness to penalise non-performance are missing.

There is no escape in the Indian context, therefore, from an adequate presence on boards for financial institutions. Yet it is precisely such a role that the Birla committee sought to deny institutions. The committee argued that if the institutions had their nominees on boards, they would be exposed to charges of insider trading. This is a specious argument to make because it would apply to family owners as well. Besides, it is not necessary that institutional investors have their employees on boards—they can entrust the job to independent professionals.

The Birla committee also contended that institutional investors could protect their interests by disinvesting their holdings in a given company or by using their voting power at general body meetings. The first option is not feasible because large shareholdings entail significant exit costs; if passive investment were effective, we would not be seeing so much concern over the composition of boards in the US. The second denies access to vital information, precludes a timely response and is cumbersome.

The governance problem in India is not the classical Berle and Means problem of dispersed shareholders not being able to control management. It is the problem of preventing the expropriation of minority shareholders by the controlling shareholders.

And there can be credible checks on the controlling shareholders only when we have independent directors nominated by institutional investors, backed by institutional activism.

It follows that the starting point for any meaningful reform of governance must be to set aside seats on the board and also on nomination, audit and remuneration committees for independent directors nominated by institutional investors. Unless space is created on boards for directors truly independent of management, we will have the forms but not the substance of governance.

November 21, 2002

Miscellany

Managerial legitimacy

The Anglo-Saxon model of corporate governance with its focus on shareholder value reigns supreme today after the disarray in East Asia and the consequent discrediting of a model in which the shareholder was not at the centre of things. But is the model capable of sustaining one of society's most important institutions—the corporation—in the long run ? There are good reasons to be wary.

First, shareholder value maximization is not readily operationalized. It is, in fact, a variant of the earlier principle of 'profit maximization' which turned out to be quite hollow. When students of business organization looked closely at 'profit maximization', they found it had little operational significance: management was always taking decisions (investment in training, increase in market share etc) which meant lower than 'maximum' profit. Hopefully, 'profit maximization' would occur at some unspecified point in the future, but today's decisions would all lead to less than maximum profit in the present.

So also with shareholder value maximization. It is quite futile to ask: what decisions does management make that will maximize cash flows to shareholder over the life of the firm. Management can only ask of any activity: what is the minimum return needed to cover cost of capital. And it must hope that if it generates that minimum return, the company's share will be valued by the market at a level that satisfies shareholders. Then management goes on adding activities all of which cover the cost of capital; it cannot realistically define a 'maximum' shareholder value that it can energetically pursue.

Return to shareholder is only a resultant that comes from doing a number of things right: satisfying customers, motivating employees, having good relationships with suppliers. Shareholders, in other words, are one of a number of constituencies the business caters to. And the most important constituency is arguably not the shareholder but the customer.

But the bigger objection to shareholder value maximization must be that it runs the risk of undermining social cohesion and thereby the legitimacy of management. In the US, the quest for shareholder value has meant corporate downsizing and massive redundancies. The markets reward such moves with huge surges in stock prices, and CEOs cart home huge bonuses as a result of bottomline improvements wrung out of firing hundreds of workers and managers. As the American economy has boomed in recent years, management may well believe it has a winning formula.

It used to be argued earlier that corporate downsizing would prove counter-productive because management would not be able to count on employee loyalty, long viewed as a key requirement for corporate performance. The robust growth in corporate earnings in recent years is seen as giving the lie to this argument.

Votaries of the Anglo-Saxon model also point out that layoffs haven't given rise to large scale social discontent because galloping growth has ensured that unemployment levels are at their lowest levels: people laid off find other jobs and without having to search for long. But this overlooks the fact that jobs are bought at the expense of wage increases: the median real wage in the US has declined since 1980. If the effects of wage stagnation have not been felt acutely in the current bull market, it is partly because 45 per cent of the American public is now exposed to the stock markets through mutual funds, and the gains in the stock market have compensated for the absence of wage increases.

Character is always tested in times of crisis. The true test of the Anglo-Saxon model will come when the business cycle reverses, unemployment rises and the 'wealth effect' of investments is no longer felt. In such circumstances, attempts by management to pursue shareholder value maximization through wholesale closures and layoffs are unlikely to go unchallenged.

And what will be challenged then is the legitimacy of management and the very requirement of profitability without which industrial society cannot function. For Peter Drucker, who saw the Second World War as arising from the failure of industrial society to further the goals of freedom and dignity of the ordinary man, the writing is on the wall: "This (top management being rewarded for laying off people) is morally and socially unforgivable, and we will pay a heavy price for it."

April 30, 1998

Family and business

Family businesses that dominate Indian industry flourished in the socialist raj despite talk of reining in "monopoly houses". It is the liberalized environment that is giving them the jitters. When Ramesh Chauhan sold out to Coca Cola, it seemed to portend an onslaught by MNCs on Indian businesses. The Asian Paints episode pointed to the enemy within. Squabbles within a family or among different promoters have caused more family groups to unravel in recent years than takeovers by MNCs. What lies in store for family businesses ?

Firms need to grow. Where the stock market drives growth, the promoter of a company often falls by the wayside. Dilution of shareholding was the original cause of doom in the US, and it led to control passing to professional managers. In recent years, takeovers have become another potent factor. As a result, the great families that were prominent in American industry at the turn of the century are no longer running the companies they founded.

In Japan and Korea, families continue to be at the helm of leading corporations. This is largely because the stock market is not as central to corporate growth as in the US. In Japan, as in Germany, banks are major shareholders in companies, and a bank, that has a significant stake in a company, is also its biggest lender. Japanese banks look upon their shareholding in a company as a means of generating income from a commercial relationship with that company; they are not looking for high returns on equity. This has allowed families that have built up relationships with their principal banks over generations to continue to run the companies they founded even while returns to equity were lower than accepted levels in, say, the US.

In Korea too, reliance on bank finance has helped preserve the hold of families over large businesses. The big conglomerates have grown mainly through soft loans provided by banks. Size and market share were the primary objectives of the large industrial conglomerates, not returns to equity. As a result, the average debt to equity ratio for the top 30 conglomerates is 4:1—

a degree of leverage that would be unacceptable not only in the US but in India as well. Neither in Japan nor in Korea, nor indeed in much of the Continent, are takeovers a big phenomenon.

Thus far, we in India seem to have adopted a variant of the Japanese or German model of corporate growth. The financial institutions, which together constitute the biggest shareholding group in several companies, have tended to be passive holders of stock over the long term, intervening only in instances where loan repayment was a problem. But with the stock market coming of age, we are drifting towards the American model. This spells trouble for family managed businesses. How to respond ?

Maintaining family shareholding at a high level will be difficult to reconcile with the requirements of growth. Nor will playing the swadeshi card help. MNCs are viewed favourably not just by domestic investors but by employees. The old arguments about national sovereignty have lost much of their sting as MNCs have learnt to use locals to run their overseas operations.

Indian businessmen can view themselves either as venture capitalists or as industrialists who are there for the long haul. If the former, they can emulate Ramesh Chauhan and Atul Choksey, that is, sell out at the highest price once their business reaches a certain size. But if they wish to continue to run their businesses, can they retain control with declining shareholding? Or are they fated to preside over their liquidation and can at best facilitate the transfer of power to professionals?

Family businesses can retain control provided they can market the brand value of the family through superior performance. They will need to marry a professional management culture with that of a family managed business. This implies two things: putting the company's interests above their own; and ceding substantial authority to professional managers. The family will then provide strategic direction, continuity in values and goodwill. We do have a model for this: the House of Tata under JRD when the Tatas exercised control at very low levels of shareholding and produced good results on the whole. India's family businesses must seek to replicate this model if they want to hold on to their businesses.

August 31, 1997

Business before family

BMW may not be a name worth dropping right now in accident-prone New Delhi or in extortionist Mumbai but in the international car industry it is truly a name to conjure with. The legendary car maker, alas, is in trouble at the moment with its acquisition of Rover in the UK having come unstuck and is in the process of defining its future direction.

For us in India, the fascinating thing about the BMW story is not its current problems so much as its success over the past four decades. Fascinating because it happens to be one of the great success stories among family managed businesses, and large businesses at that—a genre whose standards of governance and performance are a matter of concern to us.

Some of the facts about BMW reported in the Economist are worth highlighting. *One,* the controlling interest vests with the Quandt family of Germany, whose stake is as high as 46 per cent. *Two,* the family has kept just two seats for itself on the supervisory board, and let the company be run by professionals. The Chairman of the supervisory board is also a professional. The family's hands-off approach is unusual considering it's only into the third generation since it invested in BMW, and there are just two children, both highly competent professionals.

Three, the family tends to be deeply committed to its investments in general, and espcially to BMW, and is reluctant to sell out even though the shares' immediate prospects are not bright. *Finally,* 10 out of 20 seats on the supervisory board are held by workers. In case you think this must be a nuisance, the Economist points out that labour relations and productivity in Germany are better than in Detroit.

This is the stuff of which dreams about corporate governance are made. There are other examples of family businesses that have thrived by instituting similar norms. Oil major Schlumberger has an explicit policy forbidding company employment for family members. The Bergman Corporation, a leading Nordic company, has a stated policy that says there is no presumption that the CEO's job should go to a family member.

The contrast with business empires in our country could not

be starker. When business groups here talk of "professionalizing" their businesses, they mean such relatively inconsequential things as inducting a few professionals into senior positions. Or getting the younger members to acquire an MBA, even if it's from some obscure foreign university.

Business families are right to exercise control when it comes to setting the broad direction or enforcing accountability. But at least in the larger family businesses, one would have liked to see movement in critical areas, such as the constitution of formal structures to distance the family from operational management, and a process of succession planning that does not preclude professionals from being considered for the top job. Signs that they are heeding Peter Drucker's admonition: "The controlling word in 'family-managed business' is not family. It has to be 'business'."

It is, perhaps, futile to expect such vision in business groups here when the general experience elsewhere too has been to the contrary. The difference is that in the West lack of vision quickly translates into high mortality rates: less than 15 per cent of such businesses continue into the third generation in the hands of the descendants of the founder.

Here, the weakness of market mechanisms such as takeovers or institutional intervention means that business empires can carry on much longer, even if they are only muddling along. And—let's face it—promoter families prefer muddling along to letting the best people run the business because they can extract higher returns from their businesses than the returns that accrue to ordinary investors.

Is there a way out at all? There's little sense in pinning hopes on the law-enforcement machinery. Nor can we expect much from the financial institutions as they are constituted now. It's one thing for UTI to focus on a soft target like ILFS, quite another to take on politically-connected family businesses. And, in any case, the financial institutions are hardly shining examples of good governance themselves. The best we can hope for is enlightened self-interest on the part of family businesses. They need to be clear about it would take for their business to last several generations. The alternative is that inglorious repository of all failures: the dust-bin of history.

March 17, 1999

Out of joint

Suzuki can say what it likes about this or that technicality but the issue at Maruti is management control. As such rows followed sometimes by acrimonious partings have occurred often enough between MNCs and their Indian partners, the spat at Maruti provides an opportunity for MNCs to think through the joint venture option in India.

Many MNCs have opted for the JV route here while going it alone in other parts of the world. This applies, not just to the manufacturing sector, but, quite amazingly, to the financial sector where our firms are absolute dwarfs compared to MNCs. What makes world majors prefer the JV route in the Indian context, despite the issue of control this inevitably entails ?

One reason is that initial volumes in the Indian market don't quite justify the critical mass of investment required upfront. Another is that investment required for a given volume of sales is higher than elsewhere. This is because, given the country's size, the investment required in distribution is greater than what would be required in order to generate the same volume of sales elsewhere. Remember, much of the investment in distribution is in real estate where our costs are among the highest in the world.

There are two strategies available to MNCs. Target only the premium market, so that you limit your investment in distribution. But volumes in the premium market can easily disappoint—as so many MNCs have discovered. Alternatively, go for the mass market through a JV with an Indian partner who has distribution. When distribution is available at historical cost, it puts an entirely different complexion on the viability of a project. Once the volumes build up, the MNC may judge that its Indian partner is dispensable. It will also have a ready excuse for dumping the Indian partner: he can't quite match the MNC's access to capital, so he suddenly becomes an impediment to growth.

Suzuki is the source of technology for Maruti and it views itself as the prime provider of finance in future, so it would like to run the business unhindered. Is this a fair expectation? When

Suzuki tied up with Maruti, it must have been unsure about volumes, so it decided to limit its investment exposure by going in for a JV. It must also have been out of its depth in dealing with Indian workers, customers, distributors, and vendors. And it could not have been unaware of the downside to choosing the Indian government as its partner.

If Maruti has been a success, it is at least partly because it was a prestigious project for the Indian government, and very substantially because the small car idea was an extremely bright one for the time. Now that the venture is a thundering success, Suzuki thinks it right to ditch the Indian government. And it resorts to brinkmanship, hoping that support from the media and the government's anxiety not to send out wrong signals to foreign investors will help it gain control. Should the government oblige?

There are some who argue that government should not be in business, especially in businesses such as automobiles, so the government should now opt to become a passive partner in Maruti. But this is a purely ideological argument; it cannot be anybody's case that the Indian government has come in the way of Maruti's commercial success. Should the government then also get out of SAIL, SBI, BHEL and BPCL if a foreign partner can be found who is willing to pick up the majority stake or even a substantial stake?

The question is entirely hypothetical at this point. Even if you are incorrigibly anti-public sector, you cannot wish away the ground reality: no political party wants the public sector out of business altogether. So, for MNCs that wish to have total control, a JV with a public sector company is simply not the right option. With the Indian private sector too, MNCs cannot hope to get away indefinitely with what a CII spokesman had characterized as a "cowboy" mentality: use the Indian partner when it suits you, and dump him at the first opportunity. If MNCs do not want to share control, let them come in as 100 per cent subsidiaries even if that is going to take time.

September 27, 1997

Too early to celebrate

One message that has been coming through loud and clear in the ongoing debate on corporate governance initiated by UTI is that domestic financial institutions do not cut convincing figures as torch-bearers of a brave new world of governance.

These perceptions are, no doubt, proving useful to vested interests in the corporate world that would like to carry on with their old ways, unencumbered by newfangled notions of monitoring and accountability. Nevertheless, the institutions' sorry record of the past in the realm of fostering governance, on which the perceptions are based, cannot be wished away.

Can we, under the circumstances, look for deliverance to those redoubtable authors of contemporary standards of governance, foreign institutional investors (FIIs)? Tarun Khanna and Krishna Palepu of the Harvard Business School suggest we could. They find evidence that domestic financial institutions in India are ineffective monitors whereas FIIs are associated with significant monitoring benefits: firm performance is negatively correlated with the former and positively with the latter. (*Emerging market business groups, foreign investors and corporate governance, Working Paper 6955, National Bureau of Economic Research*.)

The authors use as their measure of performance a proxy for Tobin's q, the ratio of market value of a firm to replacement cost of its assets, pioneered by the famous economist, James Tobin. They find that Tobin's q is higher for firms in which FII investment exceeds the median value of such investment in a total of 1004 Indian firms in the year 1993. The authors also compare the change in Tobin's q over the period 1990-94 for a smaller sample of 488 firms and come up with the same finding: firms with higher FII investment have performed better. As for domestic institutions' ownership, the authors find that this factor either makes no difference or, worse, is negatively correlated with performance.

For those who are peddling the proposition that domestic institutions can do no good, the last correlations must seem a godsend. Unfortunately for them, the authors are careful not to mix up correlation with casuality. They are candid enough to admit that their results cannot distinguish between two possibilities: A. FIIs have improved corporate governance in the firms in which they invested; and B. FIIs have invested in firms that ex-ante showed the greatest likelihood of improving performance.

One reason it's hard to take the results seriously is that the period examined is either 1993 or 1990-94. FII investment was permitted only in September 1992, and it's unlikely that FIIs were able to exert a meaningful influence on companies in such a short period. Another ground for scepticism is the low level of FII exposure: the median value of FII ownership is 1.61 per cent for the sample of 1004 firms and 3.07 per cent for the sample of 488 firms.

But a more fundamental reason for suspending judgement would be FIIs' approach to investment in emerging markets. In the initial stages, FIIs simply to tend to buy into big-cap stocks (a hypothesis confirmed by the present study as well). The very fact of their investment tends to push up market values of these stocks—and this, not necessarily better monitoring, would be reflected in Tobin's q in the period 1990-94.

As FII investment would tend to lower domestic institutions' ownership, superior stock performance would also be negatively correlated with the latter, giving us another statistical illusion. If the study were stretched to include more recent years when the Sensex has languished, there might be surprises in store for the authors.

FIIs have compelled managements to disseminate better financial information and to think through issues of corporate strategy. But superior corporate performance calls for more. It requires an environment in which non-performing management can be shown the door through either institutional activism or takeovers. Neither of these obtains in India today, leave alone during the period covered by the authors' study. In their absence, institutional ownership cannot make a difference. From the standpoint of improving governance, it's too early to celebrate the arrival of FIIs.

Nor is it realistic to expect the situation to change materially in the near future. Political sensitivities apart, the relative insignificance of FIIs' exposures in India argues against any activist role on their part. For bringing about better governance, therefore, the challenge of structuring a suitable role for domestic financial institutions cannot be dodged. That would mean, for a start, redefining the government's relationship with the institutions.

May 27, 1999

Say 'Tata' to business ethics

The response of Union telecommunication minister, Pramod Mahajan, to the Tata group's decision to get VSNL to invest Rs 1200 crore in Tata Teleservices Limited (TTL) has been swift and hard-hitting.

Mr Mahajan has made clear that the Tatas' decision raises serious questions about the group's vaunted commitment to business ethics. He has warned that, whatever the legal fig-leaf with which the Tatas may choose to cloak their decision, the government has its own ways of penalising the group if it does not review its decision. However, by not putting forward a cogent set of arguments for his position, Mr Mahajan has allowed his detractors to paint his remarks as a peevish outburst on the part of a minister unable to reconcile himself to the exit of a blue-chip company from his fiefdom.

It must be understood, first of all, that as a shareholder with a stake of 26 per cent, the government has every right to question decisions taken by the Tata management at VSNL. Indeed, it has an obligation to do so light of the concern over the fate of valuable public sector companies after privatisation. It is absurd, therefore, to construe Mr Mahajan's response as unwarranted interference in the affairs of a private sector company.

The investment decision will transfer Rs 1200 crore from a company in which the Tata group has a 45 per cent stake to a rather small company in which the group has a 100 per cent stake. As VSNL has surplus land as well, it would be easy for the Tatas to recover much of their total investment of around Rs 2500 crore in VSNL without improving VSNL's performance in the slightest. This is not what privatisation is all about—there must be clear incentives for improvements in firm efficiency.

The proposed investment itself raises a slew of questions. Nobody should be fooled by the label 'strategic'—the use of this label is a greatly favoured gimmick at business schools.

At VSNL's most recent Annual General Meeting (by when the decision to privatise VSNL had become known), its Chairman flagged several new business opportunities that VSNL was targeting: Domestic Long Distance, Direct-to-Home services, and possibilities in the international market. He made no mention whatsoever of getting into basic services in the domestic market. The suggestion that not being in basic services would be a terrible deprivation for VSNL is, therefore, not convincing.

The argument that VSNL needs to be a player in basic services in order to get 'close to the customer' will not wash either. There are any number of players in the international market who are long-distance carriers but do not lack the ability to cultivate their customer base.

Finally, the valuation of the 25 per cent stake in TTL at Rs 1200 crore provides room for unease. The Tatas should be asked to provide details such as the P/E ratio that this translates into, the method of valuation used, the agency that did the valuation, etc.

The merits of the decision apart, questions have been raised about the manner in which it has been pushed through. If it is true that the agenda papers were not sent early enough, that would be no surprise—sending papers to a board member just as he is leaving to catch his flight to the meeting is a time-honoured technique used by companies. If there was no explicit mention of investment in TTL in the agenda, as a government nominee has claimed, that is a serious matter. Mr Mahajan should make public the relevant portion of the agenda paper so that we know exactly where the truth lies.

The ministry for disinvestment's bland statement that there has been no violation of the shareholders' agreement means nothing. What the VSNL episode has highlighted is that, where a public sector company with significant cash and surplus assets is being privatised, it is not enough to secure the right price based on the discounted cash flow method. Safeguards against asset stripping have to be built into the shareholders' agreement. One such could be the incorporation of a business plan for at least three years. Deviations from the plan would require the approval of the government as well as other shareholders.

The VSNL episode does little to allay apprehensions over the privatisation drive. A central argument for privatisation has been that it would make public sector companies more competitive by making possible infusion of capital from the private sector. The worst prospect is that, instead of funds pouring into loss-making companies, funds are transferred out of profit-making ones. The conduct of one of India's better-regarded industrial houses in this instance is warning that this prospect is by no means hypothetical.

June 6, 2002

PRIVATISATION

Introductory Note

On no issue has *The Big Picture* been as much at loggerheads with general comment in the media as on the subject of privatisation. As I have researched the subject of privatisation quite thoroughly and have written papers on it myself, I was convinced that many of the propositions being voiced in public discourse in India were at odds with the theory as well as empirical evidence on privatisation. In my own modest way, I have tried my best to correct some of these misconceptions.

One of my early observations was that while those in government freely invoked the reports of the Disinvestment Commission in support of their approach, the Commission's recommendations were, in fact, at variance with the approach towards which the BJP government was veering.

For instance, the minister for disinvestment was fond of saying that the Commission favoured strategic sales for the most part. This overlooked the fact that the Commission had opposed strategic sale in what it called 'core' industries, industries where there was an oligopolistic structure. Moreover, the Commission had sought comprehensive restructuring of public sector undertakings (PSUs) before they were privatised. The government chose to ignore this recommendation.

I was confirmed in my assessment when the chairman of the first Disinvestment Commission, G.V. Ramakrishna, wrote in to say of one of my early articles that "it was arguably the best on the subject". He added, "You have, unlike many others who have written on the subject, studied all the reports and understood the holistic and pragmatic approach of the Commission."

Even as the policy tilt in favour of strategic sales became more pronounced and it became clear that, at least in principle, all PSUs were up for sale, I began to question many of the premises on which the policy was based: strategic sale maximises revenues and efficiency; strategic sale alone can contribute to improvement in firm performance, not disinvestment; sale of PSUs will help bridge the fiscal deficit; and so on.

Every one of these premises rests on a whole set of underlying assumptions that may not—likely, will not—hold in the Indian context. For instance, auction theory tells us that if you want to maximise sales, you must have a large number of bidders. Yet firms have been sold through the strategic route even where there were only one or two bidders and this is said to have maximised revenues.

I drew on the empirical literature on the subject to make the point that disinvestment, not strategic sale, was the preferred mode of sale worldwide. It was also not true that share prices of PSUs had shot up only because strategic sale was imminent. The bulk of the increase in market capitalisation of PSUs was accounted for firms that were *not* candidates for privatisation, notably ONGC! The disregard for theory and fact in the debate on privatisation in India is truly astonishing.

I have also sought to draw attention to some other aspects of privatisation policy. *One* is the medium-term impact on employment. Privatisation is seen as a threat to jobs and this concern needs to be addressed in a context in which a safety net for workers, job retraining, etc. are non-existent. *Secondly,* we need to ask ourselves whether the cause of greater professionalism is advanced when PSUs are sold to family-managed business houses. Over time, the model for at least large firms in the Anglo-Saxon world is professionally–managed firms accountable to institutional shareholders.

The large PSUs are run by professionals, whatever the degree of political interference. Are family managed businesses, not amenable to removal thanks to their large shareholdings and to low institutional activism, really an improvement in conceptual terms? If not, how do we expect firm performance to be superior?

I note with satisfaction that today we have a coalition at the centre that has set its face against privatisation on ideological grounds and against strategic sale of profit-making what seemed contrarian—and even eccentric—yesterday is pretty much mainstream today. The swings of pendulum in public policy!

Interview: GV Ramakrishna

GV Ramakrishna joined the IAS in 1952 and rose to hold a variety of senior positions in government. He was Minister for Economic Affairs at the Indian embassy in Washington in 1972, Chief Secretary in the state of Andhra Pradesh in 1983 and India's Ambassador to the European Economic Community (European Union) in 1989.

He was Adviser in the Planning Commission in 1981 and Member in 1994. He has been Chairman of the Securities and Exchange Board of India and Chairman of the first Disinvestment Commission in which capacity he was instrumental in preparing an elaborate blue-print, running into several reports, for disinvestment of India's state-owned enterprises.

1. *Suppose we begin with the setting up of the Disinvestment Commission under your chairmanship. Until then, there was a measure of ad hocism to the disinvestment programme starting with sales through bundles of PSU (Public Sector Undertakings) shares. Could you outline how you went about drawing up a strategy for disinvestment? I imagine you considered the experiences in other countries, yet you came up with something quite distinctive.*

A. The strategy for disinvestment was evolved in an eclectic manner after studying the experience of other countries.

The taxpayer over the years had invested in the PSUs. As many as 102 out of 236 PSUs were incurring losses which have mounted from about Rs 500 crore in 1995 to Rs 13,000 crore in 2000-01. Other PSUs, though profit—making, were functioning under excessive government control which did not permit their management to take the necessary commercial decisions in a liberalized economy to compete on equal terms with the private sector.

There was erosion of the assets created out of taxpayers' money. There was need for restructuring the PSUs and for adopting a variable pattern of disinvestment appropriate to the condition and situation of each PSU.

The first thing that the DC said was that the whole process of disinvestment should be delinked from the budget. DC also pointed out that disinvestment under the compulsions of the budget will not get the best prices. It was pointed the budget deficit reduction approach had not produced any noticeable difference to the deficit but, on the other hand, had deprived the people of huge benefits. DC also said in its first report that there should be a Disinvestment Fund which could be used for creating assets for the rural poor and for various purposes calculated to resturcture the asset pattern in the most beneficial way. This has not been accepted.

The DC recommendations were tailored to the needs of then Indian public sector and were tailor-made for each PSU within the overall framework of the policy.

2. *Did the Commission have any difficulty in getting its approach accepted by the then governments?*

A. DC said that the recommendations should be taken as a whole and not piecemeal. It also said that its total approach and the general recommendations should be taken to the Cabinet. This was not done. DC was not given an opportunity to explain its total approach to the Government and it was left to the Ministries to pick and choose whatever they wanted to implement.

3. *One of the central tenets of your approach seems to have been that the public sector should be strengthened not dismantled. This requires that some of the proceeds of disinvestment should be used for restructuring PSUs. However, the present government does not appear to share this philosophy nor does it seem to believe that restructuring of PSUs is worthwhile. What, in your view, explains this departure from your philosophy? And do you see any merit in it in the present context?*

A. DC has always maintained that resturcturing, in terms of technical, financial, management changes will enhance the value of the companies. It was pointed that government as the trustee of the taxpayers' money should get the best value for the assets. The government was keen on pursuing the budget-oriented approach and found it easier and quicker to go about disinvestments without examining restructuring prospects for each PSU. It was thought that the success of the government was in getting rid of as many as possible of the PSUs as early as possible. Hence valuation suffered in several cases and the government and then taxpayers were the losers.

4. *In the majority of cases referred to the Commission, you recommended strategic sales. However, in large, well-run PSUs belonging to what you termed "core" industries, you were careful not to recommend strategic sales. Yet this distinction has been lost sight of and people insist that strategic sales are in keeping with the Commission's approach. Your comment.*

A. DC recommended strategic sales in some cases but after restructuring and proper valuation. This was not done. The DC also recommended that the bigger blue chip PSUs should not be sold through strategic sale, but that there should be process of converting them into publicly held companies; this is dealt with in detail under Q. No. 9.

5. *There is also an incorrect impression that strategic sales alone constitute genuine privatisation, that if you merely sell to the public and the government retains a majority stake or even the largest stake, that is not privatisation. Yet, we know that in the UK, public offers were the preferred mode. Do you see any reason why we in India should necessarily prefer strategic sales to public offers?*

A. This was pointed out in the context of the National Shareholding Trust (NST). The UK experience of selling shares to the public a number of their large PSUs was also pointed out. I have dealt with this in detail in my forthcoming book. The main reason for not accepting this was the strong desire of the ministers and the bureaucrats to keep control over the large PSUs. In India strategic sales would be appropriate in some cases but after proper valuation.

6. *Are you happy with some of the strategic sales that have taken place? In many cases, there have been very few bidders, in some just one. Some of this has occurred because of a reluctance to involve foreign bidders. Is it right to press ahead with strategic sales when there are very few bidders in the fray?*

A. No. Questions have been raised about the valuation of the companies before they are offered to bidders. Here, one should distinguish between valuation of assets and valuation of an enterprise. While the valuation of assets will be more relevant in the case of closure of an enterprise, the valuation of an enterprise would be more relevant in the case of privatisation of a going concern. Government should not only have competent financial advisers but also its own consultants to give it a second opinion on the advice given by the global financial advisor. These considerations will be relevant in the case of strategic sales.

In regard to the blue chip companies, the DC had not recommended strategic sale to a single bidder, either foreign or private, as in the case of other companies but the sale of shares to the Indian public with the government retaining 26 per cent of the shares.

7. *There is a perception that government ownership is simply incompatible with shareholder wealth maximization—other objectives will always intervene. So PSUs cannot compete in a liberalised environment. Do you share this perception?*

A. This is largely true. Government interference in management lowers the share price.

Other objectives like government control over pricing, contracts, personnel selection, salary scales etc. will not be conducive to getting the best talent, or to incentivise them.

Also the role of the CVC, CBI, CAG will be inhibiting factors for commercial decision making. DC had made recommendations in this regard like the creation of a pre-investigation board which has now been accepted by the CVC. But other problems have been created by the CVC asking for a role even when government shareholding is below 51 per cent. This is dealt with under NST.

8. *The Commission had argued in favour of autonomy and improvement in compensation packages for PSU management. There are those who say that no government, no bureaucracy will ever permit this. Aren't there instances abroad of PSUs enjoying a measure of both?*

A. The arrangement in Singapore similar to the NST proposal seems to provide an answer. More about this later.

9. *One of the suggestions you had made was for a National Shareholding Trust to which government shares would be transferred. This idea has been found infeasible. Another suggestion has been to float an Asset Management Company that will be run by professionals and that will manage all government holdings of shares in PSUs. This too has not taken off. Suppose we accept that government as owner cannot entirely relinquish control. Is it still possible to create governance structures that permit PSUs to compete?*

A. The NST proposal has in fact been found feasible by the legal opinion of the Additional Solicitor General, the present S G. The proposal will convert the large PSUs into publicly held, professionally managed companies which can become international companies. In Singapore they have had the TAMESEK which holds the shares of government in hundreds of companies.

TAMESEK has a broad-based board consisting of private managers along with some government representatives. It submits only an annual report to the Finance Minister and is not otherwise under the control of the government. This was sent to the government by the DC in Oct 1997.

The then Finance Secretary, Vijay Kelkar, was convinced that this was better than his proposal of an SPV. He took a paper to the Committee of Secretaries but this was buried there as neither the Ministers nor the bureaucrats were interested in giving up control. The concept of an Asset Management Company is somewhat different from NST and cannot be a vehicle for disinvestment. This proposal assumes further relevance now.

The CVC has said that even if government shareholding is reduced below 51 percent, the PSU will be managed by the government as the largest single shareholder and will therefore come under CVC. If this happens the CBI, CAG and the Parliamentary Committees will come into the picture. The solution will be to entrust the management to a Trust and for the government to withdraw from the management.

Policy

Fatal Flaw in SPV

In the period between the War and the early eighties, which saw the ascendancy of America's corporations, top management was impervious to any meaningful control. It was virtually a law unto itself. Peter Drucker has described the phenomenon in scathing terms: "unfounded, unjustified, uncontrolled and irresponsible power", and "autonomous management, accountable to no one, controlled by no one".

The phenomenon was made possible by a cozy relationship between professional managers and the Board whereby managers appointed the Board, and the Board, in turn, reappointed managers to fresh terms. It required the takeover wave of the eighties in the US, driven by fund managers' quest for capital appreciation, to bring top management to heel.

In the nineties, the newly found assertiveness of the large institutional funds has manifested itself in pressure on top management to perform even where there is no threat of takeover. As result, CEOs of the some of the biggest names in American business-IBM, General Motors, American Express, Salomon Brothers have been shown the door. Across the Atlantic, institutional funds are just beginning to come out of their torpor.

There is little to suggest that the historical experience with professional management has at all been factored into the debate on privatisation in India. The presumption seems to be that when government reduces its stake in listed PSUs to 49 percent, management accountability and performance will automatically go up. However, we do know from experience elsewhere that leaving things to professional managers will not by itself improve matters.

The fatal flaw with the SPV route is that it doesn't quite spell out a mechanism for enforcing accountability once the government's stake falls to 49 per cent or less. Either the SPV provides a camouflage for continued government control, with the government joining hands with the financial institutions that will buy up some of the 51 per cent divested. Or, the government does relinquish control, in which case we are faced with a more intractable problem: how to put in place an alternative mechanism to ensure accountability?

Professional managers accountable to an amorphous body of widely dispersed shareholders is clearly no solution. Privatisation can be allied to accountability only when alternative pressure groups in the form of non-government financial institutions arise. But the private fund industry in India has a long way to go before it attains any meaningful size, not to speak of attaining credibility. In the interim, there is little alternative to government control of PSUs in some form, with or without an SPV. This highlights a critical reality in the Indian context: the speed of privatisation is constrained by the even more tardy pace of institutional development in the financial markets.

The Disinvestment Commission (DC) Chairman, G V Ramakrishna, favours a Trust to which all PSU shares will be transferred initially; the Trust's share in PSUs will go down eventually to 26 per cent. The Trust will be managed by representatives from the finance ministry, the DC, banks and financial institutions and by eminent professional managers. This suggestion, again, is unlikely to take us very far. What we have here is a superboard; and we all know how effective Boards are. No, if the stock market is to be the key to ensuring performance, it is hard to improve upon the American Mechanism of private funds demanding returns.

There's one other flaw in the SPV scheme. PSUs in which government stakes are to be sold have an interest in restructuring themselves when they can reap the attendant benefits. The benefits are many. If the stock price moves up on restructuring, that helps validate management's approach to restructuring; it would spell rewards for managers and workers if they are offered stock options; and if the government's willing to plough back part of the gains from divestment, that's a bonus.

When 51 per cent is transferred right away to an SPV, to which the gains from divestment will mostly accrue, the motivation at the enterprise level to restructure is diminished. And the central purpose of divestment, improvement in efficiency, falls by the wayside.

October 1, 1998

Privatisation gone awry

Let's face it: the decision to get public sector oil companies to swap equity amongst themselves is dictated mainly by the government's need to manage its fiscal arithmetic. The argument that cross-holdings among oil majors make business sense would have carried greater conviction had its timing not coincided with the ending of another fiscal year in which revenues from divestment have fallen woefully short of target. The evidence points, not to a spontaneous coming together on the part of the companies concerned, but to contrived weddings.

That the buyback provision is being used to effect the swap shows that ingenuity in exploiting legal loopholes is not the monopoly of the private sector. Buybacks are intended, among other things, to return to shareholders cash for which companies don't have adequate uses. This is hardly true of the oil majors given the need for huge investments in the oil sector. The oil companies may now be forced to borrow in order to finance some of their own investments. Given the present accounting practice, this won't show up in that magic number everybody is fixated on budget day: the fiscal deficit.

This may be divestment but it's not privatisation. Both equity and bond values represent the capitalisation of future streams of cash. The presumption underlying privatisation is that future cash streams related to equity will increase because government control is removed or at least weakened.

If this latter is not going to happen, the government might as well raise revenues through additional bond sales instead of divesting its equity holdings, and that too at unattractive prices. The macroeconomic impact will be identical under the two situations. There is merit in the view that the oil companies need not be prime candidates for privatisation. But, by using their cash to dress up its budget numbers, the government merely buttresses the opposing view that wholesale privatisation alone can confer immunity from political meddling.

The frantic attempt to raise revenues without taking into account its firm-level impact is only one flaw in the approach to privatisation. Another is the premise that privatisation will, to use the tiresome cliche, "revive the capital market".

If this means somehow causing secondary market prices to perk up, it is legitimate to ask whether government should be in the business of attempting such a thing at all. There is a case for government to intervene when a crash in stock prices threatens because a crash could lead to insolvencies among market players and destabilise the market. But once prices have fallen, however sharply, there is no call for the government to intervene to prop them up: if assets are undervalued, market forces will restore them to appropriate levels.

If, however, reviving the capital market means deepening the market by attracting new investors, that makes sense in principle and indeed that was one the major achievements of the privatisation programme in the UK. But deepening the market would require offering PSU stocks at discounts to market prices to *retail* investors as happened in the UK. This is not happening here. Instead, PSU stocks are being offered at discounts to institutional investors, including FIIs!

But even the argument that privatisation will deepen the stock market is weak in our present context. The problem today is not that we lack a wide enough base of shareholders. It is the general disenchantment with the market itself. Under the circumstances, under-pricing of PSU stocks may attract savers to specific issues but it is unlikely to serve the objective of deepening the capital market as a whole.

There is disenchantment with the market partly because investors have lost heavily on the spate of premium issues in the liberalized regime but also because expectations of risk premium on equity haven't quite adjusted to the changed realities: people are still looking for returns of 25% plus in the stock market.

The market will set this right: if prices stay depressed, the risk premium will go down and this would augur well for the long-term development of the stock market. So the government would do well to let the stock market be and focus instead on its poorer country cousin, the bond market. The markets are doing their job, all right; if only governments could get on with theirs.

January 21, 1999

Privatise and be damned

The government's decision to shed 51 per cent of its equity in Indian Airlines (IA), timed to coincide with the annual World Economic Forum jamboree at Davos, sends out a clear signal that Indian privatisation has entered a new phase. What is less clear is that this will take place in a manner calculated to produce the best results.

IA is not among the 58 units on which the Disinvestment Commission (DC) has made recommendations. This raises the question of whether the DC, currently in limbo, has any place at all in the government's scheme of things and, if yes, how central the DC will be to the privatisation process. The government's initiative in respect of a vital PSU such as IA suggests that any reconstituted DC may be relegated to secondary status as privatisation gathers steam.

That would be most unfortunate. The whole point about constituting a DC is that there is a transparent framework in which the mechanics of privatisation are determined. In the absence of such a framework, there is every danger that privatisation will be driven by ad-hoc considerations, chiefly the desperation to contain the fiscal deficit, not to speak of more unwholesome considerations.

Fiscal stringency is undoubtedly why the government wants to rope in a strategic partner to whom 26 per cent of the airline's equity will be sold. For this is contrary to the approach of the Kelkar committee on IA privatisation, which had recommended infusion of government equity and other funds followed by a public offering.

It may be contended that such infusion is not feasible given the position of the fisc but that is a poor excuse. If funds are not available for restructuring PSUs, it is because successive governments have ignored the DC's recommendation about setting aside the proceeds of disinvestment in a separate Disinvestment Fund meant for such purposes.

The strategic partner is expected to usher in greater efficiency despite the fact that the government's stipulations virtually rule out the partner being a player in the airline business. The presumption seems to be that the mere transfer of control from state to private hands will make for greater efficiency. Yet there is little in the experience with privatisation worldwide that lends support to such dogma. Privatisation works in some contexts, given the right design. Not always.

The case of British Airways (BA), cited by some who have hailed the government's proposal, is instructive. One of the totems of British privatisation in the eighties, the 'world's favourite airline' as BA likes to style itself, is in bad shape today. It has run up losses and its beleaguered CEO was petitioning the UK government last week not to dismantle barriers to competition in British skies.

But the more telling lesson from BA is contained in a study of its performance over a longish period, outlined in a recent book.(*The impact of privatisation: Ownership and performance in the UK, S Martin and D Parke.)* The study analyses BA's performance over five periods: nationalisation, pre-privatisation, post-privatisation, the UK recession, and in the latest period.

The four parameters of efficiency looked at were best in the pre-privatisation period. Comparing the nationalisation and post—privatisation periods, the study found that two parameters improved while two deteriorated. In the latest period, three out of four parameters have been worse than in even the nationalisation period.

The results are not altogether surprising. Privatisation is seen to work when allied with competition. Because competition in the airline industry is restricted the world over, this would seem to limit what privatisation can accomplish. Going by the record of BA in a context in which standards of accountability are much higher than in ours, scepticism about what private control of IA can achieve is in order.

As the BA case illustrates, it is folly to expect superior performance from private ownership in every context. The cumulative experience with privatisation holds other important lessons. One is that privatisation initiatives must be periodically subjected to proof of improved efficiency.

Each proposal for selling government equity in a PSU must carry projections of efficiency levels expected following privatisation. Only if performance parameters show consistent improvement must the government proceed with further sales in each instance. In the case of IA, if the government does go ahead with its present proposal, a lowering of its stake to under 49 per cent in the second stage must be contingent on such a review.

Equally important, every proposal for strategic sale must outline alternatives, as is common with DC recommendations, and all alternatives thoroughly debated. On present showing, the auguries in these respects are not terribly promising.

February 3, 2000

Row over Rover

India's privatisation plans have run into yet another roadblock: opposition from regional parties. The Tamil Nadu assembly recently passed a resolution opposing the privatisation of the Salem steel plant. The Telugu Desam Party and the Trinamool Congress are up in arms against moves to sell the Vizag and Durgapur steel plants respectively.

Such opposition does not point to a perverse streak in Indian politicians—witness the extraordinary row that has erupted in the UK over a commercial decision by BMW, the German automotive company, to exit from its operation there.

Prime Minister Tony Blair called the chairman of BMW to express his anger over BMW's keeping the British government in the dark about its planned exit. The Secretary for Trade and Industry, Stephen Byers, flew down to Munich to seek assurances about protection of jobs at Rover Cars following the sale. Mr Byers also expressed his displeasure over the sale of the unit to a venture capital firm and his preference for an alternative buyer.

The British government is upset on account of job losses feared as a result of the sale of BMW's businesses. At least half of the 9000 jobs at Rover Cars are said to be immediately threatened. If the knock-on effects on component suppliers are included, job losses could amount to 50,000 in the industrial area near Birmingham.

Long term, more jobs could be lost. BMW's anxiety to cut its losses in the UK and run means that Alchemy, the three–year old venture capital firm to whom Rover Cars is being sold, will likely inherit the operation at a throwaway price. This increases the chances that Alchemy will scale down operations and strip assets with the clear objective of getting a return on its investment in the shortest possible time. As Alchemy lacks the resources to make the huge investments needed down the road, it could be curtains for Rover Cars if another buyer cannot be found in, say, five years' time.

Commentators will view all this as the inexorable operation of market forces. Politicians, however, find it rather more difficult to take as detached a view of job losses or an erosion of the manufacturing base, especially when these are concentrated in a particular region.

In this respect, Britain's politicians are in good company. Chancellor Schroder of Germany was quick to orchestrate a rescue package last year for an ailing construction firm in the face of criticism from home and abroad. In the free market bastion across the Atlantic, moves are afoot to shore up faltering defence firms through state support.

One aspect of the Rover drama that has been overlooked is that it is a failed privatisation story. Rover was part of the conglomerate, British Leyland, which was taken into state ownership in 1976 when it was on the verge of collapse. In the high tide of privatisation in 1988, the government sold Rover to British Aerospace, then newly privatised. Rover recovered but troubles in BAe's aircraft businesses caused the firm to sell Rover to BMW in 1994. Now on to Alchemy.

It is not as if Rover's failure under private ownership has been a costless affair so far for the British government. The state incurs costs related to social security, job retraining schemes, incentives to attract new units to make up for jobs lost at Rover, etc. The storm over BMW's exit indicates that even such an elaborate safety net is perceived as being inadequate.

The BMW-Alchemy deal raises politicians' hackles although it is wholly in the private realm. So regional parties here can hardly be faulted for opposing decisions in the public sector that they view as impacting adversely on the local economy. They see jobs being lost without a safety net being put in place. They sense a divergence between private returns and social costs. They are not sure whether, at the end of the day, the industrial base will expand or shrink.

Heading off opposition to privatisation requires support to redundant workers that goes well beyond one-off VRS packages. There must also be provisions for strengthening public sector firms where appropriate so that many of the existing jobs are protected. But by far the most important requirement is creating new jobs to absorb displaced labour. Until these concerns are addressed, expect regional parties—and politicians in general—to raise hell over privatisation.

March 30, 2000

Don't quote selectively

It is tempting but not very productive to reduce something as challenging as privatisation to one or two simple tenets. If his early pronouncements on the subject are any indication, the new minister for disinvestment, Arun Shourie, shows every sign of succumbing to the temptation.

In a lengthy interview to Rediff.com, Mr. Shourie seems to suggest that the main problem with the privatisation process so far has been the tendency to disinvest in driblets. What is required is wider use of the mechanism of strategic sale.

As a statement of strategy or even priorities for privatization, this is far too simplistic. It does not help that Mr. Shourie has got his facts muddled. Mr. Shourie quotes the Disinvesment Commission (DC), since defunct, as warning, "Don't do minority sales". He adds, "Of the 42 cases, they recommended 37 strategic sales and only five were to be minority sales. And what is the record? One strategic sale and minority sales in 39! ".

Sale of minority stakes in 40 PSUs took place in the period 1992-1996 well before the Disinvestment Commission was set up in August 1996 and before the first of its 12 reports appeared in February 1997. Of these 40 PSUs, only 21 figure in the 58 cases referred to the DC by the government. So it is incorrect to suggest that the sale of minority stakes in the 40 PSUs flouted the recommendations of the DC. The recommendations came much later and in half the instances have no bearing on what transpired.

To say that the DC generally favoured strategic sales is not an accurate characterization either. Going by the DC's guidelines, strategic sales would be possible only in non-core industries, defined as industries that do not have an oligopolistic structure. (Mr.Shourie does acknowledge the rationale for excluding such industries from strategic sales.) For the record, the DC had advised strategic sales in 33 out of 53 cases in which it had made recommendations.

Even where non-core companies are concerned, the DC had not favoured transfer of control to a private party in every instance. In the case of BHEL, which it classified as non-core, the DC had instead recommended that domestic and foreign financial institutions be induced to pick up a 20 per cent stake.

In any case, the method of sale is hardly the central issue in Indian privatisation. The issue is what privatisation is meant to achieve. The DC itself was clear on this subject: disinvestment must be "a part of a well thought out strategy of public sector reform and not made to serve merely as a means of raising revenues for the budget" (Report XII).

The DC had also repeatedly spelt out what the other elements in the strategy must be: crediting the proceeds to a Disinvestment Fund that will be used primarily for restructuring PSUs and funding VRS schemes; restructuring ahead of disinvestment; greater autonomy; better corporate governance; improvement in salaries and incentives for top management; etc.

Yet successive governments have pursued disinvestment without due regard for the other elements in the strategy. The DC mentioned this pointedly in many of its later reports. It observed ruefully that it was not aware if all its recommendations had even been taken to the Cabinet.

This is not all. In the case of Indian Airlines, the government has gone ahead with its own disinvestment proposal without reference to the DC. With Air-India, the government has thought fit to proceed with strategic sale without the prior infusion of Rs 1000 crore recommended by the Commission. This has come in for criticism from the concerned Standing Committee of parliament.

All this raises the question whether the government at all shares the DC's enthusiasm for broad reform of PSUs. Or whether it will selectively use the DC's recommendations on strategic sales to maximise revenues in the short run. By harping on strategic sales of PSUs and not mentioning the concomitant steps required for strengthening the public sector, Mr. Shourie can only reinforce the perception that the government's privatisation agenda is rather different from that outlined by the DC.

For all the talk of consensus on the subject, such a perception is unlikely to help garner support for privatisation from across the political spectrum. The government will need to demonstrate a commitment to the DC's holistic approach to privatisation if it is to fare better than its predecessors.

August 31, 2000

Air-India's case epitomises tensions in privatisation

As the contest for Air-India nears its final phase, there is every prospect of its ending up as a one-horse race. With only two bidders left in the fray, the Tata-SIA combine and the Hinduja group, the cabinet committee on security is expected to decide whether the latter is to be disqualified on grounds of national security. If the Hindujas do get disqualified, the Tata-SIA combine will walk away with the prize provided its offer is higher than the reservation price set by the government.

The government sees nothing wrong with things panning out that way. After all, the argument goes, it is not the fault of the Tatas if other bidders withdraw at various stages and if the only remaining bidder is eliminated at the final stage.

Matters are not that simple, however. When a bidder gets eliminated in the final stage on non-commercial grounds, it is bound to give rise to the suspicion that a particular group is being favoured—and indeed the Samajwadi Party has said as much. There will also be dark mutterings about the winning bid not being the highest and the government failing to maximise revenues from the sale.

But the broader issue in the Air-India case relates to the small number of bids that the offer seems to have evoked. The chances of securing the best price are improved the greater the number of bidders. An auction may fail to attract a large number of buyers because the asset in question is not attractive enough—or because the rules designed by the seller militate against efficiency.

In the case of Air-India, there is little doubt that the limitation on foreign equity of 26 per cent has restricted the number of bidders. This, in turn, limits the price the government can get and it also limits the quality of strategic partner Air-India can attract. Yet the political reality is such as to preclude a sale at the highest price to the best available party in the world. This highlights a fundamental tension in India's privatisation programme, one between the dictates of efficiency and those of political economy.

The tension needs to be resolved sooner rather than later. It is hard to think of any successful privatisation programme in emerging markets that has not been dominated by foreign capital. The only honest position for political parties committed to privatisation to take is that they are indifferent to whether the buyer is Indian or foreign. But no party today has the courage to say so no however strongly it might swear by privatisation.

Yet this is not an issue that can be glossed over even where a sale is made to an alliance in which a domestic party—in this instance, the Tatas—has the upper hand to start with. The experience with joint ventures so far has been that it is only a matter of time before the foreign player buys out the Indian partner or walks away from the venture. So when the Shiv Sena warns that the Singapore flag may be hoisted on the Air-India building before long, the issue needs to be confronted head on. Instead, all we get from political parties are evasion, obfuscation and plain dissembling.

Not taking a clear stand on the role for foreign capital can only lead to the privatisation process stretching out endlessly as more and more PSUs, including big ticket items, are offered for sale and domestic capital proves unequal to the task. In the process, PSUs will continue to be condemned to a no-man's–land where there is neither effective public ownership nor are the units privatised. This is unaffordable. The paralysis at PSUs has already taken a heavy toll of investment and output in the economy and the values of many PSUs have been eroding by the day.

Political parties must embrace foreign capital whole-heartedly. Or they must bow to political sensitivities and explore ways of strengthening PSUs through alternative mechanisms such as public sale of shares. Sadly, the will to strengthen PSUs is missing despite evidence of strong improvement in performance at several PSUs.

Air-India is said to be on the verge of declaring a profit after several years of losses. This will not be a mean achievement in an environment in which such big names as Swissair and British Airways, both under private ownership, are floundering. The turnaround will be the result of the airline making long overdue additions to its fleet and thus being able to cater to hitherto unmet demand.

This could happen in many other PSUs that have inherent strengths but have languished in the post-reform era for sheer want of capital. Give them a chance to raise capital and a measure of autonomy and they can run, if not fly. Yet the ruling elite seems hell-bent on privatisation, even by means that can only result in sub-optimal outcomes.

July 5, 2001

New Commission must first articulate its philosophy

The government's decision to reconstitute the Disinvestment Commission (DC) could hopefully mark a return to realism in its approach to privatization.

It is nearly two years since the tenure of the previous Commission lapsed. In its anxiety to expedite the process of disinvestment, the present government chose to house both policy-making and implementation in the department of disinvestment.

The two ministers who have held the portfolio have viewed their task in stark terms: Public Sector Undertakings (PSUs) were a burden on the government and disinvestment meant strategic sale. As long as the mechanics were addressed in a transparent way, there should be no problem with the process.

It is becoming clear that the government cannot hope to make much headway with disinvestment with such an approach. Only two strategic sales have taken place, Modern Foods and Balco, and both have been fraught with controversy. The proposed sales of the two national airlines have produced unsatisfactory outcomes. In the case of Air-India, there is only one bidder left in the fray while the sale of Indian Airlines is set to unravel with no bidder left at all.

SEBI's indictment of private sector management at three firms in securities fraud has compelled the government to come out with stringent qualifying standards for bidders and this threatens to seriously narrow the field of domestic contenders for PSUs. The inability of governments to hand over a large enough stake to foreign firms also limits the number of bidders—and this too may render the strategic sale route inappropriate.

There is a clear need, therefore, to revisit the issue of disinvestment in order to digest the lessons of recent experience and to evolve an approach that makes sense in both economic and political terms. The reconstitution of the DC is thus in order.

Before it grapples with the mechanics of disinvestment, the new DC must first articulate its philosophy. In particular, it must address the central issue: is disinvestment meant to dismantle the public sector or is it a means of strengthening it? The previous DC under GV Ramakrishna had addressed this issue in its very first report and emphatically thrown its weight behind the latter. The new DC under RH Patil must indicate whether it wants to build on its predecessor's approach or to reject it.

The present government has sought to justify its course on disinvestment by citing the former DC's recommendations on strategic sales in a large number of firms referred to it. It has ignored the pre-conditions that the DC had proposed, such as restructuring of PSUs prior to sale, linking proceeds of disinvestment to restructuring of PSUs and creation of a safety net for workers, improved corporate governance at PSUs etc. Merely to carry out strategic sales is to dismantle the public sector and that too on the worst possible terms.

Mr Ramakrishna's DC had ruled out strategic sale in what it called the 'core' industries (industries with an oligopolistic structure). It had also disfavoured strategic sale in firms (such as BHEL) that were not in core industries but had the potential to become internationally competitive. Its approach thus virtually precluded strategic sale in the Navratna PSUs.

If it believes in strengthening the public sector, the new DC must embrace these—and go even further. Where it recommends strategic sale, it must make out a case on the basis of under-performance relative to the private sector or inability to raise requisite capital. It must insist that superior performance in bidders be documented at the time of evaluation. In all instances, it must monitor performance following strategic sale to see whether the claimed benefits of privatization have materialized.

This is necessary because the case for privatization often rests on presumed benefits, without regard to the reality in a particular context. In the wake of the problems with US-64, the demand for privatization of UTI has been heard. Yet nobody has made out a case for this by comparing the performance of UTI's schemes (including US-64) on a rigorous basis with those of its peers in the private sector. This, in an industry in which the CRB scandal has not faded from public memory and the very mention of Morgan Stanley evokes sniggers.

The new DC confronts both a magnificent opportunity and a serious risk. The opportunity is to chart a course of disinvestment that is uniquely Indian, one that harmonises the economic imperatives with the need to build consensus in a critical area of reform. The risk is that Indian privatization will usher in an era of bandit capitalism. Mr Patil showed a remarkable capacity for innovation in the financial market. He desperately needs to produce an encore.

August 2, 2001

Adhocism and desperation in privatisation

Following the Supreme Court judgement on Balco, the government has begun to act as though it has *carte blanche* in respect of privatisation. At the same time, fiscal pressures have injected an element of desperation into the sale of public assets.

There is every danger of recklessness creeping into privatisation policy as a result, with the pursuit of ambitious targets being viewed as a sign of machismo by would-be reformers and their cheer-leaders in the pink press. While the Supreme Court is understandably reluctant to be drawn into the sphere of economic decision-making, this should not be taken to mean that anything goes when it comes to the management of public assets.

In one case after another, the government's approach to privatisation provides room for unease. In Paradeep Phosphates, a controlling stake was sold to the KK Birla group at a price below the reserve price. The argument put forward was that the company's losses would mount unless a private party stepped in quickly. But it was precisely in order to avoid such distress sales that the previous Disinvestment Commission (DC) had recommended restructuring of enterprises before sale. In the absence of restructuring, distress sales are inevitable.

In the case of Hindustan Zinc, a 26 per cent stake has been sold to the Sterlite group. The previous DC had categorically stated, "No public purpose will be served by converting a near public monopoly to a private monopoly and therefore disinvestment beyond 49 per cent is not considerable desirable at present". It suggested the induction of a strategic partner who "may be offered upto 25 per cent of the equity stake". Yet, the government has gone ahead with a sale that will reduce its stake to 49 per cent.

The inclusion of the Reliance group as a bidder for IPCL and the opposition to IOC's bidding for BPCL and HPCL have raised issues that have not been addressed satisfactorily. The two decisions are sought to be justified on the ground that, whereas the market for petrochemicals is contestable, that for petroleum products is not.

One has to be extremely wary of notions of contestability in a milieu in which corporates have formidable political clout. Besides, this is a matter that falls within the province of a Competition Commission. Until one is constituted, we should, perhaps, be guided by the extant concept of market dominance. Incidentally, the previous DC, whom the Ministry of Disinvestment is fond of quoting when it is convenient, had insisted that strategic sale in IPCL should not lead to market dominance.

In the case of Maruti, where the government wants to cede a controlling interest to Suzuki, the government is reportedly willing to lower its expectation of a control premium from Rs 1000 crore to Rs 600 crore so that privatisation can go forward. Indian Airlines and Air-India have announced plans for expansion of their fleet through suppliers' credits. One would have thought this would obviate the need for privatization as the need for funds for fleet expansion had been touted as the rationale. But no, it appears the government will still privatise these if only it can find buyers.

Meanwhile, the quadrapling of the stock price of CMC within four months of the strategic sale to the Tata group raises serious questions about the computation of the reserve price. It can be nobody's case that the Tatas have effected a stunning turnaround in this short period. Nor can any glib talk about 're-rating' of the stock following privatisation explain a rise of this magnitude. As reported in the *Economic Times* (April 4), the company's profit is slated to double. Was this projection taken into account in computing the reserve price?

The design of privatisation is absolutely critical to improvement in firm efficiency. Adhocism will not do. A carefully thought through approach of the sort espoused by the previous DC is required. Indeed, it is best that issues of policy in privatisation are deliberated upon by an independent body. Unfortunately, the existence of the new Disinvestment Commission seems to have been forgotten.

It must not be supposed, however, that the design of privatisation alone is at issue today and that privatisation *per se* is above contention. In a little noticed speech made in Guntur last month, former Prime Minister Narasimha Rao warned that, while no judicial court might set aside decisions to do away with the government's stake in PSUs, "the people's court will have to set aside these policies". If the NDA government does not wish to heed the message of the drubbing it has received at the hustings in recent months, it might at least ponder the remarks of the statesman who set in motion the programme of economic reform in 1991.

April 1, 2002

AMC for PSUs is a red herring

In the eyes of the chattering classes, the minister for disinvestment, Arun Shourie, can do no wrong. Whenever a blue chip PSU is offered for strategic sale, there is jubilation—another bastion has fallen. When a fresh bout of disinvestment is promised in IOC, GAIL and ONGC, that too is portrayed as a coup of sorts. Mr Shourie is right in pushing for outright sale; he is right also when he opts for public issues for NALCO ahead of strategic sale.

It suffices for the chatteratti that the task of dismantling the public sector is in the hands of somebody who is its sworn enemy. The dangers cannot be overstated. Unless first principles—why, what and how to sell—are thought through and applied consistently, all that privatisation will accomplish is mask the government's fiscal problems in the short-term.

The primary objective in privatisation is improvement in efficiency. It follows that the objective is best met when the most inefficient firms are privatised. As for the how of privatisation, it makes sense to list a firm through an initial tranche, followed by further tranches or strategic sale. This allows the process of price discovery, and it also allows management to focus on improving share prices through restructuring before further sale of equity is effected.

Judged by these principles, the current privatisation programme must be found wanting. The thrust is on selling some of the best-performing firms. There is virtually no attempt at restructuring firms ahead of sale. And strategic sale is the norm, no matter that the auction process ends up yielding just one or two domestic bidders.

Take the case of NALCO. It is one of the cheapest producers of aluminium and alumina in the world and among the most profitable companies in the country. The ruling dogma nevertheless requires that NALCO be handed over to private management. The first Disinvestment Commission (DC) had opposed strategic sale in NALCO, recommending instead offer of equity to domestic and international investors. The

Commission had cited NALCO's dominant share in the domestic market and the need to "safeguard against indiscriminate mining for short term financial gains" as reasons for retaining government control. These considerations are now being brushed aside.

One argument put forward for strategic sale is that it boosts share prices of the firms concerned and hence the value of the government's residual equity. This claim often rests on short-term price movements, but, more importantly, it fails to take into account the impact on share prices of factors other than change in ownership, notably ongoing deregulation. The share prices of IOC, ONGC and GAIL have all shot up over the past year although there was no hint of privatising these. The price increases are attributable to gains from deregulation.

But even if we accept that the share price will be favourably impacted, that does not by itself translate into an argument for strategic sale. Increases in share prices need not be the result of improvement in operational efficiency. They could simply be the result of actual or anticipated transfers from workers to shareholders arising from cuts in jobs. The costs to government of taking care of displaced workers must be included in any careful accounting although the human costs would still be ignored.

The ministries that run PSUs are alive to such considerations and to the performance of the better PSUs. They would, therefore, be resistant to selling off the likes of NALCO, BPCL and HPCL, not to speak of IOC and ONGC. The finance ministry can, however, use all the funds it can lay its hands on and the crusading minister for disinvestment is only too happy to oblige The move to create an Asset Management Company for government equity in PSUs must be viewed in this context.

The idea is borrowed from the first DC but the underlying motivation could not more different. The DC's proposal for an independent Trust was intended to strengthen the public sector. Today, the stated rationale for an AMC, handing over the management of government's equity to professionals, is something of a red herring.

The move is clearly aimed at circumventing opposition to privatisation of well-run PSUs from the administrative ministries and liquidating all government shareholding in PSUs. This mission will be abetted by professionals drawn from the private sector who will not be any means be disinterested parties any more than the financial advisers who determine reserve prices. To those who view privatisation in pragmatic rather than ideological terms, the signs must seem ominous, very ominous indeed.

July 18, 2002

Mechanics of Sale

Restructuring is vital

Is it a case of the left hand not knowing what the right is up to? Manohar Joshi, the minister for heavy industries, promises a white paper on restructuring of PSUs by the end of October. Arun Shourie, the minister for disinvestment, contends that attempts to restructure PSUs are money down the drain, so sell-offs to private parties is the only meaningful option.

The charitable view to take is that each minister will have a natural bias towards whatever confers more importance on his department and that the creative tension between the two departments will throw up the right compromise. Except that governments have dithered on restructuring for far too long already and this has imposed steep costs on PSUs.

The key issue before the government is whether any purpose will be served by restructuring PSUs that are certain candidates for privatisation. Many have urged that we expedite sell-offs and be done with them but this was emphatically not the course advocated by the Disinvestment Commission (DC).

The DC's approach was one of walking on two legs—plan for strategic sale but also address restructuring. The DC recognised that there would be cases where restructuring is of little use and others that can be privatised as they are. In general, however, it recommended restructuring before privatisation. Restructuring, it said, must cover three broad areas—corporate governance, business and technology.

Such an approach is necessary because the inherent strengths of many PSUs are not obvious and they will not fetch the right prices in their present condition. Many have suffered for want of capital. They cannot tap the stock market, borrowings are constrained by the failure to expand the equity base and budgetary support has dwindled. Lack of autonomy and clear commercial direction are, of course, all too common. Comprehensive restructuring – and not just infusion of funds—could make a significant difference.

Restructuring is especially required nobody can be under any illusion that privatisation is going to happen tomorrow. Even where the government has taken the decision, the whole process from appointment of advisors to tendering and eventual selection of the partner will stretch over a year or two. Unless they are restructured and prettied up and the workforce suitably incentivised, many PSUs could be rendered worthless in the run-up to privatisation. Restructuring is also necessary if PSUs are to attract strong partners, whether for strategic sale or for joint ventures or alliances.

Besides, if private parties are allowed to gain control of firms that have suffered from sheer neglect for years and are under-valued in consequence, it will not be difficult for them to show improvements in financial performance. Privatisation will then be proclaimed to have worked miracles but the benefits to the economy from improvements in firm efficiency, on which privatisation is predicated, will be meagre.

Equally important, restructuring may be required in some cases in order to take a view on whether the enterprises need a strategic partner in the first place. There are two broad categories where the DC had ruled out transfer of control to private parties: strategic sectors (such as atomic energy and defence) and core sectors (those that have an oligopolistic structure). Mr. Joshi's promised list of 'critical status' PSUs requiring majority government ownership may be expected to guided by these criteria.

However, even for non-core companies, a case-by-case approach of the sort adopted by the DC (in the case of BHEL, for instance) is warranted. Many of these PSUs are weighed down by the baggage of the past and have never really had a chance to demonstrate their mettle under a thoroughly professional management structure. The DC's view was that under the right conditions, some at least have the potential to become globally competitive firms.

Mr Joshi has given indications that he is sympathetic to this view but Mr.Shourie seems to have made up his mind that the government must exit all but the strategic and core sectors. Mr Joshi's promised white paper will, hopefully, provide an opportunity to resolve this issue once and for all and also the broader issue of restructuring of PSUs. We will then know whether the government will be guided by short-term budgetary considerations or by a livelier appreciation of the potential of national assets.

September 14, 2000

Lengthening fiscal shadow on PSU restructuring

Fiscal considerations are part of the motivation to privatise but privatisation will not be driven by short-term pressures to contain the budgetary deficit—the government has been saying this for the record. This would imply, among other things, that public sector undertakings (PSUs) would be restructured to ensure that they are in the best possible shape ahead of privatisation. The question, as the government scrambles to shore up revenues, is whether it is any longer committed to the latter objective at all.

Under conditions of asymmetric information, the price realised by the government without restructuring would, in general, be lower than the price it would get after successful restructuring minus the cost of restructuring. So, it would pay to dress up PSUs before sale just as firms can hope to get the best prices for their equity when they are doing well.

The government's pronouncements in the past have acknowledged as much. In his budget speech for 2000-01, the finance minister underlined that restructuring PSUs was a key element of the government's policy towards PSUs. "In line with this policy, during the last two years, " Mr Sinha said, " financial restructuring of 20 PSUs has been approved. As a result, many PSUs have been able to ....improve their productivity and achieve a turnaround in performance." In his budget for 2001-02, Mr Sinha went even further: he set aside Rs 7000 crore out of the targeted proceeds of Rs 12,000 crore from disinvestment for restructuring assistance for PSUs.

Now that the proceeds have fallen short of Rs 12,000 crore, will Mr Sinha have made any allocation for restructuring on a pro-rata basis? Unlikely. Far from being in a mood to make such allocations, the government has demonstrated its proclivity to raid PSUs in its growing desperation to bridge the fiscal deficit—witness the decision to cream off VSNL's reserves through huge dividends or the mechanism chosen for raising excise duties on petroleum products. Under the circumstances, the government cannot possibly be enthusiastic about injecting funds into PSUs.

There seem to be two broad objections to restructuring of PSUs. One is that such restructuring in the past has been "money down the drain". This argument fails to distinguish between funds provided to unviable units and those provided to viable ones. The wasteful kinds of restructuring have merely involved loan and interest write-offs or conversion of loan into equity in fundamentally unviable enterprises. Many of these are sick units taken over by the government from the private sector. The government continues to throw money at these because of the large workforce involved.

Where restructuring in viable PSUs has been attempted, the results have been heartening, as the finance minister's own statement, quoted above, testifies. The policy issue is whether funds for restructuring are to be provided in viable cases. By not distinguishing between the two sets of cases, restructuring is sought to be discredited.

The other objection to restructuring is that, even with good performance, PSUs are unable to meet the liquidity requirements of the government. The website of the Ministry of Disinvestment makes this point obliquely. It says that if the government were to invest the revenues of Rs 152 crore earned from the sale of its stake in CMC at 10 per cent, it would earn Rs 15.2 crore annually whereas the dividend from CMC to the government averaged only Rs 1.42 crore over the last four years. This is also what is implied when it is contended that even profit-making PSUs need to be sold in order to enable government to shift resources to areas such as social infrastructure.

Now, any sophomore at a business school could tell you that the dividend of Rs 1.42 crore represents only a part of the return to the government, the other part being capital gain. True, since government does not trade in its shares, it cannot book capital gains and hence could face liquidity problems. But there are ways out of this problem.

One would be for the government to disinvest chunks of PSU stock from time to time in the domestic market. Another was the one proposed by G V Ramakrishna. The government's holdings in PSUs could be transferred to a Trust run by professionals. The restructuring needs of PSUs as well as additional spending on social infrastructure could be met through judicious management of the portfolio without any draft on government revenues.

But either of these approaches requires faith in the capacity of PSUs to deliver, given the appropriate governance structures. Where such faith is totally eroded—as in the case of the present government—the operative credo becomes simple enough: privatise and be damned.

January 17, 2002

SEBI throws a monkey wrench into privatisation plans

Make no mistake about it, SEBI's order barring three firms—BPL, Videocon and Sterlite Industries—from accessing the capital market for varying periods has thrown a monkey wrench into the government's privatisation programme.

The companies have indicated that they will challenge the order but the matter is unlikely to resolved in a hurry. In the meantime, the government must decide how to deal with firms facing an indictment of the sort handed out by SEBI and that happen to be participants in the privatisation process.

Sterlite's acquisition of Balco, already mired in controversy, will now require re-examination. Videocon is a contender for Indian Airlines while BPL has participated in the early expressions of interest for VSNL.

The ministry for disinvestment has sought clarifications from both the Law ministry as well as SEBI regarding the implications of the SEBI order. One issue is whether the order requires the firms concerned to be blacklisted for bidding purposes and whether this applies to transactions already completed as in the case of Balco. Another is whether the ban applies to the entire group or only to specific companies.

But the issues surely go beyond legalities such as these. Assuming, for instance, that the SEBI restriction applies only to a specific company and not to an entire group, will the government hand over public assets—quite possibly, blue chips—to management facing criminal proceedings from the securities market regulator? That would take some nerve given the emotions aroused by the Balco sale.

Indeed the question needs to be asked whether the government's due diligence is at all adequate. In the case of the Balco sale, the government ought to have known that Sterlite was under investigation by SEBI. If it knew, how come it went ahead with the sale without awaiting the outcome of the investigation?

The privatisation of Indian Airlines too raises a question mark over the government's due diligence standards. With the race having narrowed down to just two parties, the government is said to be thinking of inviting fresh bids as one of them may get rejected on 'national security' considerations. How is it that the threat to national security was not detected much earlier in the selection process?

At the very least, the SEBI order underlines the need for government to improve its system of vetting bidders for Public Sector Units (PSUs). However, nobody should be under any illusion that this is insurance against deals being derailed at the last minute or even after they have been struck. India's business community does not boast of too many clean hands. So the possibility of unsavoury information about the winning bidder coming to light at any point and upsetting arrangements can never be discounted.

The SEBI order provides an opportunity to reflect on the fundamental limitations to undertaking privatisation in a context such as ours. Success in privatisation is predicated on the prior existence of both a strong law enforcement system and mechanisms of corporate governance. The first ensures that crooks do not end up in control of public assets; the second ensures competence on the part of those who acquire public assets before and after the sale. Neither condition obtains here.

These limitations have implications for privatisation policy that it would be unwise to ignore. In a critique of reforms in the former Soviet Union, Joseph Stiglitz has argued that politically sensitive privatisations of large firms must await the creation of the necessary institutional infrastructure; only small and medium firms must be privatised initially. (*"Whither reform? Ten years of the Transition", Annual World Bank Conference on Development Economics, 1999*). This argument could be apply to our context as well.

Secondly, it must be accepted that privatisation will necessarily be a long drawn-out affair, the incessant clamour for the government to 'get on with its job' notwithstanding. The timing and price have to be right, the method of sale has to be carefully determined in each case, the screening of bidders has to be thorough and there will be situations where deals are called off in the light of new information. Brushing aside these issues will jeopardise the very effectiveness of privatisation.

Thirdly, because the process will be long drawn-out, the government cannot afford to ignore restructuring prior to privatisation. To do so is to condemn public sector firms to paralysis and under-performance for years before sale actually occurs. This can only result in the government realising poor values from sale of enterprises. Clearly, a radical reappraisal of the present approach to privatisation is called for.

April 26, 2001

Rethinking PSU sell-offs

The government's disinvestment programme has run aground. The Prime Minister and his deputy can opt to go along with the self-righteous attitude of the minister for disinvestment and smother dissent. Or they can revisit the proposition in light of the experience gained so far and forge a consensus on how we must proceed with disinvestment. The former course would put the sustainability of the programme at risk; the latter requires a willingness to think through the genuine concerns raised.

The problem has arisen because the ministry for disinvestment has sought to equate disinvestment, which is the sale of government equity in PSUs, with privatization, which is the transfer of control to a private party. The government's policy is to reduce its stakes in the generality of PSUs to 26 per cent. There is no presumption that in all instances this must happen through strategic sale to a private party. This was certainly not the understanding of the first Disinvestment Commission headed by GV Ramakrishna.

It is contended that strategic sale will maximise revenues and make for superior firm efficiency. This is a moot proposition even in theory: it is true only under the most stringent conditions of auction design. It is certainly undermined by the limited experience we have had so far. The sale of airport Centaur hotel in Mumbai is a glaring example. A private group, which bought the hotel for Rs 83 crore, has sold it within four months to another private party for Rs 115 crore.

There is everything to be said in favour of having an active after-market for assets for this serves to improve firm efficiency. But one would expect a resale to take place with a certain lapse in time and consequent to the generation of information by the first buyer. Such is not the case here. When an asset is resold for a higher price in such a short period, it does mean that the auction process was inefficient in the sense of being unable to attract the highest bidder. This could well be the result of collusion among parties, a factor that the auction literature highlights as detracting from the objective of allocative efficiency.

No less troubling, although relatively unnoticed, is the sale of CMC to the Tata group. The Tatas acquired CMC in the first week of October, 2001 at a price of Rs 197 per share. A year later the price hovers around Rs 500. It cannot be that the Tatas have effected a stunning improvement in the firm in such a short period. Nor can the rise in CMC's price be ascribed to expectations of improvement following privatisation. The price of CMC touched a peak of Rs 312 in the last week of September, 2001 when TCS emerged as the lone bidder before dropping to Rs 261 after the deal was approved.

Indeed, if the change in management were the dominant factor behind the price rise, this would be reflected in a sharp rise in the price-earnings multiple. In point of fact, the multiple (using quarterly averages in CMIE's Prowess database) has increased only modestly from 18.5 in September 2001 to 20.3 in September 2002. The key factor in the price rise is the increase in the earnings per share (EPS) in the same period from Rs 16.66 to Rs 25.19. (By December 2001, just two months after the strategic sale, the EPS had risen to Rs 26.76). Between March 31, 2001 and March 31, 2002, the EPS rose phenomenally from Rs 7.46 to Rs 25.76—a rise not matched at industry majors Infosys and Wipro. This does raise the question whether profits at CMC was not understated in order to facilitate an early success in strategic sales.

Does the price at which a PSU is sold to a private buyer matter? Yes, because revenue maximisation is an objective. It is also important in so far as revenue maximisation is the result of an efficient auction process whereby an asset is sold to a party that values it the most. It follows that where there is evidence of under-pricing, the objective of allocative efficiency, which is the primary objective of privatisation, is unlikely to be met. Such under-pricing is endemic to privatisation because governments in fiscal distress are desperate to realise revenues and because the investment advisors have every incentive to see deals going through.

So when politicians, and especially ministers who oversee PSUs, express scepticism about selling a PSU to a lone bidder or voice concern about public assets being sold cheaply, they are, in their own way, articulating issues that are central to the efficacy of disinvestment. To brush these aside and to portray the minister for disinvestment as a lone hero battling assorted villains in government is to reduce matters to Bollywood terms.

October 24, 2002

Strategic sale vs public offer

The bitter tussle over disinvestment in the two oil majors, BPCL and HPCL, produced a compromise last month. While HPCL is to be offered for strategic sale, BPCL will be divested through a public offer. In HPCL, a 34 per cent stake would be sold to a private buyer and the government's equity holding would fall to 12 per cent consequent to the strategic sale. In BPCL, however, the government would hold 26 per cent of equity following the public offer, thus retaining control.

Advocates of strategic sale view the outcome as an unhappy concession to the nation's tribe of politicians. An outright transfer of control to a private party would be the best thing to happen in all cases. They need to think again. Strategic sale has *not* been the dominant method of sale in privatization sales the world over. Phased disinvestment with government control falling over time has been the preferred mode. Diehard proponents of strategic sales need to chew over this.

The empirical evidence on the methods of sale in privatisation is documented in an unpublished paper that has been widely presented. (*The choice of private versus public capital markets: evidence from privatizations, August 2002, William L Megginson, Robert C Nash, Jeffrey M Netter and Annette B Poulsen.*) The first author, Prof. Megginson, is, perhaps, the best-known empiricist in the field.

The authors distinguish between two broad methods of sale: asset sale and share issue privatization (SIP). The former involves an outright sale of a large chunk of a state-owned enterprise (SOE) through private capital markets (say, through the auction route). The latter involves sale of shares through public equity markets. What we call strategic sale in India falls broadly in the category of asset sales, with the difference that it is also being used in the cases of listed SOEs.

Using a sample of 2477 sales of state-owned enterprises that raised $1.2 trillion between 1977 and 2000, the authors found that SIPs accounted for the larger portion of proceeds, $745 billion, while asset sales produced $445 billion. The average enterprise value in an SIP was $4.6 billion whereas that in an asset sale was $641 million. (BPCL and HPCL, with a market capitalization of $1.2 billion and $2.1 billion respectively, come somewhere in between).

The authors found support for the hypothesis that SIPs were more likely in less developed capital markets, probably as a way of developing these markets. More significant in the context of the ongoing debate in the country, SIPs were the preferred mode of sale for larger and more profitable SOEs. One reason, the authors suggest, could be that asymmetric information problems are less for larger and more profitable offerings, so it is easy to attract investors to SIPs in these cases. Besides, private buyers for large enterprises would be hard to find.

The paper makes another point that is worthy of note. In the average SIP, governments sold 35 per cent of the firm's capital. (The figure was 74 per cent in asset sales.) This means that governments continued to hold a majority stake in the firms concerned following disinvestment. It is not just that governments the world over did not think it necessary to transfer control to a private party for the most part. They also did not believe that for privatisation to work, government needed to shed a majority stake in SOEs at one go.

Does privatisation of this sort work? Wouldn't the continuance of large equity holdings by government inhibit performance, as advocates of strategic sale contend?

Surprise, surprise, SIPs do work. There is a large body of research, including work co-authored by Prof Megginson, that has documented post-privatisation improvements in performance in SIPs using a variety of parameters.

Could it be that it is the existence of large institutional buyers in SIPs in some economies that makes the difference to performance? Not really. Most SIPs have targeted retail investors numbering in millions, creating extremely atomistic ownership structures. And yet the enterprises fare better than before.

Performance improves in SIPs despite continued government control because listing on the exchanges brings about a profit orientation in firms that was missing earlier. Besides, governments are careful not to interfere too much in commercial decisions for fear of upsetting millions of individual investors.

The empirical evidence speaks for itself: phased disinvestment through public offers works. It has also been the preferred method of sale worldwide especially where large, profitable enterprises are concerned. Those in government as well as their supporters outside who bang on about the virtues of strategic sale are, it would seem, a trifle out of touch with reality.

February 13, 2003

Macro-Implications

Privatisation and the fiscal deficit: what can we expect?

You have to say this for the finance minister: he has not used privatisation receipts to fudge the fiscal deficit number. While the budget shows receipts of Rs 12,000 crore from privatisation, the fiscal deficit is unlikely to be affected if the target is not met. This is because Rs 5000 crore of expenditure is explicitly linked to privatisation receipts. If receipts fall short of this figure, expenditure will be commensurately axed, so there will be no impact on the fiscal deficit.

Even the balance Rs 7000 crore is earmarked for items that are discretionary in nature. So, unless new items of expenditure pop up in the year, the finance minister will not be deflected very far from his fiscal deficit target of 4.7 per cent of GDP for 2001-02 even if privatisation does not pan out as planned.

The finance minister's approach, however, suffers from at least two infirmities. One, if privatisation receipts disappoint, budgetary support to social and infrastructure sectors will decline from the modest level at which it has been pegged. The finance minister should not win applause for adhering to the fiscal deficit target by sacrificing minimal investment in physical and human infrastructure.

Secondly, linking capital expenditure with privatisation receipts creates uncertainty in respect of the government's capital expenditure and this could inhibit the private sector's own investment plans. For these reasons, it is, perhaps, advisable to keep privatisation proceeds out of the budgetary arithmetic.

The more important issue, now that privatisation seems to be gathering steam, is the likely impact of privatisation on the fiscal deficit over an extended time horizon. Because many PSUs contribute little or nothing to the exchequer, it is blithely assumed that privatisation will automatically improve the fiscal position.

Yet even loss-making firms can have positive market values. And the condition for privatisation to result in a lower fiscal deficit is the same for all firms: the sale price must exceed a firm's market value under government control. We do know that it is difficult to determine whether this condition has been satisfied in a given case. However, what can we expect in general?

Contrary to general supposition, it is not unreasonable to expect PSUs to be sold below their market prices and the fiscal impact of privatisation to be adverse. This is because privatisation is typically resorted to when the economy is doing badly as reflected in an unsatisfactory fiscal position, depressed stock prices etc. The very urgency attendant on privatisation in such conditions tends to make for underpricing of PSUs.

Sale prices of PSUs would be lower than the market price also because of the underpricing endemic to initial price offerings (IPOs) and that is seen to be even greater in privatisation IPOs. It is suggested that the auction method addresses the problem of underpricing, hence strategic sales should be the preferred option. This is the argument put forward in the Balco sale. There was international bidding; as Sterlite came up with the highest bid, this must be close to the true value of the firm.

Alas, the literature in corporate finance does not offer certitudes of the sort peddled by politicians. The question of which method leads to better realisation of value—IPOs or auctions—remains unresolved. It is fair to suggest that in markets such as ours the auction method is beset with serious problems.

One reason is that information asymmetries would be acute in the case of public sector firms, especially since most are not listed. This makes it difficult for bidders, particularly overseas bidders who lack a feel for the hidden strengths of public sector firms, to determine intrinsic values. In the case of Balco, the very fact that the winning bid was nearly twice the other bid does point to imperfect information. One would imagine that, in a well-managed auction, where adequate information was made available to bidders, the differences in bids would not be so great.

Another problem with the auction method is liquidity constraints: at any given point, there may not be enough firms in the aluminium or related businesses with the resources to make a bid for Balco. With IPOs, firms face a wider pool of investors, both in the domestic and international markets, and this could potentially make price discovery more efficient.

There is no golden rule that tells us which method is superior in a given instance. However, in either method, a degree of underpricing appears inevitable. Governments may still press ahead with privatisation in pursuit of the primary objective of improved efficiency in the economy. But any presumption that the fiscal deficit would be favourably impacted is ill-founded.

March 15, 2001

Privatisation fancies and follies

The frisson of excitement generated by news of a great leap forward in privatization is almost palpable. Where ministers were loath to mention any target for a given year, the tantalising prospect of upwards of Rs 25,000 crore in revenues is now being dangled before our eyes. Light at last, it would seem, at the end of the fiscal tunnel. Yet the notion that privatisation is a miracle cure for fiscal problems rests on such weak foundations that it is astonishing that this proposition is heard so often in popular discourse.

The secretary for the ministry for disinvestment, Pradip Baijal, adumbrates this proposition in a recent article in the *Economic and Political Weekly* (April 27, 2002). He argues that the government has realised Rs 7164 crore from strategic sales in the past two years. Given the government's borrowing rate of around 10 per cent, this translates into an annual benefit to government of around Rs 700 crore (which would imply a corresponding reduction in the fiscal deficit).

The fallacy in this argument has to do with the conventional measurement of the fiscal deficit. Such measurement includes the government's liabilities but not its assets. If we think of the government's deficit as changes in net worth—that is, changes in debt minus changes in assets—then it should be apparent that the sale of assets makes no difference to the deficit. When the government uses asset sales to retire debt, the stream of future interest payments is reduced to the same extent as the income stream foregone through the sale of the asset.

The point was made years ago by an economist, George Yarrow, co-author with John Vickers of the classic treatise, *Privatization (MIT Press).* In his paper, " Privatization in theory and practice" (*Economic Journal, April 1986*), Yarrow went on to add, "Thus, as a first approximation, selling public assets is equivalent to selling fixed-interest debt. Both imply the mortgage of future income to improve current cash flow. For this reason, it would be surprising if asset sales represent a free lunch through which current government deficits can be financed without upward pressure on interest rates and consequent crowding out of private sector expenditure". So much for the notion that privatisation proceeds could, by retiring public debt, induce a virtuous cycle of lower interest rates and higher private investment.

In their book, Vickers and Yarrow provide two important qualifications to this proposition. The net worth of the public sector remains unchanged only if the sale is correctly priced and there are no transaction costs. Neither of these conditions is met in practice. The odds, therefore, are that privatisation actually worsens the government's long-term financial position.

The impact on public finances would, of course, be positive if the efficiency of the firm sold improved markedly under new management. But this requires competition, strong corporate governance, and an active market for corporate control, conditions not easily met even in developed markets leaving alone in the Indian context.

Indeed, it must be recognized that there is an inherent tension between the pursuit of strategic sales and the objective of improving firm efficiency. The focus on strategic sale is leading up to a disregard for the market structure implications of such sales. This was seen in the sale of IPCL to the Reliance group. It could happen again if the Hindalco-Indal combine ends up bagging Nalco. One of the paradoxes of privatisation worldwide has been that, while in principle it is intended to usher in greater competition, it has ended up creating greater concentration which militates against the objective of improving efficiency.

Strategic sales are also likely to undermine the central objective of improvement in firm efficiency by perpetuating forms of ownership that are inimical to this objective. What is required today is the rejuvenation of the public sector through an altogether new culture of governance—broad-based ownership of shares and professional management subject to control by institutional investors. Instead the emphasis on strategic sale raises the disconcerting prospect of enormous assets being handed over to precisely the narrow set of family-managed industrial groups that are themselves in need of radical change. It is hard to conceive of a greater tragedy for the Indian economy.

We need to abandon wrong-headed notions of using privatisation to manage fiscal problems and to focus instead on the central issues of governance and efficiency. Once we do so, the merits of phased disinvestment as distinct from strategic sale should become blindingly obvious at least in the case of the better-performing PSUs.

August 1, 2002

Deregulation is the key

	Market cap (31/7/02) (Rs crore)	Market cap (31/1/02) (Rs crore)	Increase in market cap (Rs crore)
BHEL	4185	3395	791
GAIL	6334	5404	930
IOC	15464	10356	5108
ONGC	49929	19457	30472
SAIL	4461	2024	2437
Total for 35 cos	152986	81925	71061
8/10			43%
(5+6+7+8+9)/10			56%

Source: *Prowess* database, CMIE

In the period January 1—July 31 of this year, the market capitalisation of 35 public sector undertakings (PSUs) listed on the exchanges has risen by 87 per cent. Privatisation enthusiasts are jubilant. They ascribe the sharp increase to Arun Shourie's success in giving a push to privatisation. The market, they say, is responding to the prospect of improved returns at these PSUs consequent to privatisation.

Sorry to spoil the party but an analysis of the data does not quite bear out this hypothesis.

Of the increase in market capitalisation in the period, nearly 43 per cent is accounted for by one company, ONGC, alone. And ONGC is *not* a candidate for privatisation.

If we include four other companies that nobody has thus far talked of privatising—BHEL, IOC, GAIL and SAIL—then 56 per cent of the increase in market capitalisation is accounted for PSUs in which we can expect further disinvestment, not privatisation.

Even if assume that all the rest are certain to be privatised, the certainty of privatisation has contributed only to the smaller proportion of the increase in market capitalisation—44 per cent.

It would be fair to conclude, therefore, that the rise in prices of PSU stocks is more a vote for disinvestment at some of the biggest companies in the list than it is for privatisation at the rest.

There are only two companies in the list whose market capitalisation has declined, FACT and VSNL. The writer does not wish to be as blinkered as some of the votaries of privatisation and claim that the decline at VSNL is on account of the firm having been privatised.

It could be contended that, while the five companies cited above are not due to be privatised in the near future, the market knows they will be privatised eventually. It is this happy prospect that has got factored into their prices. If this is true, then all the companies should have seen a sharp re-rating related to an impending change of ownership—the price-earnings multiple at all companies should have gone up significantly. This is not the case.

Over the period examined, the price-earnings ratio for ONGC has risen steeply from 3.33 to 8.06. So also at BHEL—from 5.74 to 9.29. The increases at GAIL and IOC have, however, been modest—4.83 to 5.41 and 4.50 to 5.35 respectively. (SAIL has been incurring losses, so we cannot compute the ratio in its case). Either the omniscient market has concluded that ONGC and BHEL are due for privatisation whereas GAIL and IOC are not. Or, which is more plausible, the re-rating has to do with improved profitability under government ownership, the extent of improvement varying from firm to firm, and not with privatisation.

The price-earnings multiple has almost doubled for HPCL—from 6.45 to 12.66. For BPCL the increase has been only from 8.86 to 10.87. Will somebody explain why the market is ecstatic about the prospect of a change of ownership at HPCL but not at BPCL?

It should be apparent that the attempt to relate the behaviour of PSU stock prices to the recent thrust towards privatisation is far too glib. The rise in market capitalisation at the petroleum companies accounts for 65 per cent of the increase in total market capitalisation. This rise is more likely a response to deregulation in the oil sector, which impacts favourably on the bottomlines of oil companies, than to the prospect of privatisation.

But the self-serving interpretation of PSU stock price behaviour should not come as a surprise. The bane of many of the studies on privatisation has been their inability to disentangle the ownership effect from that of deregulation. Privatisation is very often one component of a larger deregulation package that tends to stimulate economies and improve firm performance. However, very few studies separate the two effects and advocates of privatisation have been only too eager to ascribe all the improvement to withdrawal of state ownership.

Price deregulation has, of course, been a big factor in the improved performance of PSUs in which disinvestment has taken place. But other factors too that have contributed—greater autonomy, the induction of independent directors and the increased focus on profitability that has come with listing. To argue that the phenomenal improvement in performance at the bigger PSUs that has resulted must, nevertheless, not come in the way of privatisation points to ideological cussedness of a high order.

August 29, 2002

INTERNATIONAL ECONOMY

Introductory Note

When I began writing my column in 1997, I suffered the blues that most columnists go through. Would there be a topic for me to comment on? Would I have something to say? I need not have feared. The East Asian crisis burst upon the world in all its intensity within a few months of beginning my column and it offered plenty of column fodder, Even as the countries in the region and the IMF scrambled to find a suitable response, we were inundated with diagnoses and prescriptions for East Asia's maladies. The issue has, of course, been analysed threadbare since, so I have not included all the articles I wrote on the subject.

Looking back, I notice that my immediate reactions have been vindicated by much scholarly comment since, especially the position taken by people like Joseph Stiglitz. I questioned the view that there was a fundamental problem with the growth model followed by East Asian countries or that 'crony capitalism' was responsible for the crisis. I argued that state intervention had, in fact, produced spectacular growth rates in the region and that openness to capital flows was what had caused problems. India's policy makers, by implication, had been right to be cautious about capital account convertibility

I was critical of moves to get the East Asian countries to close down failed banks, saying that this would exacerbate the downturn. Bank management needed to be replaced but the banks needed to be kept going. I pointed out that the IMF was imposing on East Asia prescriptions that had not been followed in the case of bank failures in the industrial countries. I would not think it necessary to change any of these assessments today.

The vicissitudes of the American economy and the international economy came to be duly chronicled in my column. As I happened to be in the US when some of the pieces were written, I had the advantage of being able to watch developments closely. The resilience of the American economy in the face of sharp stock market declines or shocks such as the attack on the World Trade Centre was a recurring theme. The soundness of the American banking system and the readiness of the federal authorities to follow a loose monetary policy the moment growth is threatened, I argued, were reasons why falls in the stock market would not seriously undermine US economic growth.

In keeping with the general tenor of my column, I drew on academic or policy research to highlight trends or to provide explanations. I cited a paper in the *American Economic Review* that debunked the belief that the chairman of the US Fed, Alan Greenspan, had superior insights into the US economy that informed his deft moves on interest rates. The paper showed that Greenspan was, in fact, following a simple monetary policy rule.

The *World Economic Outlook,* published twice every year by the IMF, was a rich source of summaries of research on international economy. One interesting finding was that business cycles in the industrial world had become more benign, with longer periods of expansion and shorter periods of recession in a given business cycle. Denizens of the industrial world would be justified in thinking that the world had become a better place to live in. Another insight provided by the *Outlook,* following the bursting of the dotcom bubble, was that equity price busts are to be less feared than housing price bursts and that bank based financial systems are more vulnerable to the latter. As India happens to be more of a bank--based financial system, the absence of a housing price bubble is a matter of comfort.

Interview: Lawrence J White

Lawrence J White, who obtained his doctorate in economics from Harvard University, is the Arthur E. Imperatore Professor of Economics at Stern School of Business, New York University. His primary research areas include financial regulation, anti-trust, network industries, international banking and applied microeconomics, and he has published numerous articles in leading journals. He is the author of *The S&L Debacle: Public Policy Lessons for Bank and Thrift Regulation*, among other books and he is the co-editor (with John Kwoka) of *The Antitrust Revolution*, the fourth edition of which is in preparation.

While at Stern, Professor White has taken three leaves of absence to serve in the US Government: on the Senior Staff of the President's Council of Economic Advisors (1978-79); as Chief Economist of the Antitrust Division of the US Department of Justice (1982-83); and as a Board Member of the Federal Home Loan Bank Board (1986-89).

1. *Let us begin with the East Asian crisis, a phenomenon that has been analysed threadbare by now. So what finally is the bottom line—was there a fundamental problem with the growth model followed by those economies or was the problem mainly the result of unbridled financial liberalisation?*

A. I don't think that the growth model was wrong; it's hard to argue with high rates of savings that generally are put to productive uses. But some investments and loans clearly were badly conceived, and the prudential regulation of banks and similar depository institutions was inadequate. Prudential regulation is not easy to do properly. Most people don't understand banks to begin with, and the prudential regulatory issues are even harder to grasp.

2. *Do you believe that East Asia has overcome its problems and growth is back on track? Or are the days of high economic growth a thing of the past?*

A. I think that the problems are largely in the past. But as economies mature, it's increasingly hard to maintain high rates of growth—because it's hard to maintain high rates of savings and to find good places to invest those savings. Also, the easy sources of growth—e.g., transferring individuals out of low-productivity agricultural positions into higher productivity manufacturing positions — are largely used up. And then there's the issue of how to deal with services (as well as measuring output and productivity in services, etc.)

3. *Is there a recognition in the IMF today that it may have got some of its responses wrong?*

A. I'm not the right guy to ask about that.

4. *One of the issues raised in the wake of the East Asian crisis was whether the IMF itself might not be in need of reform. What reforms, if any, do you believe are needed at the IMF?*

A. The mission of the IMF needs greater clarity. I believe that the original Bretton Woods vision is a good one: to provide short-term adjustment liquidity to countries that are basically sound and are pursuing sensible policies (or are tangibly moving toward sensible policies). Anything more fundamental should be handled by the World Bank. The analogy to the Federal Reserve (or other central banks) as a provider of short-term liquidity to solvent banks, and the FDIC as the agency that deals with the fundamental structural problems of insolvent banks, is a good one.

5. *What of the other initiatives that were talked about for some time—lender of last resort for countries, an international bankruptcy mechanism, standstill and so on? Are these relevant at all?*

A. Yes, lender of last resort is relevant; see above. But I was not an enthusiast of the international bankruptcy mechanism. Yes, there needs to be an orderly way that creditors to defaulting countries can have an orderly process for resolving their claims. But the bankruptcy model, where liquidation is a possibility, and there is a court with legal jurisdiction, doesn't apply to sovereign countries.

6. *Let us turn now to the US economy. Much of the euphoria over the New Economy has since died down but, at the same time, there is a sense that there has indeed been a modest improvement in productivity growth. Can we expect the US economy to grow faster than the trend before the nineties?*

A. Yes, my guess is that the US will grow faster, but probably not achieve the rates of the 'golden age' of 1945-65. Part of the issue is surely measurement of services, of quality improvements, and of new-product introductions. Also, a higher rate of domestic saving would likely help, as new ideas and innovations more readily get embodied in new investment.

7. *There is a perception abroad that, no matter how good US economic growth might be, the old protectionist enclaves will remain—agriculture, textiles, steel, etc. Would you agree?*

A. The old protectionist enclaves are indeed powerful, because the mercantilist model still has a powerful hold on the political process, as well as there being only imperfect ways in which 'winners' can compensate 'losers'. Nevertheless, over a longer sweep of things—say, since 1945—it is amazing, how much has been accomplished. But when I see the US's distorted agricultural system, and steel protectionism, and textile tariffs, I sometimes get discouraged.

8. *Corporate governance may well have been the great disenchantment of the new millennium, with some of the biggest names in the US corporate world turning out to have feet of clay. Even before the present bout of scandals erupted, there was a school of thought in academic that believed that the governance issue was overdone and that competition is what will really work. Has this school been proved right or is governance back on track with Sarbannes-Oxley?*

A. No, competition is not a solution to governance problems. It's all about asymmetric information (between shareholder-owners, and senior managers), and competition doesn't cure that. Senior managements can make a lot of bad decisions—e.g., engage in a lot of value-reducing mergers—and they can dissipate rents (producer's surplus) even in roughly competitive industries (e.g., US banking). And some industries are oligopolistic, giving senior managers even more room.

I am not a great fan of Sarbanes-Oxley. It's probably a modest move in the right direction. But we need a better incentive structure to keep boards of directors responsive to the shareholder-owners' interests and to keep auditors responsive to parties other than management, and S-O provides too little of that. Reducing the power of poison pills and other protective devices and strengthening the takeover market for corporate control would help. So would expensing of executive options.

What about institutional shareholders or even minority shareholders appointing their nominees to boards instead of leaving it to management to select board members?

9. *The flip side to the heightened concern over governance is said to be a diminished appetite for risk-taking in corporate management? Do you believe this is a serious problem?*

A. No. That's not the problem. It's just that managements are often excessively optimistic and too focused on increasing the sizes of their enterprises, willy-nilly.

10. *There is also some rethinking over the role of high-powered incentives for top management, chiefly stock options. There was always the possibility that such incentives could cause management to take undesirably high risks in the knowledge that somebody else would suffer if things went wrong. Are high-powered incentives perceived to be part of the problem?*

A, The problem was their short-term nature, the absence of expensing, and the incentives that they generate for reinvestment rather than dividend payment.

11. *Finally, a question about India. As a student in the US in the late eighties, I found to my dismay that India was not on the American radar screen at all. Now, thanks to our successes in software, we seem to be registering in the US consciousness. From the detached perspective of an academic, where do you see India figuring in the overall American scheme of things?*

A. Yes, India has not been a major focus for US foreign economic policy—partly because India itself was not open until the mid-1990s or later. But the outsourcing of software, customer servicing, etc., is increasing the effective trade between the two countries. And I hope that a receding tide of protectionism in both countries will increase economic interchange and the consciousness of each country in the other's economic policies (for the good!).

Country Perspectives

Wobble, wobble

Until recently, the industrial economies and, particularly the US, could afford to look on while the East Asian miracle unraveled in the wake of the currency depreciation in those economies. Firms with East Asian exposure would have to trim their earnings forecasts, but the growth story, particularly in the American context, would not be fundamentally altered.

Now that the crisis has engulfed South Korea and Japan, the eleventh and second largest economies in the world, complacency is giving way to a touch of alarm. And the alarm is not entirely on account of American security concerns in the region. If the threat to the Korean won had not been countered by an infusion of capital, it could have triggered a further bout of devaluation in the region, this time embracing China and Hong Kong as well. That, in turn, raised the prospect of the American trade deficit widening to a point where protectionism, already resurgent, would become impossible to rein in.

Moreover, any collapse of the South Korean economy would drag down Japan, given Japanese firms' considerable exposure to Korea. The tottering Nikkei would fall even further. A fall in the Nikkei threatens the solvency of Japanese banks because of their large holdings of equity. If the holes in the balance sheets became too large, the banks would have no recourse but to dump their holdings of international paper. Interest rates worldwide would shoot up and derail growth in the other industrial economies. The Americans are breathing down then necks of the Japanese government to make sure that doesn't happen.

It's important to understand what's common to East Asia, Korea and Japan, and what is not. In East Asia, there is both a solvency problem and a liquidity problem. The solvency problem arose because there were huge inflows of capital in recent years, much of it going into non-tradeables such as real estate, that could not be serviced because of a slowing down of exports. The liquidity problem relates to the high proportion of short-term liabilities in foreign inflows, and to gross imprudence on the part of banks and has resulted in funds drying up for industry.

South Korea has primarily a liquidity problem. On the external front, the problem has been caused again by excessive short-term borrowings. Domestically, there is a shortage of liquidity because the slowing down of growth has led to a steep increase in non-performing assets of banks—understandable in an economy in which the leading conglomerates are highly leveraged.

It's hard to argue that Japan has either a liquidity or a solvency problem when it happens to be the world's biggest exporter of capital: Japan's reserves of gold and foreign currency are estimated at around $220 billion. No, it's not that the Japanese economy as a whole has a problem comparable to East Asia or South Korea; it's just that the Japanese financial sector has a major problem. This problem cannot be left to market forces because huge sales of American securities could lead to deflation being exported to the other industrial economies. The solution that the West wants is one that would minimize pain to itself: the re-capitalization of the stronger Japanese banks by the government.

It's an axiom with even the most fervent advocates of the market that a big bank cannot be allowed to fail. Governments applied this doctrine within their respective countries. But now, as a corollary to financial integration, the doctrine is beginning to mean that a big bank in another country, that is a holder of my country's paper, cannot be allowed to fail.

Both in South Korea and in Japan, the problems are the creation of the private sector; it is not fiscally irresponsible governments that have created a problem tailor-made for the IMF. This is being interpreted to mean the failure of crony capitalism as distinct from the real thing. Banks were forced to lend to favoured industrial groups, there was fudging of accounts (abetted by the local affiliates of leading international accounting firms), regulators were willing to look the other way, and high leverage was a standing invitation to disaster. It is contended that in a more efficient market, such lapses would not have been possible. But would the market have delivered phenomenal growth rates in the first place? That deserves a column to itself.

December 6, 1997

Limits to market

Many commentators have been quick to suggest that the problems in South Korea and Japan stem from the state creating distortions in the market. The lesson for these economies is to allow freer rein to market forces. This is debatable. Recent events in many ways reinforce the case for state intervention. And they certainly argue for caution in opening economies to international flows.

Both Korea and Japan have followed a strategy of corporate growth through reliance on banks, instead of on the stock market. In the process, banks got over-exposed to a few industrial groups, and companies ended up getting highly leveraged. Critics say that, in a more efficient market, there would have been a better balance between debt and equity and hence the economies would have been less susceptible to financial turmoil.

True, but it's doubtful that the stock market could have facilitated the phenomenal growth rates of these economies. First, the stock market in its early stages could not have matched the funds provided by the banking system. Secondly, family businesses that have powered growth of industry would have been inhibited by the dilution of control necessitated by the equity route. Most importantly, the single-minded focus on growth at the expense of return on equity would not have been possible in the stock market model.

Growth in South Korea and Japan will slow down in the next few years, but the growth story over a longish period (including the next few years) would still be a compelling one. It would be a different matter if the problems in the financial sector were so grave as to lead to a prolonged recession akin to Latin America's "lost decade" of the eighties. But if the banking sector's problem is merely the obverse of high economic growth, that hardly constitutes a repudiation of the growth strategy. Indeed, the growth strategy would be valid even if we accepted that Japan and Korea need a course correction at this point.

In both Korea and Japan, banks will need to be recapitalized by the government. The government will thus be indirectly picking up some of the tabs for the private sector. This is government spending in industry by another name: the banking sector will, in effect, have acted as a conduit for government funds to the private sector.

The important lesson that emerges is that, over a reasonably long period, government funding of industry is critical to sustaining a high growth rate and building a strong industrial base. Until recently, Korea and Japan were viewed as essentially market-driven economies in which government merely backed bright ideas in the private sector. After the present bout of government bail-outs, this view is hardly tenable.

The form that government funding takes will be specific to each context. In a totalitarian context (such as Korea's) or a polity dominated by one party (such as Japan's), the government can opt to provide funds to a few private groups. In a democratic set-up, it is difficult for a clutch of politicians and bureaucrats to narrow down availability of public funds to a select few. Yet, following from the above, government has to be an important mover, if not the prime mover, of industrial growth. That leaves us in India with no choice other than the public sector as the receptacle for government funds earmarked for industry. We need to question whether return on equity constitutes an appropriate basis for judging the public sector's role in propelling growth.

Of the prescriptions urged on Korea, the most dubious is greater openness to foreign flows into the financial sector. It was a speculative run on the won that greatly magnified the problems of the financial sector and devastated Korean industry. So what Korea needs at this stage, perhaps, is less integration with international markets, not more.

The experiences of Japan and Korea underline the limits to market, and they reinforce the view (propounded by, among others, Prof. Robert Wade in *Governing the Market*) that state intervention can often yield better results. The point about curbing short-term inflows and moving cautiously in respect of capital account convertibility has been made by many. But the need for state participation in industry is, perhaps, the more striking lesson to have emerged from the recent crisis.

December 11, 1997

Medicine that kills

Not for the first time, the IMF is drawing flak over the cures it has prescribed for a sick economy. The appropriateness of fiscal and monetary tightening for South Korea, a country whose internal and external deficits are not really out of control, has been questioned; so also the IMF's asking for opening up of the financial sector after the havoc wrought by international speculators.

But the IMF's focus this time is different. It's on financial sector restructuring. Many elements in its restructuring package make sense. But in asking for the closure of unviable banks, the IMF is on shaky ground. Administering strong medicine to a patient who is already debilitated can kill; sometimes, you need to wait for the patient to recover a bit.

When a firm has gone bust, it makes sense to let it go to the wall. Applied to a bank, however, the logic of liquidation isn't as straightforward as it seems. For the economy, the costs of liquidating a bank tend to outweigh the costs of keeping it afloat through recapitalization.

What happens when a bank is wound up? Assets are realized, and deposits redeemed. These deposits would then head for other banks; new loans would replace the sound loans erased by the closure of the failed bank. In effect, deposits from bank A will have migrated to banks B, C and D; so also loans. From the standpoint of the economy, what has changed? Very little. This is the best case scenario. In reality, there will be transaction costs; and costs of dislocation to the economy in the period that deposits of the failed bank find new havens. Hence the general reluctance to let a big bank fail: such failures impose huge costs on the economy.

But what about the costs of a bailout? The issue came to the fore when the Savings and Loans disaster occurred in the US and there was a hue and cry over taxpayers' money being used to bail them out, in many cases after deposits had fled. Martin Feldstein, Harvard Professor and former Chairman of the President's Council of Economic Advisors, argued that because most of the bailout funds would go towards reconstructing deposits at failed S&Ls, there would be no impact on US income and employment.

Private savings tapped by government bonds would go back to the same pool as redeemed deposits, and duly show up as loans. Savings and investment after the bailout would thus end up at the same level as before the S&L failures. This is an exaggeration, but because equity in a bank is small in relation to assets, the costs of recapitalization are far lower than the gains to the economy. That explains why recapitalization is preferred to liquidation of a big bank.

Then why not recapitalize every time a bank fails? You can't afford to because that would create moral hazard: bank management would have no incentive to prevent failure. And bank failures do imply loss of assets in the economy. It's a different matter that, once the loss in assets has occurred, recapitalization imposes lower costs relative to liquidation. But the original loss in assets must be prevented. It becomes necessary, therefore, to let banks fail, so that managers know that failure implies a cost to them.

It's one thing, however, to enforce this penalty in good times or when the odd bank has failed; quite another when the economy is in the throes of asset deflation and when several banks face closure. South Korea's economy will recover faster if banks are recapitalized instead of being closed: what was good for S&Ls in the US is surely good for Korean banking as well.

But the IMF must address moral hazard because that is the price its donors will demand for helping out the beleaguered country. There are other ways to improve a financial system, and these have been proposed for Korea: better disclosure, norms for ensuring quality of loan assets, competition from foreign banks etc. Now is not the time to close down banks. Besides, the IMF should be wary of pushing moral hazard too far: after all, an important motivation behind its rescue package is saving private lenders in the West from their own follies in Korea.

December 25, 1997

Lesson from Jakarta

There is a lesson that's common to two unconnected events, the fall-out of the Indian explosions that shook the world and the upheavals in Indonesia that shared the headlines in the same week. It has to do with the relationship between an open economy and a nation's sovereignty.

The Indonesian economy has been brought to its knees in a matter of months. The economy, which grew at 4.7 per cent in 1997, is projected to contract by 7-10 per cent in 1998; inflation will rise from 6.6 per cent to around 50 per cent; the rupiah has fallen from 2600 last year to around 12000 today. The mobs are out on the streets.

It's easy to fall for the line plugged by the Western media, about President Suharto's brand of crony capitalism and how it proved to be Indonesia's undoing. Like good dictators everywhere, Suharto, no doubt, lined his pockets. But the train of events that plunged his country into turmoil and eventually unseated him cannot be ascribed to his excesses. The fault lay elsewhere—in Indonesia's openness to capital flows and its high level of foreign debt, mostly in the private sector, which together rendered it vulnerable to speculative runs on its currency.

It's true that a poorly regulated banking system saddled with a high proportion of non-performing assets magnifies the impact of an exogenous shock. But the trick is to minimize the shock in the first place; and, next, to cushion its impact. Absent capital controls, Indonesia could not have avoided the shock. But the impact would have been less severe but for two significant acts on the part of the IMF—one of commission, and, the other, of omission.

The act of commission was the IMF's insistence on the closure last November of 16 banks, a move that aggravated the panic and sent the rupiah hurtling to new lows. Governments are reluctant to close banks at the best of times: the French government is currently engaged in the umpteenth bail-out of Credit Lynonnais. To close banks when an economy is tottering is criminal.

The IMF's act of omission was its failure to address the problem of privately held foreign debt. The IMF ought to have given priority to getting foreign lenders to arrange a quick rescheduling. It didn't, hoping that its rescue package would bolster the rupiah and mitigate the problem of foreign debt. That expectation has since gone up in smoke.

Contrast the woes of Indonesia, buffeted by speculators and international donors, with the dexterity with which India could contain the fall-out from its nuclear explosions. In a context of full convertibility, it would not have been difficult for the international community to orchestrate a run on the rupee and to mount pressure on India to renounce its nuclear status.

Instead, we had the heart-warming spectacle of the RBI keeping speculators in check, and the UTI and the SBI intervening in the stock market to stave off the possibility of a steep fall. The policies that made such intervention possible—limits on capital flows and a dominant presence for the public sector in the economy—impose costs in terms of efficiency, but for a country of India's size, ambitions and stage of development, they are critical to preserving national sovereignty.

There's talk now of baiting foreign investors by opening up the economy in a bigger way. That makes sense after we have established an industrial base and gone nuclear, and given that foreign capital has been thus far been marginal to the economy. Had foreign capital loomed large in the economy today, we may not have had the same leverage.

We are familiar with the trade-off between democracy and economic efficiency. But, equally, the demands of sovereignty entail their own trade-offs with economic efficiency and growth. The point is well made by Sunil Khilnani in his perceptive book, The idea of India. Elaborating on the rationale for Nehru's reliance on the public sector and his preference for heavy industries over consumer industries, he writes, ".. for Nehru, a rapid growth rate was not an end in itself. It had to be reconciled with independence and with democracy." It is this breadth of vision that is missing in our latter-day reformers.

May 28, 1998

Flu or pneumonia?

Asia's economies are poised either to shrink or to crawl. Negative GDP growth is forecast in 1998 for Japan, Hong Kong, South Korea, Malaysia, and Indonesia. Elsewhere—in China, Taiwan, Philippines and Singapore—GDP growth will slow down.

None of this is news after the turbulence of the past few months. The worry, given the battering of the yen in recent weeks, is that the pain may last longer than thought earlier; according to some, upto a decade. Asia's 'flu threatens to become a case of full-blown pneumonia.

The latter denouement could well come about, but there is no fatal inevitability to it. Bad as the situation is, it can be managed. Provided the governments of the region muster the courage to defy the ruling wisdom. The West must go along as the costs to itself of a protracted Asian slump could be prohibitively high.

Europe bounced back after two savage wars in this century. On both occasions, the industrial capacities created over decades had merely to be reactivated; the entrepreneurial culture and the industrial work ethic were in place. Asian economies, which have been laid waste by currency speculation, have these things going for them plus high savings rates, but sceptics say that over-capacity and poor governance make a rebound more difficult.

Huge capacities were added during the Second World War, but nobody talked of over-capacity. Nor can Europe's post-War recovery be ascribed to superior corporate governance. The focus on shareholder return driven by large institutional investors is a post-seventies phenomenon in the US, and it is only now beginning to touch Europe. And it arose out of concern over the quality of corporate governance in those economies.

Two factors underpinned Europe's rapid recovery: the Marshall Plan, which provided capital needed for reconstruction; and the opening up of markets through freer trade. For all the fears of a protectionist backlash, the present trade environment can hardly be judged more hostile than that which facilitated a

European recovery. The issue, then, is infusion of capital. This has been self-evident; not so the use to which capital must be put.

The IMF, whose expertise is in handling short-term balance of payments crises, has focused on propping up the currencies of the region by making war chests available to the beleaguered governments. And it has mandated measures meant for fiscally irresponsible governments when the problem was caused everywhere by the private sector. The IMF also insists its assistance must be tied to improving governance in the financial and corporate sector—through wholesale closures of industrial units and banks.

But economies cannot be revived by destroying industrial capacities and cutting off credit flows . Except for hopelessly unviable cases, banks and industrial enterprises must be recapitalized. Local businesses would have a limited ability to do so; foreign private capital can be used only selectively because no government can hand over domestic assets at bargain basement prices to foreigners. Nor can the government provide capital to businesses while leaving them in the hands of existing management. That would allow owners and managers to get away with mismanagement; foreign lenders and the IMF would never agree to such abetment of moral hazard.

That leaves only one alternative: nationalization of banks and industries. Nationalization alone would facilitate recapitalization without compromising on moral hazard. It could be accompanied by a commitment to privatize at the first opportunity down the road. Secondly, foreign lenders must share some of the pain through rescheduling, write-offs and concessional rates. When a firm fails, creditors can only claim the underlying assets; at today's deflated values, this would certainly entail a loss. Let the lenders bear this loss instead in ways that would utilize industrial assets.

The governments of the region need not rely entirely on foreign funds for recapitalization; funds can come out of budgets as fiscal deficits are generally within acceptable limits. Once industrial activity revives and exports pick up, currencies will strengthen and confidence will return. The trick is to get the wheels of industry moving.

When you are down with 'flu, self-medication is superior to rushing to a five-star hospital. Asia's stricken economies stand to recover faster if they rely on homespun wisdom instead of looking to the West for advice.

June 25, 1998

Virtual realities

On the face of it, news of the imminent demise of the US economy—and its knock-on effects on the rest of the world—appears vastly exaggerated. Despite disappointing numbers in the second quarter, the US economy still promises to notch up growth of 3 per cent in 1998. When you factor in projections for other major chunks of the world economy— 2.8 per cent for the European Union and 7 per cent for China-, it's hard to see where all the talk of a global recession is coming from.

If, nevertheless, economists shudder each time the Dow sheds a couple of hundred points from its vertiginous heights, that's because growth in the real economy is being powered to a disconcerting degree by what's happening to the virtual economy represented by financial assets of individuals and firms.

The Fed Chairman, Alan Greenspan, stated recently that $12.5 trillion (or 1.8 times America's GDP in 1997) had been added to wealth since 1994 primarily because of the rise in share prices. This virtual wealth is causing consumers to spend like crazy. By holding down costs of worker benefits under 'defined-benefits' pension programs, it's translating into bigger profit margins for companies.

The combination of consumer spending and soaring profits is boosting capital spending by companies. The virtual economy, in turn, has been bolstered by purely financial factors: foreign funds have sought refuge in the US following the East Asian meltdown even as American institutions have cut asset allocations outside the US.

As valuations have raced ahead of fundamentals, the stage is set for the asset bubble to be pricked. The concern now is that when share prices fall, the impact on the real economy will be as shattering as it was salutary in the first instance. This is, of course, typically what happened to economies in the past. The most recent parallel being cited is the protracted slump in Japan following the asset bubble of the late eighties. Such pessimism can, however, be overdone, for it ignores the strengths of America's real economy.

Suppose we pursue the comparison with Japan. The Japanese asset bubble was largely the result of enforced monetary laxity: In 1987, Japan was persuaded to cut interest rates in order to shore up a sagging dollar. Tokyo's stock market touched a record high in early 1990—and Japan's still paying for that excess. It's argued that the US Fed should have raised the interest rate over the past year to head off an asset bubble, but its carefully calibrated judgement, based entirely on the needs of the US economy, hardly qualifies as laxity on a comparable scale.

Even if the Fed was mistaken, its mistake may not prove as costly. Japan's financial institutions, with their mountains of bad loans, were acutely vulnerable to falling asset prices because of their huge exposures to the stock market. Inevitably, they radiated their problems to an over-leveraged corporate sector, thus pushing the Japanese economy into a downward spiral.

America's banks are in much better shape (and are not as exposed to stock market volatility). So is the American corporate sector, notwithstanding the wave of mergers in recent years. That's because mergers have been financed to a greater degree by stocks than by borrowed cash. So the risks of corporate and bank bankruptcies meshing together and paving the way for a recession are much lower. Another striking improvement in fundamentals is the federal budget moving into surplus, which limits the potential for a debilitating interest rate rise once inflation reasserts itself.

To be sure, consumer spending will reined in sharply once share prices in fall, but setbacks to consumers don't impair the productive capacity of an economy the way firm failures do and are easier for an economy to take in its stride. Finally, the risks of overshooting because of faulty market mechanisms (which underlay the crash of 1987) or because of lack of transparency in businesses (which caused panic in East Asia) are minimal in America's highly efficient markets. America appears largely exempt from the virtual reality that other economies have to defer to: if there is no crisis, the financial markets will invent one.

August 20, 1998

Not quite irrational

The story is by now familiar to all. At the first signs of crisis, "irrational" investors stampeded out of East Asia, causing currencies to collapse and interest rates to shoot up, which, in turn, set off a wave of bankruptcies. Yet, a close look at the composition of flows into the region in 1997 and 1998 points to differences in the behaviour of different classes of investor that suggest that each class behaved quite rationally in its own way.

According to the World Bank's *Global Development Finance,* private capital flows into East Asia and the Pacific (which includes China but excludes Korea) fell from $105 billion in 1997 (and $101 billion in 1996) to $77 billion in 1998. The decline of $28 billion is overwhelmingly on account of a $24 billion decline in private loans which fell from $31 billion to $7 billion in the period.

But other investors have responded differently. Foreign direct investors, for instance, have emphatically defied the herd mentality to the extent of being contrarian. FDI inflows into East Asia and the Pacific amounted to $64 billion and $61 billion in 1997 and 1998 respectively compared to $59 billion in 1996. Even the modest decline in 1998 over the previous year was largely because of a $2 billion decline in inflows into China.

Portfolio equity investors, widely believed to be fickle-minded, have proved only slightly less defiant. Net equity inflows declined from $14 billion in 1996 to $9 billion and $8 billion in 1997 and 1998 respectively. The slight decline in 1998 over 1997 is deceptive because it conceals a sharp fall in inflows into China from $8 billion to $1 billion; in the problem economies of East Asia, inflows actually increased by $7 billion in 1998 over the abysmal level of $800 million in 1997.

This pattern of behaviour among different investors is easily explained. On a long-term view, which is what matters to FDI inflows, the logic of investment in emerging markets remains irresistible. Returns to investment there are higher than in industrial countries; besides, nothing has happened to overturn the principle of portfolio diversification. If anything, the convergence of economic policies in industrial economies only strengthens the case for such diversification. In the present context in East Asia, an added attraction is that assets can be bought at bargain prices.

The last factor applies to portfolio equity flows as well, given that valuations are a key determinant of such flows. Another reason why equity flows into East Asia have rebounded strongly from the dip in 1997 is that at the large instutiutional funds, exposures to emerging markets are incredibly low— in general, less than one per cent of total assets.

Fund managers can routinely make such allocations without losing sleep over potential losses.

Bank loans, however, are a different proposition. Unlike FDI or equity investment which can be liquidated in a crisis only at great loss, at least that component of bank credit that is due to mature (notably short-term loans, which formed a big chunk of debt in East Asia) can be withdrawn or renewed at higher rates. Secondly, bank credit has no upside possibilities that can tempt lenders to sally forth in troubled times.

Thirdly, banks' exposures to emerging markets are quite significant (nearly 25 per cent for American banks), so banks can't afford to be as indifferent to losses in emerging markets as equity funds. Last but by no means the least, provisioning and capital adequacy requirements mean that non-performing assets in emerging markets might cause banks' balance sheets in the industrial world to shrink and erode profitability even further. Banks, therefore, acted quite rationally in cutting back flows into East Asia until such time as the economies got their acts together.

In doing so, banks sought to minimize the costs to themselves even as their actions inflicted huge costs on their host countries. It's been suggested that rational behaviour would have been different if the IMF were not around to provide bailout packages. Banks would then have been compelled to reschedule payments or sell loans at steep discounts. But these processes are time-consuming and can not only spell higher costs for the affected economies but pose grave risks to the international financial system. Measures proposed such as 'standstill' or 'lending into arrears' have little chance of acceptability because they fail to appeal to banks' self-interest. Economies that wish to avoid the havoc caused by volatile flows are wise, not to look for benevolence from international investors, but simply to keep a lid on such flows.

April 15, 1999

Japan at the receiving end

For a nation that happens to be the world's second biggest economic power, it is amazing how much advice Japan gets on running its economy. The world's revenge, no doubt, for the times when it had to take sermons on Japanese management.

Exhorted in recent weeks by the markets and the media (but not the G-7) to rein in the surging yen, the Bank of Japan has agreed to factor the exchange rate into its monetary policy. Whatever the short-run outcome of such intervention, the markets must not count on long-term weakness in the yen if Japan's economic recovery endures.

There are two, quite different reasons why monetary intervention has been urged on the BoJ. The less persuasive reason is that the yen must weaken in order to promote export growth in the short-run. Exports are not responsible for the current revival. The 2 per cent growth in the first quarter came from domestic demand that grew at 2.2 per cent while exports actually declined by 0.2 per cent.

Public investment has been the biggest factor underlying domestic demand but both private consumption and business investment, which declined in 1998, have grown in the first quarter. Private spending, in turn, has been spurred by the revitalization of the banking sector that has boosted confidence all round.

It is argued that the present level of public investment cannot be sustained given the magnitude of the fiscal deficit but at least the IMF believes that public spending must continue "as long as the recovery in private demand has not firmly taken hold". The US Treasury Secretary, Lawrence Summers, too has been quoted as saying that Japan must find ways to base growth on domestic demand which suggests that currency intervention to push exports is not a priority in his view.

The more plausible case for monetary intervention focuses on its impact on domestic demand. This centres on the "liquidity trap" argument, namely, that people have no incentive to loan funds to banks in the face of the near-zero nominal interest rates obtaining in Japan today. The way to stimulate activity in such circumstances is to target a modest rate of inflation (or a weaker yen) so that consumers start spending their cash hoards.

The IMF has joined the clamour for monetary intervention but in its *World Economic Outlook* of October 1998 it had expressed scepticism at least about the second argument. It had then contended that the lags in effects on policy instruments could be as long as six years and that " an early resolution of the problems of the banking system is more likely to enhance confidence and boost domestic demand than a strategy of expanding the monetary base". Precisely what the Japanese have done.

Targeting the exchange rate may work in the short-run by pushing both exports and domestic demand but the key issue is whether Japan needs such a target over the long haul. This depends on Japan's choice of economic strategy going forward.

Japan has a structural current account surplus arising from the excess of savings over investment. Some contend that the latter gap—and hence the current account surplus—must widen as Japan needs to take out capacity in several inefficient sectors, not maintain investment at today's level of 17 per cent of GDP. So Japan must rely on exports, not on domestic demand, to deliver growth—and this requires sustained currency weakness.

In making this argument for yen weakness, people are really laying down a model of growth for Japan. This raises the issue of whether Japan is obliged to close down businesses and suffer a wrenching dislocation in order to conform to some abstract notion of efficiency. Japan has long had two sectors—an efficient, export-oriented sector and inefficient, small businesses. It must not be presumed that the Japanese polity favours the latter's disbandment in order to expedite economic recovery.

Japan's G-7 partners have been indifferent to the yen's recent strengthening because it neither signifies a secular weakness in the dollar nor impedes growth in the world at large. It is a purely Japan problem. But if Japan now opts for a growth strategy that curbs its capital outflows and implies a stronger yen, that could make the yen a competitor to the world's favoured reserve currency, the dollar, and upset hopes for the euro. That is not something to which the G-7 will be indifferent.

September 30, 1999

From reform to crisis: tales from another continent

This year the world economy will crawl at around two per cent. The US and Europe will both slow down, Japan will probably shrink, and the recovery in East Asia will have sputtered to a halt. There will be two luminous exceptions. China will grow at 7.5 per cent and India at around 5.5 per cent.

If that is not consolation enough, you need only to look at a continent that has gone from crisis to reform to crisis, namely, Latin America. The IMF recently announced an $8 billion stand-by credit package for Argentina just days after it had announced a $15 billion loan for Brazil. Argentina had received $40 billion from the IMF only last year.

The new US administration and, particularly its Treasury Secretary, Paul O'Neill, have had to resile from their public positions on the subject of IMF-led bailouts. With good reason. American banks have significant exposures to Latin America (although these no longer threaten their balance sheets) and would take big hits if Argentina were to default on its external debt. Secondly, the US reckons there is a risk of contagion in emerging markets arising from any collapse in Argentina at this point. Thirdly, there is every danger that a major crisis in Argentina would discredit the free market principles that the US and the IMF have preached to emerging markets.

The big question, however, is whether IMF assistance to Argentina will do more than defer the day of reckoning. Argentina's external debt of $130 billion—under 40 per cent of GDP—would not normally be viewed as formidable. But doubts about the country's ability to service even this level of debt have arisen because of poor export performance—the country's debt is over 300 per cent of export earnings—and the dismal outlook for world trade in general.

Of the $8 billion being extended to Argentina, $3 billion is said to be intended for 'voluntary' restructuring of debt. This could take the form of new and cheaper debt to replace old debt or write-downs by foreign investors or both. But most observers believe that $3 billion is too small a sum to make a difference to the debt overhang. They fear that a default on debt is almost impossible to avert and that this will be followed by a steep devaluation that will devastate the financial sector.

We in India need to understand what exactly has gone wrong in much of Latin America. Argentina has been in the vanguard of countries that embraced the market-oriented principles enshrined in the Washington Consensus. It has opened its doors wide to foreign investment; it has gone the whole hog on privatization; and it has liberalized both trade and the capital account. In other words, over a decade of reforms coinciding with our own, it has done everything that the advocates of "second-generation reforms" insist will take us to high-growth nirvana. Yet, at the end of the decade, Argentina finds itself peering into the abyss.

Some would blame Argentina's decision to go in for "dollarisation" (whereby the government undertakes to back every peso with a dollar, in effect forsaking a sovereign currency) for the mess it is in today. This is strictly hindsight. When dollarisation was introduced, it was supposed to be the answer to both currency risk and hyper-inflation.

By addressing the threat of devaluation, it would enable the country to borrow at lower interest rates abroad. By taking away the government's control over monetary policy, it would ensure that irresponsible politicians did not cause inflation to get out of hand, and this would cause interest rates to decline at home as well. Both foreign and domestic investment would rise and propel economic growth. These hopes have proved delusional.

Reforms based on the Washington Consensus seem to provide an impetus to growth initially but this does not last. For much of the nineties, Argentina did experience an average growth higher than that in the eighties. But volatility in growth rates was also higher. From 1999 onwards, economic decline set in. Even without a full-blown crisis, the jury will be out on whether reforms produced a higher and sustainable growth rate over the entire period.

It is contended that dollarisation in a period in which the dollar ruled high led to an overvalued peso. This, in turn, rendered exports uncompetitive and constrained growth. But reforms should have generated strong domestic demand. Privatisation and foreign investment should have increased competitiveness of the country's products. Dollarisation should have produced greater integration with the American economy with its attendant benefits. Those who insist that further liberalization, more reforms will take us to a higher growth trajectory must first explain why big-bang reforms have not produced the expected results in Latin America.

August 30, 2001

Where China lags behind India

Look at China, see how far down the reform path they have gone—the refrain, not always well-founded, has become the staple of discourse on the Indian economy. Yet, as is evident from a recent paper, there is at least one area where the Chinese lag behind us, namely, banking. (*John P Bonin and Yiping Huang, Foreign entry into Chinese banking: does WTO membership threaten domestic banks? World Economy, August 2002*).

The paper focuses on how China has been slow to open up its financial sector to foreign competition because of the perceived threat to state-owned banks. For long, foreign banks in China were confined to doing foreign currency business, that, too, with foreign enterprises. It was only in 1996 that foreign financial institutions were allowed to accept local currency deposits from foreign-funded enterprises and extend local currency loans to them. The experiment was confined to a district of Shanghai but was later extended to Shenzhen.

In addition, foreign banks have been subject to stringent locational restrictions. In 2001, 65 foreign banks were operating a mere 157 branches in the country compared to the network of 125,000 branches of the top four state-owned banks alone. Foreign banks' shares of total loans and deposits were just 1.8 per cent and 0.5 per cent respectively. To put matters in perspective, the comparable figures for India are 8 per cent and 4.7 per cent.

Following China's accession to the WTO in December last year, the country is committed to opening up its banking sector but foreign entry will be carefully phased in. Foreign banks were allowed to conduct all types of foreign exchange transactions with foreign clients with immediate effect and with Chinese clients in designated cities in a year's time. Two years after entry, foreign banks can make corporate loans in local currency; five years after entry, foreign banks can deal with individual Chinese customers. As with privatization and capital account liberalization, so with banking sector reform, China is determined to go its own way.

Can China's banks cope with foreign competition? As the authors note, the experience of central Europe shows that foreign banks do not end up gaining a large share of the market unless domestic banks are sold to them. One might add that this is the Indian experience as well. But the challenge for China's banking sector is not so much withstanding foreign bank competition as keeping state-owned banks from imploding as a result of other pressures that will be released by deregulation.

As in India, there are big positives in Chinese banking: the existence of an extensive branch network, the absence of a credible threat of disintermediation on account of under-developed financial markets, and a huge, untapped retail market, including a large market for housing loans. But the negatives loom larger than in India.

One, interest rates remain regulated. *Two*, an inter-bank market is yet to develop. *Three*—and this is most critical—the size of non-performing loans, estimated at between 45-55 per cent of GDP, is way above ours (5 per cent), even if we accept that the official figure for non-performing loans in India is an under-estimate.

Four, the average capital adequacy ratio at the four top banks was a mere 5.6 per cent in 2002 whereas most Indian state-owned banks have a capital adequacy ratio of more than 9 per cent. China's low capital adequacy ratio, along with the high proportion of non-performing loans, means that recapitalisation will pose enormous burdens on the national exchequer.

International accounting standards were introduced only in 1998, whereas India had instituted crucial international standards by 1994. As in India, an independent bureau for financial supervision has been created within the central bank. Unlike India, China has moved to set up asset reconstruction companies to deal with problem loans at the top four state-owned banks. Given the primitive state of financial markets and the problems in recovering loans from state enterprises, the authors are rightly skeptical as to whether the ARCs will be effective.

The Chinese economy is growing faster than India's, with a vibrant industry component, and this is a big plus for China's banking sector. But where China has missed out relative to India is in not having a culture of private entrepreneurship in banking, including a stronger foreign presence, as this makes for rapid diffusion of skills and technology within the system consequent to deregulation.

'Take care of the banking system and the economy will take care of itself' was one of the central lessons of the East Asian crisis. For those accustomed to viewing India as an eternal loser in the economic race with China, here is a tantalizing thought: might our head start in banking just help us pip China at the post?

December 5, 2002

Economic Outlook

Crash and rebound

On October 19, 1987, the Dow Jones Index fell by 22.6 per cent, surpassing the fall of 12.8 per cent on October 28, 1929, and the fall of 11.7 per cent the following day, which together constituted the Crash of 1929.

The response in the media was hysterical. Some talked of apocalypse; others saw it as the beginning of the end of capitalism; yet others pontificated about how greed on Wall Street had met its nemesis.

One man stood amidst the ruins unfazed by the tremors the stock market crash had caused—Ronald Reagan. President Reagan's response: "It's one of those stock market things." For this remark, he was lampooned by intellectuals on both sides of the Atlantic.

Events were to prove President Reagan right and the intellectuals dead wrong. The Dow Jones Index stood at 1739 on October 19, 1987. It recovered to its pre-crash levels by the second half of 1989, and is now hovering around 7500, a gain of over 200 per cent in eight years. The Dow crashed again last month, but it has rebounded pretty quickly, in effect shrugging off the problems in South-East Asia.

Markets will fall; sometimes they may crash. There is such a thing as 'over shooting' in markets, be they stock markets or currency markets. But a market crash need not necessarily translate into recession in the real economy. Whether that happens or not depends on how sound the economy is.

The association in the public mind of a crash with a prolonged economic slump has to do with residual memories of the Great Depression in the US that followed the 1929 stock market crash. At least for the US, the correlation is rather weak today because the American economy has undergone structural changes that help insulate the real economy from falling stock prices.

Government spending as a proportion of GDP has risen sharply which makes for a degree of stability in demand. Companies rely less on the stock market for capital relative to retained earnings, so the impact on investment is not very large.

The banking sector is sounder, which diminishes the possibility of a crisis in banking following any bankruptcies among firms; besides the Fed is willing to bail out a major bank, which was not the case in 1929.

The 'wealth effect' on consumer spending is not such a potent factor as consumers are now sophisticated enough now not to raise or lower spending dramatically in response to the ups and downs of the stock market. But, perhaps, the most dramatic change is in the stance of the monetary authorities.

The failure to adopt an aggressive monetary policy at a time of general deflation led to high real interest rates following the crash of 1929. This, along with the misguided Smoot-Hawley tariff, did more damage than any other factor. Today's monetary authorities are a wiser lot, and, with inflation having been routed in recent years, will not hesitate to cut interest rates or expand money supply.

All this explains why a stock market crash no longer holds terrors for the US and why the markets have displayed resilience after the 1987 crash and last month. There is another recent instance of a market staging a dramatic recovery from a crash, namely, Mexico since January 1995, but there the economy did suffer before being turned around.

This does not mean that South-East Asia can emulate Mexico. Mexico is special to the US, so the US was willing to go all out in terms of providing financial support and market access. Besides, the Mexican political class was willing to make the public pay a heavy short-term price for recovery.

None of these conditions obtains in South-East Asia. Nor are the banking systems in those countries anywhere near attaining the soundness of their American counterpart. They are, perhaps, closer to the US banking system of 1929. Another crucial difference is that the US, with its huge domestic base, did not have to rely on export-led growth. The South-East Asian economies do, and may find it difficult to recover in the present global environment.

Stock markets may not mirror conditions in the real economy. Bubbles will occur, followed by crashes. But the impact the crash has on the real economy certainly mirrors the soundness of the underlying economy.

November 8, 1997

Revisiting the crash

In my last column ('Crash and rebound', ET Nov. 8), I argued that a stock market crash need not translate into an economic crisis if the underlying economy is sound. I'd like to explore a few related themes.

A crash need not reflect weak fundamentals, true; it could mean that a bubble has been pricked and prices have been restored to realistic levels. But is an orderly correction preferable to a crash? The impact on the real economy should not be very different in the two cases. Long-term investors have no cause for concern if a sharp fall occurs in conditions such as those obtaining in the US until the recent crash.

Yet, in the absence of sound market mechanisms, a crash could scar the economy for reasons analogous to a bank failing because of a run on the bank. As stock prices trend downwards, panic sets in and 'sell' orders tend to snowball. This is especially true of sophisticated markets such as the US, where 'portfolio insurance' strategies mandate a certain ratio of stocks to cash at each specified level of stock prices, and such trading strategies are heavily concentrated in a few players. Each drop in stock prices automatically starts a huge wave of selling. This puts severe pressure on the liquidity of the principal market players and on the clearing systems, which could translate into bankruptcies.

Another problem caused by a precipitous fall in stock prices is that linkages between different markets—the stock market, the futures market and the options market—through such means as index arbitrage tend to be disrupted, and this also exacerbates panic in the markets. The Presidential Task Force on Market Mechanisms set up in the US in the wake of the 1987 crash focused on these aspects of the crash, rather than on the macro-economic factors, and made a number of recommendations about strengthening the microstructure of the market to enable them to cope with a sudden fall in prices. The lesson is that a stock market crash, while not necessarily harmful in itself, could turn out to be disruptive if the market mechanisms are not sound;

and the more sophisticated the markets, the greater is the need for sound microstructures.

A second theme that has come to the fore is the impact of globalization. Because American companies and institutional investors are exposed to South-East Asian markets, there were fears that the 'contagion effects' would cause the American stock market to come crashing down.

It's turned out that the impact was exaggerated. The American stock market is off by about 10 per cent from its 1997 high; given its high valuations, that seemed the right thing to happen anyway. American GDP growth, projected at 4 per cent earlier, will shed about one per cent, even when the impact of Latin America (which has been badly hit) is factored in. "Mild but not negligible"—that's how the Fed Chairman characterizes the impact on the US.

But the possibility of being impacted by happenings elsewhere does not constitute an argument against globalization. The logic of portfolio diversification is that, for a given return, risk is reduced—as long as markets are not positively correlated. And long-term correlation is what is relevant, not temporary volatility. So, investors in the advanced economies can shy away from emerging markets only if they believe that growth rates there in future will be lower than in their own economies or that the advanced and emerging markets are beginning to be highly correlated.

Finally, it's necessary to be clear as to what a sustained bull market implies. If stock prices rise sharply year after year, that could mean an increase in the expected return on equity. This may sound great to investors, but it's bad news for firms because it means that the cost of capital is going up. It's particularly bad for small firms that depend heavily on external funds relative to retained earnings. Over time, a high cost of equity could inhibit innovation and erode the competitiveness of industry. That would inevitably cause returns to equity to decline, perhaps sharply if the bull run has gone on for too long. So investors ought to welcome corrections in stock prices, and even the odd crash if the market mechanisms are strong enough.

November 22, 1997

Virtual realities

On the face of it, news of the imminent demise of the US economy—and its knock-on effects on the rest of the world—appears vastly exaggerated. Despite disappointing numbers in the second quarter, the US economy still promises to notch up growth of 3 per cent in 1998. When you factor in projections for other major chunks of the world economy—2.8 per cent for the European Union and 7 per cent for China—it's hard to see where all the talk of a global recession is coming from.

If, nevertheless, economists shudder each time the Dow sheds a couple of hundred points from its vertiginous heights, that's because growth in the real economy is being powered to a disconcerting degree by what's happening to the virtual economy represented by financial assets of individuals and firms.

The Fed Chairman, Alan Greenspan, stated recently that $12.5 trillion (or 1.8 times America's GDP in 1997) had been added to wealth since 1994 primarily because of the rise in share prices. This virtual wealth is causing consumers to spend like crazy. By holding down costs of worker benefits under 'defined-benefits' pension programs, it's translating into bigger profit margins for companies.

The combination of consumer spending and soaring profits is boosting capital spending by companies. The virtual economy, in turn, has been bolstered by purely financial factors: foreign funds have sought refuge in the US following the East Asian meltdown even as American institutions have cut asset allocations outside the US.

As valuations have raced ahead of fundamentals, the stage is set for the asset bubble to be pricked. The concern now is that when share prices fall, the impact on the real economy will be as shattering as it was salutary in the first instance. This is, of course, typically what happened to economies in the past. The most recent parallel being cited is the protracted slump in Japan following the asset bubble of the late eighties. Such pessimism can, however, be overdone, for it ignores the strengths of America's real economy.

Suppose we pursue the comparison with Japan. The Japanese asset bubble was largely the result of enforced monetary laxity: in 1987, Japan was persuaded to cut interest rates in order to shore up a sagging dollar. Tokyo's stock market touched a record high in early 1990—and Japan's still paying for that excess. It is argued that the US Fed should have raised the interest rate over the past year to head off an asset bubble, but its carefully calibrated judgement, based entirely on the needs of the US economy, hardly qualifies as laxity on a comparable scale.

Even if the Fed was mistaken, its mistake may not prove as costly. Japan's financial institutions, with their mountains of bad loans, were acutely vulnerable to falling asset prices because of their huge exposures to the stock market. Inevitably, they radiated their problems to an over-leveraged corporate sector, thus pushing the Japanese economy into a downward spiral.

America's banks are in much better shape (and are not as exposed to stock market volatility). So is the American corporate sector, notwithstanding the wave of mergers in recent years. That's because mergers have been financed to a greater degree by stocks than by borrowed cash. So the risks of corporate and bank bankruptcies meshing together and paving the way for a recession are much lower. Another striking improvement in fundamentals is the federal budget moving into surplus, which limits the potential for a debilitating interest rate rise once inflation reasserts itself.

To be sure, consumer spending will reined in sharply once share prices in fall, but setbacks to consumers don't impair the productive capacity of an economy the way firm failures do and are easier for an economy to take in its stride. Finally, the risks of over shooting because of faulty market mechanisms (which underlay the crash of 1987) or because of lack of transparency in businesses (which caused panic in East Asia) are minimal in America's highly efficient markets. America appears largely exempt from the virtual reality that other economies have to defer to: if there is no crisis, the financial markets will invent one.

August 20, 1998

Triumph and tragedy

Writing in the inevitable millennium-related edition of *Newsweek* (Issues 2000, December 5), Fareed Zakaria, Managing Editor of *Foreign Affairs,* gives eloquent expression to the triumphalist mood in the American establishment." For almost a half century, the West has struggled mightily to spread capitalism and democracy around the world. Now it has gotten what it wanted—unbridled market and people power...... ."

Triumphalism in the US has given a boost to the doctrine that the developing world's hope for economic advancement lies in applying a set of free market principles, referred to as the Washington Consensus. Mainstream economists such as Joseph Stiglitz have questioned the blind application of the Washington Consensus to the developing world, saying these principles won't work. (Mr Stiglitz reiterates his position in the same issue of Newsweek.)

Others have raised more fundamental objections. They argue that the industrial economies, including the United States, themselves did not achieve economic success through adherence to the principles they urge on the developing world today, least of all free trade. Commenting on the case for "an unrestricted and uncontrolled global free-market economy" in his magisterial survey of the present century, *Age of Extremes,* the leftist historian, Eric Hobsbawm, writes: "Until the 1970s national and world capitalism had never operated under such conditions or, if they had, had not necessarily benefited.... its (the twentieth century's) economic miracles were not achieved by laissez-faire but against it."

Let us suppose that the historical record is of little relevance to today's world. Let us also suppose that the "unbridled market power" that Mr Zakaria celebrates does work, contrary to what Mr Stiglitz thinks. We still have to deal with another fundamental objection, namely, that the market economy causes inequalities to widen unconscionably both within nations and between nations, with a great many people becoming worse off in absolute terms. The marginalisation of large numbers of people in the global economy can only set the stage for a tragedy of epic proportions.

These arguments are made forcefully in a recent book, *Profit over people*, by Noam Chomsky, the liberal-left thinker and MIT professor, who has been a long-time critic of America's political and economic system. Chomsky cites several instances of how the leading economic powers of today systematically used protectionism to bolster domestic industries.

But the most important departures from free market doctrine in the US, Chomsky notes, related to the use of subsidies, often made available to industry through the Pentagon. He cites the civilian aircraft industry as a striking example of success made possible by large-scale public subsidy and adds that "the same pattern prevails in computers and electronics generally, automation, biotechnology, communications, in fact just about every dynamic sector of the economy".

Chomsky quotes *Foreign Affairs* as saying of the Reagan administration, widely credited with ushering in the market revolution, that it "presided over the greatest swing towards protectionism since the 1930s". He mentions a study of transnational corporations that found that " at least 20 companies in the Fortune 100 in 1993 would not have survived at all as independent companies if they had not been saved by their respective governments". So much for free market doctrine.

Chomsky's book is not for the squeamish. It abounds in facts that will be unsettling to all but the most closed minds (example: Britain has experienced poverty " on a scale not seen since the 1930s" as a result of Thatcherite policies). It is scathing in its examination of the impact of the free market gospel on Latin America. Its dissection of the workings of American democracy and its media will be deeply troubling to many who find much to admire in the American system.

But the book will have served a greater purpose here if it causes people to ponder the future direction of economic reforms, a subject on which there has been more hype than genuine debate lately. One obvious lesson is that we need to be alert to the costs of integration with the global economy and its potential for disruption.

Another is to recognize that our relatively low level of integration is a strength especially given the size of the domestic market. Most importantly, there will remain a significant role for the state both in order to cushion the impact of globalization on those adversely affected and to sustain large-scale economic activity independent of the vagaries of the global market.

December 23, 1999

Twice, the ground shook beneath the feet

The floor seemed to swing to one side, then to the other. Next, an overpowering dizziness. Was this what they called a heart attack? Or might it be a stroke? As the brain raced to make sense of it all, there rose screams of 'earthquake, earthquake'. Within seconds, we were in the open ground outside.

It was only when we tuned in to the radio bulletins a few hours later—for the cable had blanked out—that the full horror of the Gujarat earthquake began to sink in. That was at the beginning of the year and the omens were unsettling.

Later in the year, in a distant land, the ground again seemed to shake beneath the writer's feet; only, this time the tremors threatened to engulf most of the world. The writer had just emerged from the subway onto Greenwich Village in Manhattan when he found hordes of men and women stampeding down the street. A bemused bystander offered an explanation that sounded absurd, "The World Trade Centre's gone".

On Fifth Avenue, his meaning became clear. There were only dark clouds of smoke in the distance where New York's beloved landmark had once been. As the scenes were played over and over again on TV screens through the day, the American nation woke up to an altogether new sense of vulnerability. Weeks later, when the anthrax scare erupted, that sense was to deepen and give rise to something close to despair.

America was not alone in mourning the acts of destruction. When a French newspaper declared, "We are all New Yorkers now", the sentiment found a resonance amongst many, including Indians, who could readily identify with America's pulsating and extravagant cosmopolis.

Within the US itself, three different strains were discernible. As the investigations unravelled the identities of those involved, there was an almost palpable hostility towards non-white immigrants. If you had a Muslim last name or Middle Eastern looks, you had reason to feel sorry in the immediate aftermath of September 11. The US administration rose magnificently to the occasion and the racial fall-out was quickly contained but the seeds of distrust have been sown.

Then, there were the calls for retribution. As President Bush vowed action in his address to Congress, members rose to their feet repeatedly to cheer him. The media and the general public rallied around. Americans were united in believing that a vital threshold had been breached and that justice needed to be done, whatever the costs and however uncertain the outcome.

But there was yet another theme on which America remained fixated for weeks on end: why do they hate us so? Not everybody was willing to buy the glib talk about envy and resentment towards the world's richest country. There seemed to be a recognition that America's stance towards Israel, for instance, and its support to autocratic regimes in the region were important causatory factors; that the developed world could not be indifferent towards failed states such as Afghanistan; that, perhaps, there was a message in the anti-globalisation protests at Seattle and Genoa that needed to be taken seriously.

The Bush administration's immediate responses themselves held out the hope that a new ordering of international relations was possible. Gone was the unilateralist approach that had threatened a rupture with the European Union. There was a reaching out to the Soviet Union, an effort to mend fences with China, an affirmation of an independent state of Palestine.

In the economic realm, the boost to public spending, the expansion of the safety net and the bailouts of the airline and insurance industries pointed to a willingness to forsake doctrines considered sacrosanct and for long urged on other nations. The American position at the WTO talks at Doha suggested a degree of flexibility that had seemed unlikely earlier.

With the war in Afghanistan drawing to a quick close, one is not so sure. The western world could well conclude that it has the capability to put down recalcitrant peoples in a 'war against terrorism' without having to address any underlying grievance. Israel's stridency in recent days, backed by the US, is a disturbing pointer. The American decision to walk out of the ABM treaty hints at a new triumphalism. The US Congress' insistence on bringing labour standards into the WTO and the move towards higher protection against steel imports mock the promise of a new deal for developing countries.

More disconcerting for us, we cannot be sure that terrorism in South Asia evokes the same outrage in the US. With the citadel of Indian democracy coming under attack, many in India will be forgiven a sense of ending the year as they began it—on shaky ground.

December 20, 2001

Throttles open, the world's airlines struggle to take off

The outbreak of hostilities in Afghanistan is bound to add a thick layer to the pall of depression that has hung over the world's airline industry ever since the attacks on the US on September 11. The issue is no longer one of staving off bankruptcies, it is holding down the costs of bailouts. Those who fume over the government's inability to privatise Air-India might contemplate an interesting fall-out of the crisis in the industry: the re-nationalization, partly or substantially, of some of the world's leading carriers.

The disruption that has followed the events of last month has threatened to push virtually the entire industry in the US into bankruptcy. In Europe, well-known flag carriers, such as Swissair, British Airways and Sabena are in dire distress, as are lesser names in Italy, Ireland, Greece, Portugal and Poland. Air New Zealand had gone over the brink even before the recent turmoil.

Perhaps the most dramatic of the collapses that have occurred is that of Swissair. Having suffered the ignominy of seeing its operations grounded last week, the erstwhile paragon of customer service could not even provide refunds for tickets to thousands of passengers stranded at airports. The Swiss government was constrained to inject $277 million in cash in order to enable the airline to keep flying.

The collapse of Swissair has had a knock-on effect on the Belgian carrier, Sabena, in which Swissair has a 49.5 per cent stake. Sabena has had to be bailed out by a $115 million loan provided by the Belgian government even as it sought protection from creditors.

Air New Zealand is being saved by the government at a cost to the tax payer of $360 million. The infusion will give the government of New Zealand an 83 per cent stake in the airline, twelve years after it was privatized. One of the two principal shareholders in the airline as it hurtled towards bankruptcy had been Singapore Airlines with a 25 per cent equity stake. Mr Shourie, please note.

In the US, faced with the prospect that most of the airline industry would go bankrupt, the administration and Congress took barely 10 days to agree to a rescue package of $ 5 billion in cash and $10 billion in loan guarantees. The government is giving itself warrants over the carriers' shares, thus making it a potential owner if the airlines' fortunes revive in the future.

It is not that America's airlines would have been viable but for the recent crisis. Many of the leading airlines were headed for huge losses even before the fall in traffic consequent to September 11. The critical consideration underlying the bailout seems to be that a collapse in the airline industry could have wider effects, including a generalized loss of confidence at a time when the US economy seems headed for recession. The reckoning was that the systemic effect needed to be contained first, restructuring of the industry could come later. Makes you wonder what the hullabaloo over the UTI bailout was all about.

The airline industry must strike anybody as a graveyard for privatisation—it probably has more failed privatisation stories than most industries. The reason is not far to seek. The industry fails to meet what is, perhaps, the most important requirement for success in privatization: unhindered competition. The world over, the industry is hemmed in by regulation, typified by national ownership laws and bilateral arrangements.

Nor does it appear likely that governments in Europe and the US will dismantle these in the near future and do what it will take to put the industry on a viable footing, namely, allow consolidation not only within Europe but across the Atlantic as well. Emotional attachments to flag carriers apart, the heightened concern today over airline security will impede movement in that direction. It looks as though state presence, whether through direct ownership or through subsidies, will continue to be a factor for a while.

In many ways, India's flag carrier is better placed than others. Several airlines, notably Swissair, have failed because they found themselves unable to generate demand after having expanded capacity. Air-India's problem is not excess capacity but the lack of it. It is not in a position to meet demand fully because it has lacked the capital required for fleet expansion.

The turmoil in the airline industry means the government may have to find ways to raise capital for Air-India other than through the induction of a strategic partner. It should be understood, however, that the government's tortuous and, in all probability, futile efforts at privatisation over the past few years will have imposed their own costs on the hapless airline. One hopes the lesson is well learnt.

October 11, 2001

Test of nerves for kingpins of the financial world

As people everywhere watched on television the World Trade Centre, the familiar landmark of New York's financial district, dissolve into rubble, it must have been hard for many to avoid a sense of looming economic catastrophe. Provided, however, the kingpins of the financial world keep their nerve, the world economy can ride out the present storm.

The nightmare scenario that haunts the world economy following the assaults on the American mainland has five key elements. One, the flight to safety will cause American investors to dump stocks in favour of government securities, which would cause interest rates to soar. Two, foreign investors will stampede out of the American market, accentuating the collapse in stocks.

Three, the devastation suffered by the leading financial institutions in terms of hardware and personnel will make transactions difficult and give a further jolt to investor sentiment. Four, insurance companies, unprepared for losses on this scale, will collapse and this would wreck the financial system. Five, consumers, apprehensive about what is in store, will curb spending and this will slow down the US economy even more than was forecast earlier.

Yet, the odds are that the gloom and doom in the aftermath of September 11 will turn out to be overdrawn. For one thing, the capacity of central bankers, proved at the time of the 1987 stock market crash and again during the East Asian crisis, to act in unison at the prospect of a meltdown must not be underestimated. Any rise in the risk premium should be offset to some extent by cuts in interest rates across the leading economies. The cuts in interest rates should serve to check any fall in stock prices.

It is also hard to see foreign investors abandoning their perception of the US as a safe haven. It is not just that neither Europe nor Japan today is a meaningful alternative. Despite the publicised failures in the technology sector, all indications are of a genuine improvement in productivity and in the long-term rate of growth in the US, although these figures are lower than thought earlier. To ignore these improvements in the wake of the collapse of a couple of buildings in the financial district would call for more than the normal fit of irrationality in evidence in times such as these.

The disarray in leading financial institutions will not be inconsiderable. But the good news, going by early reactions, is that most institutions have enough back-ups on the operational side to help them cope with the dislocation. The suspension of trading for one day, which could be extended as the authorities take stock, provides market players just the breathing space needed to digest all relevant information. It is possible to hope that, as the immediate shock wears off, the market reaction to recent events will be sober.

Insurance companies, including re-insurers, are bracing themselves for a clutch of claims on an unprecedented scale. But leading companies, including the world's largest re-insurer, Munich Re, have been quick to announce that they have built up provisions even for a disaster of the present magnitude. With central banks ready to infuse any amount of liquidity into the system, a general collapse in the insurance sector seems a remote possibility, although this will not be a great time for shareholders of these companies.

Provided a collapse in the financial markets is averted, consumer spending should not be impacted any more adversely than had already been forecast. Even if there is some impact, this will be balanced out at least in part by government spending as the work of rebuilding the financial district of New York and the Pentagon gets under way in right earnest.

Over the longer term, the havoc wrought by relatively low–tech warfare on the United States might serve to put the brakes on the Bush administration's plans for an ambitious missile defence system. Already calls are mounting for a greater focus instead on the conventional security apparatus. If this shift occurs, fears that spending on high-tech weaponry will turn the American budgetary surplus into a big deficit in the years ahead might abate and confidence in the US economy would get strengthened. This could be the positive thing to come out of the week's horrors.

There are two risks to this optimistic scenario. One is a loss of nerve in the leading players in the financial world that propels them into ignoring fundamentals. The second—and more fearful—possibility is that the US administration forsakes a measured response to the bombing outrage in favour of a protracted, no-holds-barred war in the event that any state (or states) is held responsible. Should the latter come to pass, it will have incalculable consequences for a world economy that was not lacking in sources of crisis even before this week's events.

September 13, 2001

Business cycle is more benign

Shrugging off not only the collapse in high-tech stocks but also post-September 11 blues, the US and the other industrial economies have bounced back from last year's downturn. The IMF's *World Economic Outlook* (April, 2002) expects the world economy to grow at 2.8 per cent in 2002 and 4 per cent in 2002 compared to last year's growth rate of 2.5 per cent.

Last year's downturn put paid to the notion that, in the brave new economy world, the business cycle was dead. But the quick recovery since underlines a trend evidenced in recent years: business cycles have been getting more benign, with longer periods of expansion and shorter periods of recession in a given business cycle.

The *Outlook* has an excellent survey of the empirical evidence on business cycles in the industrial world (Chapter 3, "Recession and recoveries"). It highlights four key changes in the nature of business cycles. The most striking change is that recessions have become less severe and less frequent over time.

The average decline in GDP from peak to trough was 4.3 per cent in the period 1881-1913 and 8.1 per cent in the period 1919-1938. In the Bretton Woods era (1950-72), the decline fell to 2.1 per cent, increasing slightly to 2.5 per cent in the post-Bretton Woods period (1973-2000). The proportion of years in expansion increased from 75 and 71 in the pre—and inter-war years to 95 and 87 in the two subsequent periods.

A *second* change is that synchronization in business cycles has increased across economies. *Thirdly,* the role of investment in recessions has increased over time. In recent years, virtually all recessions have been accompanied by investment contractions while that of inventories has declined. *Fourthly,* since World War II, deflation has rarely been a feature of recession.

There is one statistic, however, that the report does not comment on: the average growth rate in the most recent period is the lowest in the four periods. We are, of course, comparing growth rates on very different bases. However, since the overall tone of the chapter is self-congratulatory, one wonders if there a presumption here that a lower growth rate is preferable if accompanied by lower volatility. It would be useful to know because this is not a presumption that appears to inform the IMF's policy prescriptions for the developing world.

The *Outlook* cites three factors that account for the lower amplitude of business cycles: the structural shift away agriculture and manufacturing towards services, which tends to be less cyclical; greater use of counter-cyclical fiscal and monetary policies; and greater financial stability. The last is, of course, debatable, given the frequency of financial crises in recent years, but one could argue that such crises have not been frequent or severe in the biggest economy, the US.

The report does note, in a separate box, that economic fluctuations in the developing world are more severe than in industrial countries. One reason is financial systems are not sufficiently developed to play a stabilizing role. Indeed, where they are exposed to volatile capital flows, financial systems may exacerbate macroeconomic instability. It is worth asking whether the Indian experience on output volatility has not been different because the much-maligned Indian financial system has been rather more stable

Another interesting observation is that stock prices rebound from their lows faster than in the past: it takes less than a year for stocks to regain their previous peak compared with two years in the past. It does look, however, that the experience in the current cycle will disappoint in this respect going by trends in the US stock market.

After swiftly erasing the losses sustained in the wake of September 11, the US market bounded back in the remainder of 2001. It has fallen by about 8 per cent this year despite the good news about the economy. The perception, following the string of corporate scandals, is that price-earnings ratios will be higher once earnings are adjusted for bogus accounting. But, more fundamentally, the market seems to have woken up to the realization that the gains in productivity noticed in the past decade tend to be competed away among firms, so it is consumers who benefit, not investors.

The ongoing global recovery is, of course, good news for the Indian economy, but it is mixed news for the Indian stock market. The high-tech stocks that are linked to the US market are likely to see modest gains, given the prospects for the US market. To the extent that industry benefits from the global recovery, however, the old economy stocks should be doing better in the coming months. If that sounds unexciting, well, things could be a lot worse.

May 23, 2002

A spluttering world economy

Table: Recovery in slow gear

Growth in (per cent)	Average 1985-94	Average 1995-01	2002	2003
World	3.2	3.6	3.0	3.2
Advanced economies	3.0	2.9	1.8	1.9
USA	2.9	3.3	2.4	2.2
Developing countries	5.1	5.1	4.6	5.0
India	5.4	6.0	4.9	5.1
Transition countries	-2.6	2.2	4.1	4.0

Source: *World Economic Outlook*, April 2003

The swift end to the Iraq war has removed a major source of uncertainty about prospects for the world economy. But, as the IMF's latest *World Economic Outlook* makes clear, economic recovery will be slow in coming—and is threatened by uncertainties on other counts.

The IMF projects world economic growth in 2003 at 3.2 per cent, up from 3 per cent last year and about the same as in the decade that preceded the mid-nineties boom, 1985-94. Developing countries will grow in 2003 at around the same rate as in 1985-94 as well as 1995-01, namely, 5 per cent. Growth in the advanced economies is way below that in both the periods. The boost to world growth, as the table shows, comes from the transition countries.

The IMF's forecasts are a hardy bi-annual and notoriously prone to error. The more interesting part of the *Outlook* is an essay, "When the bubble bursts", that documents the boom-burst pattern in the industrial world in the past and attempts to fit the slump in 2001 and the ongoing recovery into this pattern. This gives us an insight into why we must expect recovery to be slow and what risks beset the recovery.

In the 19 industrial countries covered by the essay, equity price busts occurred on average every 13 years , lasted for 2.5 years and were associated with GDP losses of about 4 per cent of GDP. A bust is defined as a peak-to-trough decline where the price change fell into the top quartile of all declines during bear markets; similarly, a boom is defined as a trough-to-peak rise where the price increase was in the top quartile of all increases. The way booms and busts are defined, every boom need not be followed by a bust. To qualify as a bust in the sample, a bear market contraction had to exceed 37 per cent. It turns out that only one-fourth of booms ended in busts.

Although equity busts tend to capture the public imagination, it is housing busts that are the real killer. They last longer—about four years. At 40 per cent, the probability of a housing boom being followed by a bust is disconcertingly high. Output loss has been 8 per cent in a housing price bust or twice that in an equity price bust.

A striking conclusion about the impact of sharp asset price declines on the macroeconomy is that the structure of the financial system matters. During housing busts, bank-based financial systems tended to suffer larger output losses than market-based financial systems. The latter suffered larger output losses during equity price busts.

The Outlook finds broad similarities between the present wave of equity busts that began in 2000 and those in the past. The magnitudes and lengths of declines are consistent with past episodes; so is the cross-country synchronisation. However, the decline in output has been larger this time round, thanks to sharper falls in private fixed investment in most countries. The IMF thinks this is because over-investment was even more pronounced in the last boom.

Past over-investment is one constraint on recovery after a bust. Another is that corporates find themselves over-leveraged. A positive in the present scenario is that stock market valuations remain above pre-bubble levels and this makes for lower debt to equity ratios than is normal in such periods. *Secondly*, because interest rates have been cut sharply, interest coverage is reassuringly high. *Thirdly*, the steepest declines in valuation were in the IT sector which relies more on equity than on debt and this has limited the impact on the banking sector.

The upbeat implication of the *Outlook's* analysis is that the consequences of the equity price bust appear manageable. The bigger worry today is that housing prices in many countries have crossed the threshold for a boom. This raises the prospect of a housing price bust that could drag the world economy down. A sharp fall in the dollar too would derail economic recovery. The *Outlook* concludes gloomily that the risks to the world economy outlook are "principally on the downside".

Extending the analysis to the Indian context, the 56 per cent fall in the Sensex in 2001 from the high of 2000 certainly qualifies as a bust. But India's is a bank-based financial system and hence more vulnerable to a housing price bust. Despite the boom in housing loans, we have not had any price bubble, so a crash in housing prices is not in sight. We can expect, therefore, to be spared the vagaries that go with asset price bubbles.

However, growth possibilities will undoubtedly be circumscribed by sluggishness in the world economy. The IMF's projections for India of 5.1 per cent and 5.9 per cent for calendar years 2003 and 2004 thus appear realistic. This will not tickle those who dream about a growth rate of 8 per cent. But, in the present environment, we should be grateful for small mercies.

May 21, 2003

Policy Issues

Great Helmsman

It is possible that when future historians talk of the twentieth century's Great Helmsman, they will be alluding, not to Mao Zedong, but to the man who has presided over the US Federal Reserve since 1987 and is poised to see it into the new millenium, Alan Greenspan.

In his first decade, Greenspan steered the US economy through the stock market crash of 1987 and oversaw a period of unprecedented expansion with low inflation. But his greater triumph has come in the period since July 1997. He has ensured that the US economy—and, by implication, the world economy—has kept ploughing ahead in the wake of the turbulence unleashed by Asian markets.

The US economy's growth has hinged on consumer spending driven by high asset values. Mr Greenspan's task of keeping the US economy cruising along has thus boiled down to shoring up its stock market without engineering an asset bubble. He has managed the feat with aplomb.

He has twice fended off pressure to raise interest rates, in September 1997 and in March 1998. The first time, the worsening of Asia's situation towards the end of that year showed that he was right not to deflate the stock market earlier and slow down the US economy. On the second occasion, the spread of the contagion to Russia and Latin America dealt heavy blows to the American stock markets. Thanks to Mr Greenspan, they could come off their high levels without impacting severely on the real economy. To keep them from sliding further, Mr Greenspan has effected three cuts in interest rates—in September, October and November. The rate cuts in Europe earlier this month suggest that central banks elsewhere believe Mr Greenspan has got it right again.

Mr Greenspan's success stems from making three crucial judgements. *First*, he has assessed that in a context in which growth has been throttled in much of the world, with unpredictable implications for the industrial economies, there has to be a bias towards expansion in the Fed's policy, even if US macroeconomic indicators themselves point to caution.

Secondly, while analysts have fumed that Mr Greenspan has risked abetting an asset bubble, Mr Greenspan believes the risk is worth taking. He's convinced the Fed has digested the lessons of the crashes of 1929 and 1987 and that the American financial sector is in better shape today. So even if his actions brought on a stock market crash, that need not translate into another Depression.

Thirdly, he's been quick to recognize that conventional models that suggest the American stock market is overvalued are inappropriate in the present context. The models factor in only the base Treasury rate and ignore the spreads on corporate bonds. This is fine for comparing valuations over time as long as spreads stay within a narrow range. That is emphatically not the case now: spreads have widened considerably since the Russian default.

Of course, it's not enough for a central banker to get his assessment right. He has to have credibility with the markets and a sense of timing. Mr Greenspan scores on both counts.

This is the art of central banking at its best. But by keeping the US economy going, Mr Greenspan has met only one of two requirements for rescuing the world economy. The other requirement, putting the capsized Asian economies on course again, eludes. The soft option is to ignore it, but that's to overlook the icebergs that loom in the distance—say, a collapse in Japan or a major setback to China. The second option is to put the onus squarely on Japan, but the Japanese can't be pushed beyond a point.

The third option is for the industrial economies to shoulder some of the pain. A US government-led bailout is simply not on, given the mood in Congress. But it's possible for the international banks to lighten Asia's burden through write-offs, rescheduling etc, and this is an area where Mr Greenspan is not without clout. If he can lean on the banks and get Asia going sooner rather than later, Mr Greenspan's chances of snatching Mao's title will be a lot brighter.

December 24, 1998

Exit Joseph Stiglitz

Joseph Stiglitz, the distinguished Chief Economist of the World Bank who ruffled feathers at the highest levels in Washington, has been shown the door. Writing in the letters column of the *Financial Times,* Jagdish Bhagwati says the economist's recent resignation is "known to all as a dismissal with a fig leaf".

Prof. Bhagwati seems to hold Mr Stiglitz's public criticism of the IMF and the US Treasury, rather than his dissent *per se,* responsible for the development. Others, however, will view Mr Stiglitz's departure as the inevitable outcome of the formidable challenge he mounted to the orthodoxy represented by the Washington consensus.

On three issues in particular, the Washington establishment could not have countenanced Mr Stiglitz's positions any longer: the diagnosis of the East Asian crisis and the prescription required; financial market liberalization; and privatisation.

Mr Stiglitz questioned the view that the East Asian crisis pointed to fundamental flaws in the economic strategies adopted by those countries in recent decades, strategies that accorded an important role to state intervention. Mr Stiglitz's ringing judgement deserves to be quoted: "Certainly, for three decades it (the system) delivered the most impressive level of increases in GDP ever attained in such a short span of time. ...These increases were far more impressive than those delivered in any major country following solely the prescriptions of the so-called Washington Consensus."

Mr Stiglitz was strident in his criticism of the IMF's response to the crisis. He argued that the standard IMF prescription of fiscal and monetary tightening in response to a depreciating currencies was inappropriate in a context of pronounced weaknesses in the financial sector. When some talked glibly about staying the course as Mexico had done in 1994, Mr Stiglitz retorted acidly that Mexico had been smart in choosing the US as its neighbour. He also underlined the social costs of exacerbating the crisis and the weakness in Mexico's non-export and financial sectors that persisted after the economy recovered.

While these views could not have been music to the ears of the Washington establishment, Mr Stiglitz's denunciation of financial and capital market liberalization must have been particularly jarring to those eager to prise open economies to America's financial companies.

The case for reining in capital flows into developing countries, which Mr Stiglitz strongly argued, seems to have found grudging acceptance but Mr Stiglitz views this as only part of a broader argument for measured deregulation of the financial sector in developing countries. He believes that capital adequacy norms by themselves cannot make for stability in weak financial systems and has favoured protecting profitability in banking by keeping deposit rates below market-determined levels.

Mr Stiglitz's critique of the IMF's reform programmes for Russia must have been equally discomfiting to the Washington elite for, in the process, he targeted the holiest of all cows in the Washington establishment, privatisation. Mr Stiglitz has long held that privatisation is undesirable where regulatory and legal frameworks are not strong enough and he has cited the chaos in Russia as vindication of his contention.

In general, Mr Stiglitz's writings point to a preference for gradualism in economic reform as distinct from a Big Bang approach. He views institutional development and popular support as important pre-conditions for success, a point that seems to have been lost on some of our more impatient reformers.

Mr Stiglitz's views could have been brushed aside had his stature in the economics profession not been as high as it is. This is not some besotted Marxist mouthing the shibboleths of a bygone era but a mainstream economist who has his feet firmly planted in information economics, a field in which Mr Stiglitz has been a pioneer.

Mr Stiglitz questions not the need for a vibrant market economy but the belief that there is a universally applicable formula for moving towards one. Precisely because this viewpoint calls into question the priorities ordained for developing countries by the Washington establishment and the dominant economic interests behind it, men such as Mr Stiglitz are dangerous. They have to go.

Professionals in high positions are faced at some point in their lives with a critical choice: they can allow themselves to be co-opted into a system whose core principles they are uncomfortable with or they can rebel and be rejected. Mr Stiglitz has chosen the path of the brave. As he returns to the salubrious environs of Stanford University, many in the developing world and in East Asia will salute this intrepid intellectual giant and look to him for continued guidance.

December 9, 1999

Narrow agenda

Larry Summers, America's brilliant and combative Treasury Secretary, must be pleased. Under constant prodding from the US, the G-7 countries have agreed to a reform of the IMF's lending policies. Mr Summers' elation will, however, not be shared by the developing world.

One proposal agreed to by the G-7 is for the IMF to raise the prices of some of the loans it provides to middle-income countries. Another is for a reduction in the interest rate on loans provided under the Contingent Credit Line (CCL) facility introduced in April 1999. The facility allows countries that qualify by meeting acceptable standards of economic management to draw a significant amount of credit in times of crisis.

In the recent past, Mr Summers has clearly articulated the rationale for these proposals. The IMF must scale back long-term lending, leaving the area to the World Bank. It must focus instead on objectives more in line with its original mandate: providing short-term loans to countries in crisis, and preventing financial crises in the first place.

Secondly, the Fund can best meet its re-defined objectives by incentivizing better economic management among developing countries. The way to do so is to assure well-managed countries of a large supply of credit under the CCL facility in the event of a crisis.

The idea that the overlapping of functions between the IMF and the World Bank should make way for a clearly demarcated role for each based on their respective strengths is beguiling. But there are negatives to it.

It is not clear what a shrinking of the IMF's role implies for overall long-term lending to the developing world. Will the World Bank's lending rise commensurately? Not if the next US government were to go by the recommendations of a Congressional commission headed by the economist Allan Meltzer. The Meltzer Commission has asked for a reduction in loans to middle-income countries from the Bank as well on the ground that official flows are, in any case, dwarfed today by private flows.

This is true but even developing countries that can access the capital markets find it difficult to obtain funding of more than five year maturity—the sort of funding required for, say, infrastructure. Moreover, the gap between middle-income and developed countries remains unconscionably wide. While the case for official flows has thus not disappeared, there is every danger that "restructuring" of the multilaterals will become a cover for whittling down such flows.

Joseph Stiglitz has argued that an overlap in jurisdictions of the two institutions is useful. It helps throw up alternative approaches to crucial economic issues, which makes for better decisions. Further, Mr Stiglitz contends that, given the links between macro—and micro-issues evidenced in the East Asian crisis, it may be unwise for the institutions to focus on one area to the complete exclusion of the other.

The proposal to use the CCL facility to foster better macro-management in developing countries is also not problem-free. Will qualifying countries lose their privilege when their economic indicators deteriorate? If yes, it could bring on the very crisis the facility is meant to avert. This is why the facility has had no takers over the past year.

The flaws in these proposals apart, the bigger concern in the developing world must be that the US seems to be pursuing a narrow agenda of scaling back the activities of the Fund and the Bank. It has shown little appetite for broader reforms needed for ensuring financial stability. These include: encouraging taxes on short-term inflows; getting lenders to assume a bigger share of the costs imposed by a systemic crisis; and a greater say for developing countries in decision-making at the IMF.

Given the asymmetry between the sizes of their economies and the magnitude of capital flows, the developing countries today face a situation that is inherently destabilizing. Without a commitment to broader reform of the international financial system, it is hard to see how their vulnerability to crises can be reduced.

Perhaps because the industrial world (barring Japan) has emerged unscathed—or even benefited—from the most recent crisis, such a commitment is missing today. Yet the biggest lesson from past crises surely is that in safeguarding the stability of the international financial system, there is little room for complacency.

July 20, 2000

Competition policy: Europe begs to differ with the US

As though the Microsoft case was not enough, the European Commission's (EC) decision to block the merger of two American companies, General Electric and Honeywell, has provided more grist to the mill of competition policy economists. The EC ruling in the case has thrown into sharp focus contrasts in the application of competition policy in the US and in Europe.

The EC's decision, which came earlier this month, has had a big impact in the US. An adverse ruling by the WTO could not have attracted greater attention. The decision has upset the Bush administration which was keen to see the merger cleared as it had already secured the approval of regulators in the US. It has raised concerns among American transnationals about strategic decisions being undone by overseas regulators. Not least, it is seen as a rare setback to GE's charismatic boss Jack Welch who seemed all set to bow out in a blaze of glory.

Many saw the EC ruling as merely underlining Europe's reluctance to expose its national champions to serious competition. This perception was reinforced when the European Parliament recently voted—albeit by a majority of just one—against a measure that would have made takeovers easier. The measure called for management to consult shareholders on takeover bids instead of unilaterally resorting to poison pills aimed at thwarting hostile bids.

It is true that many of the European Union's constituents are not ready yet to go the whole hog on competition. But this certainly not the position of the EC (the European Union's executive arm) that sponsored the takeover measure. No, the EC ruling on GE-Honeywell is not about protecting Europe's national champions. Rather, it reflects a European approach to competition policy that is different from that of the US.

In reviewing the deal, anti-trust authorities in the US asked whether the deal would have the immediate effect of hurting the consumer. The answer was 'no'. The EC, on the other hand, focused on whether the deal would hurt competition. The answer was 'yes'.

Some economists think the EC's focus on the impact on competition is altogether misplaced. Writing in the *New York Times* (June 28), Hal Varian, author of a standard textbook on microeconomics, pointed out that this was a case of firms producing complementary products: airplane engines (GE) and related aviation equipment (Honeywell). And economic theory is quite clear that a merger of firms producing complementary products in highly concentrated industries (such as aviation) leads to lower prices for the consumer. This is the "Cournot effect", named after the French economist who wrote about strategic interactions between firms way back in 1838.

The EC acknowledged the relevance of the "Cournot effect". It, nevertheless, seems to have judged that the attenuation of competition would turn out to be bad for the consumer over the long run. This essentially reflects the profound distrust of concentration of economic power that shaped competition policy in both the US and Britain in the last century.

Attitudes in the US have changed since but not as much in Europe. American regulators these days are more relaxed about market dominance and reluctant to guess the impact of a given market structure. However, at the first sign that market power is being abused, they swing into action. Unlike in Europe, the anti-trust authorities in the US cannot issue a ruling themselves; they have to take the concerned firm to court.

But then the wheels of American justice grind swiftly. They also grind relentlessly small:

abuse of market power renders firms liable to "triple damages" (that is, three times the damage suffered by victims). Lacking a comparable history of deterrence, the Europeans seem to prefer taking pre-emptive action against abuse of market power to reacting after the event.

The debate on competition policy in India has echoed this dilemma: to rein in at the outset or to react where required? In the SVS Raghavan committee report on competition policy, a dissenting view was expressed that we do not need a competition policy at this stage where the imperative is to usher competition into a cloistered economy. A Competition Commission could, in fact, become the handmaiden of vested interests and end up throttling, instead of promoting, competition.

However, it is just as likely that, in the absence of competition policy, entrenched firms could use their financial and political muscle to limit future competition. This is not a matter that is easily resolved. The theoretically neat compromise, favoured by the Raghavan committee, would be to go ahead with a Competition Commission but to ensure its independence and the highest quality of staff. The deed is about to be done, we can only keep our fingers crossed.

July 19, 2001

Bush's early moves on economy fail to enthuse

To Americans, the first 100 days of a Presidency has a mystique of its own. This period is seen as setting the tone for the rest of the term and giving early cues as to whether the newly elected President has a grip on the job.

President George Bush has wasted no time in his first 100 days in giving a vigorous push to key elements of the Republican economic agenda: cuts in taxes, an emphasis on producing greater energy rather than on conservation, reform of Social Security.

More controversially, he has refused to be drawn into any short-term initiatives for solving the power crisis in California. He has met with early success but his moves have failed to enthuse the experts.

Bush's efforts in the first 100 days have yielded what Republicans would regard as a glittering prize: the most sweeping cuts in taxes since the time of Ronald Reagan. The final package agreed to by Congressional negotiators will produce reductions in taxes worth $1.35 trillion over a ten year period.

Tax reductions by themselves are not an issue in the US today but there are differences over what magnitude of reductions is appropriate. There are even bigger differences over what form the tax cuts should take. The administration has trumpeted the fact that all taxpayers can expect to see a cheque from the Treasury department by the end of the year—$300 for individuals and $600 for a married couple.

But no amount of packaging can disguise the fact that the real plums in the tax bill are for the super-rich. The top rate will drop gradually from 39.6 per cent to 35 per cent by 2006. (Bush had wanted the rate to go down to 33 per cent). The estate tax will be phased out by 2010.

Most galling to many is the provision relating to the alternative minimum tax (AMT) that will make nonsense of the vaunted deductions in the bill and that will mostly hit upper middle-class people. The tax bill is designed so that the impact of this provision is felt gradually. This year 1.4 million will qualify for the AMT. The number rises to 5.3 million by 2004—when the next Presidential election is due—and then starts rising sharply, touching a peak of 36 million in 2010. The AMT is seen as shifting the tax burden from the super-rich to the merely well-off.

Equity considerations apart, the overwhelming impression created by the tax bill is that the tax cuts are simply unsustainable. That is why some of the biggest cuts are deferred until late in the ten year horizon. It is also the reason why, astonishingly, the bill contains a "sunset" clause that causes the whole bill to expire in 2010, bringing taxes back to their current levels in 2011!

In a scathing attack on the tax bill in the *New York Times* (May 29), Paul Krugman wrote, "In short, the tax bill is a joke.....The administration,, knowing that its tax cut wouldn't fit into any responsible budget, pushed through a bill that contains the things it wanted most—big tax cuts for the very, very rich—and used whatever accounting gimmicks it could find to make the overall budget seem smaller than it is."

Bush has not won plaudits for his response to the California energy crisis either. On a visit to the state last week, Bush bluntly conveyed to Governor Davis that he did not favour capping of wholesale prices of power—that is, prices charged by generators to distributors. (Retail prices are prices charged by distributors to customers.)

The steep rise in wholesale prices even while retail prices were fixed by law has bankrupted many of the state's utilities and has led to demands for caps on wholesale prices to limit the use of market power by suppliers of electricity. Bush set his face against these demands, arguing that addition to power supply was the more meaningful long-term solution.

Implicit in Bush's stand is a refusal to recognize that deregulation of the power sector, as practised in California, has failed. Many believe that, in the short-term, a bailout of utilities is required so that power suppliers find them creditworthy enough to resume normal supplies. Temporary caps on wholesale prices are also needed in order to limit damage to the Californian economy. This is a course that is advocated by, among others, Alfred Kahn, the Cornell university professor who was the author of airline deregulation in the US.

By refusing to intervene, Bush may have gladdened the hearts of the faithful in the Republican camp but he will not have won any marks for deftness in matters economic.

June 7, 2001

Demystifying the 'maestro'

After fifteen years as uncrowned czar of the world's financial markets, Alan Greenspan, Chairman of the US Federal Reserve, is in danger of losing some of his aura of greatness just a year before he steps down. Media analysts see the threat to his stature as arising from the bursting of the asset bubble of the nineties in the US. Greenspan's critics contend that, by not pricking the bubble early enough, he may have contributed to the severity of the subsequent slump in the real economy.

In a recent paper, two academics attempt what is, perhaps, a subtler chipping away at Greenspan's larger-than-life image. They show that his success in sustaining the American economic boom can be ascribed to a simple monetary rule. (*The Fed and the New Economy, Laurence Ball and Robert R Tchaidze, American Economic Review, May 2002).*

This contradicts folklore that invests Greenspan with extraordinary acumen. He pores over reams and reams of data and picks up the tiniest inflexions in these. He makes it a point to interact with business leaders in order to stay clued in to changes in the economy. His vast experience in forecasting makes him adept at synthesising information. He is, to use the ecstatic title of a biography by journalist Bob Woodward, the 'maestro', the man who "spotted productivity growth in the 1990s and refused to raise interest rates when the traditional economic models and theories cried out for it".

Many academics have been sceptical of such claims. They have long held that Greenspan's actions can be explained in terms of simple monetary rules that any central bank would follow these days. The best known is, of course, the Taylor rule that says that interest rates should respond to inflation and economic slack (say, the "GDP gap" or the unemployment rate). When inflation rises, interest rates would rise; when real GDP falls below its natural rate, interest rates would fall.

Ball and Tchaidze first ask whether monetary policy in Greenspan's tenure can be explained by the simplest rule or whether the Fed deviated from such a rule in the late 1990s.

One distinguished economist, Gregory Mankiw, has contended that a Taylor rule, using the unemployment rate as the slack variable, explains the behaviour of Greenspan's Fed.

The authors examine the stability of such a rule over two periods in Greenspan's tenure—the "old economy" period (1987-95), and the "new economy" period (1996-2000). They do so without adjusting for changes in changes in the non-accelerating inflation rate of unemployment (NAIRU), the unemployment rate to which the economy gravitates in the long-run. They find that the simple Taylor rule explains the Fed's behaviour in the first period but not in the second. The actual interest rates in the second period were lower than what the simple Taylor rule predicts.

The authors next employ a Taylor rule in which NAIRU changes over time, and use the deviation of unemployment from NAIRU as the measure of economic slack. They find that the modified Taylor rule explains the Fed's behaviour well in both the periods. Clearly, the Fed realised that NAIRU was falling and, therefore, did not respond to falling unemployment with a major tightening.

Under changing economic conditions, the Fed used, not the simple Taylor rule, but a modified one. As an explanation for the Fed's success, this falls well short of crediting Greenspan with divine insight into the economy. The authors conclude, tongue in cheek, that future policy makers could replicate such a rule "even if they do not possess Alan Greenspan's special skills."

While this conclusion might seem to dim the Greenspan charisma somewhat, it might yet provide the beleaguered Chairman of the Fed with his best defence against criticism that he did little to contain the asset bubble. By following a sensible monetary rule, Greenspan was able to preside over the longest expansion ever in US history. While there has been the inevitable slowdown since, it has so far been mild by historical standards. Unless, therefore, the US economy goes into a prolonged slump, Greenspan's policies will have been vindicated.

Even if the slowdown stretches out, it is not clear what the Fed could have done to prevent it. Greenspan has argued recently that it is hard to tell an asset bubble until it has burst. Even if a bubble is identified, it cannot be preempted except through a substantial economic contraction, precisely what policy seeks to avoid. Thus, a prolonged slump would merely underline the limits to monetary policy in an economy that long ago learnt the limits to fiscal policy. For policy-makers, that would be a very humbling moment indeed.

October 10, 2002

The lure of imperialism

Whatever the officially stated reasons for the Iraq war, most people are convinced that Iraq's oil riches are the principal motivation for the United States. They see the US as gaining economically from access to the world's second largest oil reserves. Yale professor of economics, William D. Nordhaus, thinks otherwise. He argues that America risks huge losses on account of the Iraq war. (*The economic consequences of a war with Iraq, NBER Working Paper 9361*).

Nordhaus evaluates costs to the US in two scenarios. In one, the war is short, that is, it lasts 30 to 60 days. In the other, the war stretches out over a year. There are the military costs, costs of post-war occupation and reconstruction, humanitarian assistance, and costs arising from the impact on the US economy.

Nordhaus places the military costs at \$50-140 billion or about 0.5-1.5% of GDP (the first for a short war and the second for a longer one). These costs are negligible by historical standards Major wars in American history cost more than 50% of GDP; the Vietnam war cost 15%.

Postwar occupation would cost \$75-500 billion. The costs of reconstruction and nation-building would be \$30-105 billion depending on how serious America is about this objective. Humanitarian assistance spread over a two to four year horizon would cost \$1-10 billion.

The economic impact of the war would be two-fold. First, the impact of oil prices on the US economy. Secondly, the impact on aggregate spending of psychological factors that affect consumption and investment. In the worst case, Nordhaus assumes that oil prices triple in 2003 and gradually fall back to the pre-shock level. The loss of real national income would be \$778 billion over a decade. In the optimistic scenario, prices dip marginally below the trend, yielding a benefit to the US economy of \$40 billion.

Finally, the impact on aggregate spending of psychological factors. In the pessimistic case, a sharp rise in oil prices would be accompanied by a fall in consumer and business spending